Praise for Successful Onboarding

In *Successful Onboarding*, Lilith and Mark demonstrate the financial impact that the onboarding process can have on your organization and provide a road map for improving your return on investment. The book has already changed the way we think about onboarding in our organization.

—**Andrew Blocher**, Chief Financial Officer,
Federal Realty Investment Trust

This book has the potential to change the way we think about new hires and what is possible from this group. With the instruction provided, you can migrate onboarding from the administrative to the strategic, and deliver far greater value for your enterprise.

—**Betty Thompson**, Senior Vice President,
People Services, Booz Allen Hamilton

This is an important book for business leaders who want to assure employee engagement from day one! Practical and instructive, the book gives leaders everything required to plan and implement an onboarding strategy that provides maximum organizational benefits. Not only does the book convincingly build the business case for excellence in onboarding, the authors lay out in the clearest of terms a recipe to assist practitioners to plan and implement a strategy that will contribute the results we are all looking for—engaged employees who choose to build a career in our organizations and contribute to organizational success in the long term! Well done!

—**Bonnie DuPont**, Corporate Director and former Group
Vice President, Corporate Resources, Enbridge, Inc.

An approach to transforming your organization's onboarding process from a one-time transaction to a sustained and integrated employee experience that drives performance and engagement right out of the gate.

—**Matt Motzkin**, Director, Organizational Development,
Disney-ABC Television Group

A comprehensive and highly practical guide to the critical—but underappreciated—practice of onboarding new employees. The authors make a convincing business case for strategic onboarding and then outline a step-by-step process for a positive and enduring outcome.

—**Max Stier**, President and CEO, Partnership for Public Service

Successful Onboarding could easily be titled Maximizing Your ROI. If you adopt the authors' perspective and follow the best practices they present, your organization will get the greatest possible return on its investment in new talent. Stein and Christiansen's work will shift your focus from activities to results.

—**Scott Eblin**, Executive Coach; author, *The Next Level: What Insiders Know About Executive Success*

This is a terrific resource for anyone wanting to create an effective onboarding program.

—**Mindy Moye**, Ph.D., Manager, Employee Engagement, John Deere

Every company leader who is serious about delivering results through people should read this book. *Successful Onboarding* not only gives a roadmap to successful hiring and retention but also addresses the common pitfalls that lead to adjustment struggles, discouragement, and skepticism from new hires. This book rings true to those of us who coach leaders in the onboarding transition.

—**Kate Ebner**, Co-Director, Georgetown University Leadership Coaching Program; Principal, The Nebo Company

People are a company's most important asset. *Successful Onboarding* makes the case for the importance of effective onboarding in setting up employees for success.

—**Stephen Squeri**, Group President, Global Services, and Chief Information Officer, American Express Company

Goodbye old school orientation and hello to onboarding. A great reference to tailor your onboarding based on your culture and strategy. This book demonstrates how sound and creative onboarding can prevent a lot of voluntary off-boarding from high performing employees.

—**Sonia Narang**, Director, Leadership and Organization Development, Sony Pictures Entertainment

Hiring employees is the biggest investment most organizations make. Understanding how to make sure that investment sticks is what onboarding is about, and *Successful Onboarding* shows you how to do it right.

—**Peter Cappelli**, Director, Center for Human Resources, The Wharton School, The University of Pennsylvania; author, *Talent on Demand*

SUCCESSFUL ONBOARDING

A Strategy to Unlock Hidden Value Within Your Organization

Mark A. Stein and
Lilith Christiansen

New York   Chicago   San Francisco   Lisbon   London
Madrid   Mexico City   Milan   New Delhi   San Juan
Seoul   Singapore   Sydney   Toronto

ISBN   978-0-07-173937-5
MHID   0-07-173937-8

Onboarding Margin is a trademark of Kaiser Associates, Inc.

McGraw-Hill books are available at special quantity discounts to use as premiums and sales promotions or for use in corporate training programs. To contact a representative, please e-mail us at bulksales@mcgraw-hill.com.

This book is printed on acid-free paper.

CONTENTS

122830

ACKNOWLEDGMENTS

It's nice when work—the day-in, day-out stuff we do in the course of making a living—turns to produce ideas and solutions that offer promise and returns far greater than client fees. Onboarding, because of its character as a high-prospect and hugely under-focused management issue has provided us with just that. And the intellectual, professional, and client impact return is not only a result of these circumstances, but also the fantastic work and support of colleagues at client organizations, peers in the industry, colleagues within our management consulting practice, and finally the interests and support of our friends and family. In particular we would like to call out—in no particular order—the specific and significant contributions of many who have assisted us over the past years in this endeavor and for more broadly shaping our professional thinking and providing us with encouragement and support.

Those names include our colleagues at Kaiser Associates: Parkin Kent for his early (and intense) work in our client delivery on the onboarding front, for also helping us develop and distil so many of our core models and frameworks, and finally for his assistance in development of our original outline for this book; Sarah Fiorillo for her tireless energy, and highest of work product standards for both client engagements and too-numerous, small but necessary pieces of this book; Adam Goldstein for his ideas and analytical prowess associated with several of our basic frameworks, and his contributions to various client outcomes; Megan MacLennan and Sravan Narayan for their support on our economic impact analysis; Lars Wensel for his client contributions and for keeping us so thoughtfully on tack with our professional efforts; Nina Trinca for early encouragement and support in keeping our heads on straight; Matt Laughlin, Karim Nhedi, Scott Albrecht, and Emile Chin-Dickey for their collaboration on our first client facing onboarding work; David Gibson and John Wilhelm—for introducing our work to so many great companies and helping our intellectual capital see the light of day in so many new communities within the commercial world. To Kate Ebner for her best-in-world faith and trust in our abilities and ambition, let alone her intellectual contributions in supporting our aspirations to develop as greater professionals in the field, and her collaborations in solving some very challenging client challenges. To Aimee George Leary for her confidence and trust in allowing us to contribute to such a great effort and critical function at a client organization. To Lillian Pacheco for her partnership in doing heavy lifting and working through "change management" issues with finesse and optimal stakeholder outcomes in mind. To Chris Holmes for her leadership and assistance in ensuring the Booz Allen Hamilton story told inside was thoughtfully presented and instructive for other change agents. To Jonathan Jordan who worked hard as an initial advocate of our methodologies. To Vince Gonzalez, Terry Bickham, Mary Andrade, Brenda Brophy, Eric Nilsson, Tricia Dirks, and Cinda Jensen among numerous other client professionals for your trust, ideas, partnership in ensuring great outcomes, and for making our work fun.

We would also like to thank the 4,000 plus members (and growing) of our onboarding network for your ideas and contributions, not only to elevate the thinking around onboarding in companies across the United States and globally, but also for sharing your experiences to help illustrate the ideas included in this book. To the latter point, we specifically want to call out the contributions of Mindy Moye of John Deere and Beth Kavelaris, Kimberly Thekan, and Karen Berenson of Robert W. Baird & Co.

With regard to actually pulling this work together—both commercially and the specific content—we thank and will forever appreciate the tireless efforts, energy, and backing of Lorin Rees our dedicated agent, Seth Schulman our terrific and tremendously patient editor and world-class sparring partner. Without you two this book would not exist, for better and for worse. We thank Gail Ross for providing valued counsel in the world of book publishing—an area that we simply did not have experience. Additionally we thank our research assistants John Landry, Lin Qing, and Dan Berger. We also want to thank Daniel Lombardi for his style and artistic eye in driving simplicity and elegence to the graphical representation of our frameworks. We thank the team at McGraw-Hill for their support and efforts in the process of bringing these ideas into print on this wide scale.

Professionally, we thank our partners in our consulting practice for helping produce an environment that stimulates great work and intellectual stimulus.

On more personal notes, I (Mark) thank my partner in life, my wife Lisa, for everything that you have ever said (and not said) to support me and help me achieve what I have, and hope to in our future. You make the hard stuff worthwhile and always put me in my place when I most need it. I thank my parents for their support throughout the years and of great particular contribution my father for inspiring me, and causing me to truly enjoy and understand—at a wonderfully early age—the thing that makes the world go round—*business*. I thank Sylvia Eskind for inspiring me to not wait for the ship to come in, and for everything else that she gave me. I thank Tim Ogilvie for being my first, truest, and greatest mentor—onboarding me like no other into a successful career in management consulting—giving me the cultural, social, strategic, and early (and often) career support that has proved so meaningful to my career.

I (Lilith) thank my husband, Brett, for all of your support. Your encouragement, love, and perspective are invaluable. I could not have accomplished half the things I have in life if not for our partnership. A special thanks on this endeavor for being our first reader and giving us the frank feedback. I thank my parents for all of their encouragement and support from an early age to aspire and achieve whatever I set my mind to. I also want to thank Pam Knox, for taking on many new responsibilities at Kaiser Associates allowing me to transition from my development role to that of author and back to consultant. I thank Kevin Dell'Oro for encouraging my return to Kaiser Associates.

Together, we thank our kids—Mark's (Ainsley, Sarah, Abigail) and Lilith's (Tyler and Bryce)—for making life fun (and teaching us that a self applied haircut is just a haircut, not a referendum on our ability to parent, consult, and write a book at the same time) and for giving us feedback when we most need it—in the form of hugs and smiles—that we are doing the right things.

INTRODUCTION

How well would your company be doing if less than a third of new customers felt positive about their first year of interactions with your company?

How would you feel if after six months a full third of your customers were seeking a new place to buy their products or services?

Would your Senior Vice President of Manufacturing have a job today if a third of new manufacturing plants were not working (and he repeated this performance year after year)?

At many companies, such outcomes would prompt a shareholder to call for new management. We believe that onboarding of new hires should meet the same, if not higher, standards. Over the past 10 years (and especially during the past five years), a number of Fortune 500 companies and small- to medium-sized businesses have reviewed traditional orientation programs and begun to embrace "onboarding" as a means of increasing employee productivity and engagement levels, reducing turnover, and elevating a company's employment brand in the eyes of prospective hires. Yet despite millions spent on these initiatives, many firms have experienced a modest return on investment. Companies continue to absorb new hires less effectively than they otherwise might, and as a result they experience longer new hire time-to-productivity, higher attrition, frustrated hiring managers, and a mediocre return on investment. Consider these facts:

- A full third of external hires are no longer with the organization after two years.
- Less than a third of executives worldwide are positive about their onboarding experience.
- Almost a third of executives who join organizations as an external hire miss expectations in the first two years.
- Almost a third of employees employed in their current job for less than six months are already job searching.[1]

Companies need to take a serious look at how they are integrating new hires into the organization. Although onboarding has received attention in human resources circles, typical programs remain haphazard, limited in scope, and disconnected from a firm's larger strategy. Onboarding usually amounts to little more than old and tired orientation programs—sometimes dressed up in new clothes. New hires are pulled through maybe a half-day of company introduction focused on corporate history, compliance policies, and employee benefits. They're given basic job direction, introduced to a few peers and company leaders, and made aware of available training resources. They're provided with security access and basic work tools (e.g., phone, computer, instruments, etc.). And that's where the formal process ends. Firms offer little inspiration nor specific challenge, direction, or commitment to new hires. During the rest of the new hire's first year—a make-or-break period in an employee's tenure—firms leave it to overwhelmed and under-prepared hiring managers to address informally the critical needs that all new hires face, including help with job preparedness, development, assimilation, networking, and career planning. Senior leaders typically regard such activity as a mundane part of filling positions, not as a strategic opportunity to renew the company and its prospects.

Most onboarding programs have other shortcomings as well. Companies will present the same orientation material to every new hire, irrespective of their level of career experience, defined role or responsibilities. In many cases, no single department oversees or retains accountability for the onboarding process. Therefore companies have little idea how successful the process is, and what metrics do exist are too broad and not tied to specific program goals. Administered by Human Resources, Recruiting, or Learning and Development, most programs do not possess buy-in from functional or business line management. Finally—and this is hardly an exhaustive account—most organizations do not keep themselves apprised of best practices, nor are they equipped to determine if and how to apply them. Onboarding programs, as a result, tend to remain static and unresponsive to newly adopted company strategy, marketplace changes, or new measures adopted by competitors.

This book will help enterprises remedy these shortcomings—and realize a far bigger return—by introducing a *strategic and systemic* approach to onboarding, one that leading companies are already applying to great effect. Onboarding can and should be far more than a glorified orientation program, and in fact a number of progressive organizations have already begun to design and implement strategic programs that bring diverse stakeholders together to engage new hires over the first year plus of their tenure. These programs incorporate an array of content, including what we refer to as the four organizing pillars—early career support; orientation to the firm's culture and its performance values; insight into the firm's strategic position, intent, and direction; and activities and experiences that enable the new hire to build beneficial relationships. Strategic programs include important structural elements, including clear diagnostics and a system of feedback and accountability, and are customized for unique segments of new hires. They are also tightly integrated with the enterprise's primary business and operating processes. On the most basic level, firms adopting strategic programs have begun to craft seamless first year experiences that, by taking seriously the perspective of new hires, hiring managers, and the enterprise in whole, address the ongoing needs of the business more effectively than ever before.

Systemic programs have many benefits, not least that they can be more cost-effective than the disjointed programs commonly in place today. As we will demonstrate, strategic onboarding not only reduces operating costs, and helps new hires improve their personal contribution to the enterprise; it also reduces regrettable attrition, and helps the organization deliver against its strategic goals. The discipline can uncover immense new value—what we term the *Onboarding Margin*™—even as it improves the enterprise's employment brand in the eyes of employees and prospective recruits. Through real-world examples from our work with Chief People Officers, onboarding leaders at renowned universities, Fortune 500 HR executives, and other pioneers of the field, *Successful Onboarding* teaches the fundamentals and state-of-the-art practices that can improve the onboarding performance of any enterprise. Read on, and you'll discover a framework for analyzing and understanding the opportunities available. You'll also take your first step toward designing and implementing a best-in-class system for your own organization.

Broken Promises

To understand how unhelpful standard onboarding experiences are, consider what happened to Charles Weber. After 13 years as a Learning and Development Leader with two large multinational corporations, Charles decided to pursue a leadership role with what he understood to be an up-and-coming, high-growth company. Charles had grown frustrated by bureaucracy that had thwarted several human capital initiatives he'd spent years developing. At his last company, his promotion path was impeded by the firm's L&D vice president, who seemed determined to stave off retirement as long as possible. It was time for a change.

Charles spent months searching and interviewing for a new job, and he received several attractive offers. After many dinner table conversations weighing options with his wife (and contemplating the merits of his existing job), Charles accepted a role with a well-respected international financial services firm. Charles' only reservation, the job's slightly lower title and pay grade, was assuaged by a promise from his soon-to-be manager. "You're our best candidate. Give me 6 months," she promised with a wink and a nod. "I'll make you a Director and you can be in charge of our Learning and Development programs. I just can't bring you in as a Director." Together, they crafted a set of responsibilities and an exciting initiative that Charles alone would design and lead. Charles enjoyed the early collaboration with his hiring manager and eagerly accepted the new position. The firm's lead recruiter got word and was excited to have finally filled the position after 6 months of process and search. Things were looking good.

What transpired next surprised Charles. After packing his family up, moving to a new home in a new city, and completing a week-long centralized orientation program, Charles arrived at his office eager to catch up with his new boss. Yet his boss' office was empty. His boss, it turned out, had been conducting a personal job search, too. After waiting two weeks to meet with his boss' replacement (an internal transfer), Charles discovered that the accelerated promotion timeline promised to him had not been communicated to anyone else in the company, nor was the new boss much enthused about taking up the political fight associated with an accelerated promotion. To make matters worse, Charles discovered that the specific initiative and associated responsibilities that sold him on the job belonged to another group within the company—and it was not going anywhere. In the blink of an eye, Charles' excitement for his new role vanished. After weeks spent seeking a remediation path or support resources, Charles sat down at his new computer and restarted his job search. A month later, he was gone.

Charles' experience casts light on just a few of the common shortcomings of standard, non-strategic and non-systemic onboarding initiatives. Lacking any formal collaboration between recruiting, the hiring manager, senior management, and other parties in the firm—lacking, too, a process for addressing new hires' career planning needs—Charles' firm quickly wound up disappointing him. Even further, it broke "the hiring promise" it had made during the recruiting process. Charles in turn questioned his new company's values and the support it would provide over the course of his career. Without anywhere to turn to figure out a solution, he could only conclude that a position with a smaller high-growth firm could be every bit as frustrating as his previous job with an established industry player. The best choice now was to leave.

Charles was not the only one hurt by the lack of an adequate onboarding program; the company suffered, too. Charles was a supremely talented guy whom the firm had spent 6 months wining and dining and whom it had also engaged an external search firm to find (paying 20% of a year's salary in a finder's fee). Lost for good were the recruitment expenses, as well as the funds the firm had invested in his signing bonus, his moving expenses, and other administrative costs associated with his hire. In addition, the company had to spend even more money recruiting someone else to fill Charles' position. Productivity suffered, since after six months of recruitment, two months of unenthused work on Charles' part, and a subsequent search of undetermined length, the job position Charles was to have occupied would be filled by another person who would also likely require an adjustment period before being able to work at his or her best. Most damagingly of all were the long-term, indirect costs. When top-notch people like Charles become disillusioned, a firm's brand becomes tarnished in the eyes of prospective employees (after all, Charles actively participates in online social networks), and it becomes even more difficult to attract the best talent. Also, the firm's strategy suffers. How do you propel an organization forward if you have a revolving door atmosphere, with key people leaving after short tenures and new people entering, bringing with them different skills, agendas, and commitments?

Even if Charles had stayed, his hiring firm's onboarding program would have failed to satisfy the organization's needs. By limiting to a short program that merely familiarized new hires with the culture and helped them with some basic administrative tasks, Charles' firm failed to acclimate new employees to their organization and its broader business goals. As a result, Charles would have been unable to connect his efforts with the firm's strategy as creatively and proactively as he otherwise might. And if there were elements of the onboarding experience that caused Charles to get excited about a future at the company, there is a chance that Charles would have forgiven the company over his their initial entry snafus. Finally, by failing to explore with Charles over a sustained period how the organization defines success and how this could relate to the specifics of his own career, Charles' firm was failing—by a long shot—to maximize its return on human capital.

Strategic Onboarding: A Burning Need

The sub-par performance of non-strategic onboarding programs seems especially troubling for firms when we consider the broader business context. Managers have long understood the financial and strategic challenges of integrating new talent. For decades, firms have wrestled with how to reduce time-to-productivity for new hires and increase retention. Yet today, it is not uncommon for organizations to battle 10 to 15% annual attrition, and they face the daunting prospect (or opportunity, depending on your perspective) of replacing over 50% of their employee base in a three- to five-year period. This phenomenon has received much attention in the business press. In 2008, in the midst of a weak economy and rising unemployment, *BusinessWeek* ran an article entitled "The Global Talent Crisis," which cited "attracting and retaining talent" as one of the top threats to business success perceived by the over 850 C-level executives surveyed.[2] "Competition" was the only threat that ranked higher.

The broad trend facing hiring managers today is a dramatic increase in demand for high-potential recruits. Most large companies have highly tuned, albeit expensive, recruitment engines. Companies that recruited regionally now routinely conduct national searches with increased sophistication, support, and investment. Governments and non-profits are rethinking their recruitment and retention strategies given increased availability of top talent from the private sector. Although these organizations have increased access to A-level recruits, the focus must reside on retaining these new hires for the long term rather than risking high attrition.

Of course, long-term social trends have made retention more difficult. Responding in large part to firms' almost complete abandonment of pensions, young entering employees have shifted their attitudes toward prospective employers, with lifetime employment at a single firm becoming a stale and uninteresting concept. As we have all experienced, today's younger workers have different—and in some ways, grander—expectations about employment. They seek meaningful careers, not merely well-paying jobs. As a result, the best and the brightest give weight to the prospective employer's employment brand, and more specifically to the company's plan for them during their first year on the job and beyond. Even during hard economic times, these recruits are thinking beyond the first 30 days and focusing instead on what employers can do to address their long-term aspirations.

To meet recruitment and retention challenges, leading firms are exploring how to redefine the employer-employee compact. To that end, they are pursuing state of the art onboarding programs even during recessions, when job markets are tighter. For some human capital teams, it's a question of preparing for the inevitable economic upswing that will also incite a hiring uptick; a recession presents an opportunity to revamp and revitalize onboarding programs. Additionally, recessions produce a surplus of top talent, and companies that are selectively hiring want to ensure that they can retain these high achievers once bad times end.

Beyond the challenges of recruitment and retention, productivity is perhaps the most important reason onboarding has taken on such immense strategic relevance for progressive firms. In today's service-based and knowledge-based economy, new employee onboarding provides organizations with a critical means to retain the value and increase the productivity of one of their most important assets: human capital. And if done right, onboarding provides companies with the opportunity not only to accelerate time-to-productivity of new hires, but also to elevate standards of productivity for all employees. The average organization replaces half of its employee base over a five- to 10-year period (because of 5 to 10% annual attrition). Imagine the impact if all of these new employees were better developed and prepared with a more comprehensive set of role expectations. Elevating new hire productivity levels through robust onboarding programs helps companies do more with less—a key business imperative in our dynamic, hyper-competitive 21st century economy.

Elevating Onboarding ... and Human Resources

Despite the strategic importance of attracting, retaining, and maximizing the productivity of top talent, too many companies continue to neglect onboarding. Human Resources in general remains somewhat marginalized in the boardroom, all too often seen as a "soft" discipline. Some firms publically proclaim human resources a critical function only to limit the investment behind closed doors, treating human resources as a functional necessity rather than a true strategic value-add. This is a huge mistake; as our book argues, talent management and onboarding in particular should be on the radar of cross-functional managers as well as a firm's senior leadership, up to and including the CEO.

Many North American companies invest as much or more on *new* labor every year as they do in manufacturing infrastructure, yet management devotes far less time figuring out how to drive performance from this labor. This is true, even though, and probably because, it is actually far harder to engineer a positive outcome from human capital than from traditional capital investments. Management is simply more focused on areas that are perceived to be easier to tackle. Let's look at the situation in another way. A 10% attrition rate means that, not even considering growth factors, your company will turn over nearly one third of its workforce in $3\frac{1}{3}$ years (i.e., 40 months)—a timeframe approximately in line with many firms' product line refreshment, and also in line with average capital investments (with many assets having a 10-year life). Annual recruiting and intake has become the normal course of business, yet we don't see company leadership recognize the fantastic strategic opportunity this investment represents, nor have they developed the management techniques to take advantage of it.

We were once onboarding skeptics ourselves. We came to the discipline as business consultants whose Organization Development practice focused first and foremost on improving companies' strategic and business performance—bottom line stuff. Earlier in the decade, one of our clients—a Fortune 50 company—asked us to help conceive a state-of-the-art onboarding program. We were not all that familiar with the term "onboarding," and the very concept seemed a bit lightweight and over the top to us. Early investigation on supposed best practices highlighted—as an example—attention to providing "white glove" service to new hires. As we saw it, our client was supposed to be hiring mature and responsible adults, people who were motivated to perform and who would be faced with all kinds of job requirements and standards. Why should the company spend money designing a sophisticated system to bring these employees into the organization? Shouldn't a reasonably intelligent new hire be able to figure things out for him or herself? That's what we—and most people that we knew—had done upon starting our own careers.

We told our client that they were going down the wrong path. They should work harder on hiring better people rather than integrating new hires. In this, we took inspiration from Howard D. Schultz, Starbucks' long-time leader, who has been reported by management guru Tom Peters to say, "We don't train our people to smile, it is far easier for us to hire people who smile."

But it was not long before we changed our tune. Howard Schultz does not leave the customer experience to chance, nor does he leave the employee experience to chance. Instead, Starbucks and other leading companies apply "design thinking" to ensuring winning outcomes. Analyzing the process of integrating new hires as well as the needs that new hires brought to the table, we realized that onboarding was actually a tremendous business opportunity, even more exciting for being virtually unexplored by the large majority of firms. What most people associated with onboarding—the initial welcome and the initial orientation, getting new hires familiar and set up—turned out to be the least of the opportunities that a solid program could address. New hires will forgive you for not showing them where to park, or how to locate the supply rooms or the company's history and mission statement; this we know from our research. But if they fail over the first year to discover enough that will excite and enable them, that's where you suffer your loss. Lost insight. Lost productivity. Lost ideas. Lost retention. In other words, lost profit and prospect.

The more we probed into onboarding, the more we understood that this nascent discipline was actually, at its core, about business performance and the prospect for improving profit and profit potential. Our research into the state-of-the-art confirmed that most companies' onboarding approaches were disconnected from the actual needs of new hires (their personal needs and their needs associated with their ability to deliver against the company's aspirations). Also, these programs lacked buy-in from managers outside of human resources and unfolded over too short of a period to have any meaningful impact. If we could make our clients better at onboarding—if we could help them develop a program that was more comprehensive, systemic, and strategic than other firms' programs—we could truly give them a sustainable competitive advantage (the Holy Grail for management consultants) that would affect their top and bottom lines.

We've since engaged in more exhaustive best practice research, studying the operating conditions at firms such as Microsoft, Procter & Gamble, Deloitte Consulting, Target, Booz Allen Hamilton, Boston Scientific, Lockheed Martin, Verizon, FedEx Office, IBM, Best Buy, Ernst & Young, Deutsche Bank, and John Deere, among many others, including smaller firms. We've met with and collaborated with organizations in the public sector and diverse private industries and have addressed issues for both corporate knowledge workers as well as front-line employees. At each step, we've concerned ourselves with designing programs that support the companies' human capital needs based on their strategic plan and operating environment.

Findings from our broader organization development practice and our study of onboarding effectiveness have pushed us toward development of a strategic approach to onboarding. We learned early on that onboarding actually includes *every experience* that the new hire has in the course of the first year, not just the few that are owned and managed by centralized HR functions. It is this full set of experiences to which the new hire synthesizes and responds. Virtually all large and medium-sized organizations could benefit by creating onboarding programs that bring together stakeholders from across the enterprise, span at least the entire first year of the new hire's tenure, provide a comprehensive, designed integration into the firm, and address both new hires' diverse needs and the firm's strategic goals.

We've written *Successful Onboarding* to get the word out about strategic onboarding's potential, and by extension, about that of the broader human resources discipline. We hope that senior leadership will support onboarding as a worthy initiative that really can create new value for their firms. Experience has shown that best outcomes occur when decision makers throughout a firm get excited by the value, buy into the program, participate in supporting the requisite systemic changes, and feel personally invested in the program itself. We therefore have sought to provide readers with information that can help drive successful discussions with important participants in the system. Additionally, we've written this book because we want every hiring manager in every organization to understand the onboarding process better, and because we want to raise awareness and know-how among HR leaders, many of whom still remain unfamiliar with strategic onboarding's promise.

There is a significant need for more clarity on this subject. As we've worked in our own practice to give onboarding more depth and rigor, we've encountered a great deal of confusion—a situation that's gotten worse as more players have sought to jump on the onboarding bandwagon. Over the last few years, a number of vendors have developed valuable off-the-shelf software for use by human resources professionals. But this software as implemented usually serves merely to automate the administration of orientation activities. Given the wide promotion and availability of this software, managers interested in learning about onboarding often develop a limited impression of the subject as a result of the information they find when they Google the topic.

One software vendor's web site, for instance, defines onboarding as a process that involves the following exchanges with a new hire: Hiring Documents, Employee Handbook, Drug Screen, Relocation, Computer, Network Access, Workstation Setup, ID Badge, Security Access, Parking Permits, Business Cards, Expense Account—all "first-day" activities. Then the vendor talks about attrition activities: Security Deactivation, Asset Recover, and Exit Interview—"last day" activities. It's ironic (or tragically comical) that this model completely ignores all of the important elements—the things in between the first and last day of employment. And this example, although a bit extreme, is truly representative of the senti-ment associated with most solutions and published material in the public domain.

To many people, onboarding seems to involve nothing more than handing tools out and then collecting them back during an "off-board-ing" phase. You can imagine our frustration. A number of human capi-tal and business magazines have covered onboarding and reported on "best practices," but they typically fail to distinguish between a progres-sive practice and *proven* best practices, and they also fail to explore the operating conditions that define which practices should apply when. As a result, many managers have adopted practices that give the firm a sense of being "progressive," but that lack the requisite rigor to make them impactful. The result, sadly, is a modest to negative return on investment.

We've designed this book to give readers at any level of an enterprise the understanding they need to take advantage of onboarding's strategic and financial opportunities. Even when firms recognize their existing pro-grams' shortcomings, their redesign efforts often come up severely short; in framing the new hire's experience, companies tend to over-emphasize the fun, the welcome, and the service side of things, often presenting an unrealistic sense of what the firm is all about and setting unsustainable expectations. Additionally, companies tend to apply insufficient diagnos-tic and design techniques and pay insufficient consideration to what is required to govern, update, and sustain onboarding programs over time. As a result, many efforts enjoy a great first release before losing energy, leading to decreasing returns.

Human resources professionals need a deeper understanding of how to design human capital programs that cut across functional silos to create value. This book provides that understanding by describing the funda-mentals of robust, year-long onboarding programs. Chapter 1 presents the business case for onboarding, while Chapter 2 presents the general char-acteristics of a world-class, strategic program. Chapters 3 through 7 explore the contents and administrative features of strategic programs in consid-erable detail. Presenting examples and anecdotes from our practice, we describe the best-in-class principles firms are now using to help meet the pressing needs efficiently and effectively. The final two chapters focus on how to develop a strategic onboarding program. We discuss elements of diagnostic, planning, implementation, and ongoing operations, and conclude the book with an extended case study of a successful onboarding program's design and implementation.

Rethinking the Metaphor

Before embarking on our journey through state-of-the-art onboarding, let's reflect for a moment on this term itself. "Onboarding" is a metaphor, and a rather obvious one at that; it evokes a process for bringing a person onto a ship. The staff of a cruise ship, for example, would "onboard" a ship's guests by getting all of the luggage to the correct cabins, conducting a safety drill, showing them around (dining room, casino, movie theater, etc.), and describing what activities they might enjoy so that they feel welcome and familiar.

This book argues that we need to redefine this metaphor if we are to have any hope of unlocking the potential of this important process. As talent managers, we're not welcoming visitors to a company; we are employing and deploying employees or human capital investments—people that we should expect to stay and make a difference. We need to go beyond the superficial and take care to teach new hires things vital to the organization's successful performance—how to steer the ship, what makes it go, the ship's and the cruise line's business model and competitive environment, the intricacies of how one department works with another to create a good customer experience, the long-term goals of the ship. The only way a guest can get off a cruise early is to jump ship, and we don't want our employees to do that. Rather, we want them to make a big contribution. Thus we need to do more.

Strategic onboarding is a process by which a workforce is reconstituted and enrolled to align with a firm's primary emerging business strategy. From a new hire's perspective, onboarding encompasses everything a new hire experiences that defines his or her entry and orientation into an organization and that sets him or her up for success. From an organizational perspective, it's the experiences and programs that can be designed to set up employees as well as meet the needs of the new hire manager to have staff become productive quickly. If you embrace strategic onboarding, your enterprise won't see as many new hires frustrated by a boss who knows little about what the recruiters have suggested about career advancement (nor will you have recruiters making promises that may not be delivered). Your firm won't have new hires struggling to introduce themselves to managers and other people critical to their career. Your firm won't have high-potential recruits disillusioned because they've waited too many weeks to get their first assignment. Instead, your firm will have motivated, inspired employees who adjust quickly, remain enthusiastic, and are empowered to contribute at levels not usually delivered—giving you a competitive advantage that can produce top- and bottom-line results. What could be more desirable and worthy than this?

Part One

RETHINKING ONBOARDING

1

THE BUSINESS CASE FOR ONBOARDING

An R&D manager at a large consumer electronics firm wanted to improve the time it took to get new hires working at their best. This manager felt that a more comprehensive onboarding program would help new hires gain better and quicker access to the specialized knowledge they needed to excel in their jobs. Yet when our client tried to get his chief technology officer to invest in new hire onboarding, he received an unenthusiastic response. More effective onboarding seemed like an intriguing idea, but it wasn't worth funding over other priorities and wasn't clear what the payoff could be.

Few operating leaders today appreciate the full value that effective onboarding can deliver. This is understandable given onboarding's position as an emerging discipline with only a short history. This is a shame because on an intuitive level, onboarding makes a good deal of sense. The dollars we spend to recruit Grade A talent have mounted over the past 20 years because of a number of factors, including tightening of the labor force and the increasing value of knowledge workers in a service-based economy. Other factors, as some have argued, are the wider emergence of external recruiters who have an economic interest in fostering higher salaries; talent shortages; the never-ending cycle of hire, attrit, and rehire; and the associated stream of finders' fees. In fact, the cost of attracting talent approaches 30% of a new hire's annual salary. Imagine the added value if firms possessed a centralized, focused, properly resourced function to incorporate talent into the firm, so there was less of a need to rehire.

It's one thing to talk about adding value, and quite another to provide hard numbers and explain exactly where those numbers originate. This chapter builds a quantitative business case for dramatically enhancing and broadening the way firms bring new hires into the fold. It begins by examining the economics of onboarding, quantifying typical returns that can be expected. It then describes in more detail the specific business objectives and results firms can achieve with a strategic program in place. But this is only part of the story. The second half of the chapter attacks the problem from the employee's viewpoint by examining the new hire's personal needs. Employees who are enthusiastic about their work and their careers are usually strong and productive, and a well-designed onboarding experience satisfies them far better than an inconsistent, haphazard one. The chapter closes with a detailed and thorough economic analysis across industries. Using benchmark data from 25 leading companies across six industries, the prospective impact for your company and your shareholders is measured and illustrated.

It is hoped that this chapter will provide change agents inside organizations with the business case they need to spark serious discussions about onboarding with senior decision makers. If most leaders today believe their firms can't afford an effective onboarding program, this chapter's material is designed to convince them of the very opposite: Their firm cannot afford *not* to invest in one.

The Economics of Onboarding

The first step in building the case for onboarding is to estimate the hidden value that typical firms can hope to recover via a strategic program. To arrive at some hard numbers, we took a sample of Fortune 500 companies across six major industry sectors.

We assessed the impact of attrition of new hires on the overall cost structure and its impact on profit. Based on our research, on average across industries we believe that companies experience approximately 13% attrition of new hires in the first year, and some of that constitutes "regrettable" attrition (productive recruits with great prospects who choose to leave) as opposed to "non-regrettable" attrition (unproductive and low prospect workers leaving the firm). We asked ourselves, what if a strategic onboarding program could invert the common ratio of regrettable attrition? That is, instead of having 65% of our attrition made up of regrettable losses, what if we had 65% of our attrition made up of nonregrettable losses?

We determined that an approximate 25% reduction in total attrition levels was a reasonable goal and would represent a clear savings to a firm in terms of the *replacement cost* the enterprise would have to pay to recruit new employees. Yet this was only the beginning of the value effective onboarding could bring in this model. To get a more complete measure of this value, we also factored in the *opportunity costs* of regrettable attrition. When you put a new hire in, say, a quality improvement job and she or he doesn't make it in the role because of poor onboarding, the loss includes all of the improvements to your quality program that are not happening during the failed ramp-up period, the departure period, and the new search—value that is lost forever. This loss may show up as rework cost, warranty cost, and a reduction in brand equity as customers grow frustrated with your company's products or services. Although difficult to quantify in a simple analysis, these losses are significant, and they need to be reduced through more effective onboarding.

As the preceding discussion suggests, onboarding does not just offer an opportunity to reduce the overall attrition *level*. Rather, it also aims to improve the overall attrition *mix* (regrettable versus non-regrettable loss, as represented by Figure 1.1), which can have an even greater impact.

The objective of onboarding now includes retaining more of the people you want to keep, and reducing the proportion of your head count loss that is made up of *regrettable* attrition (i.e., retain more people you want and lose more people you are happy to see separate). The most exciting part of this attrition gain is that although it will affect the short-term, day-to-day productivity of the organization, its larger impact will be in the form of what the retained employees—who otherwise would have been regrettably lost—will do for your business in years to come. This is potentially a non-linear relationship, as some of these new hires may provide a truly big impact down the road. This is the game you need to be changing.

Another gain from onboarding relates to the productivity of all new hires. Effective onboarding can shorten the time it takes for the average

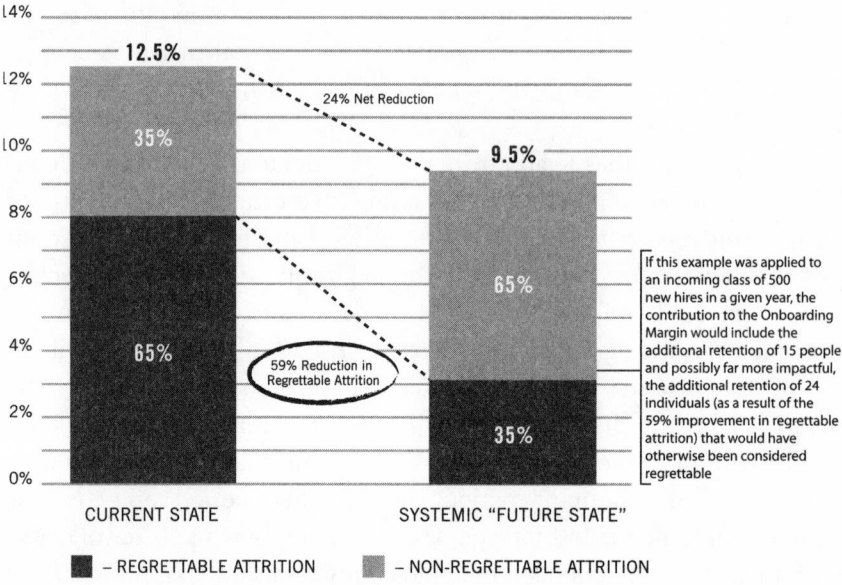

Figure 1.1 The Gain from *Both* Level and Mix of Attrition to the Onboarding Margin

employee to achieve expected productivity levels. The time (and level) will vary depending on the role, function, and company in question.[1] To quantify the potential gain from strategic onboarding, we calculated what it would be worth if we could reduce the *time to productivity*. We then asked what it would be worth if we could improve the average *level of productivity*—in effect, redefine what we expect out of a prospective new hire with regard to overall productivity, or contribution. Consider the situation in which, before an effective improvement, a firm deemed a new customer service representative "productive" when he could handle eight calls an hour. What if we were able to produce an entirely new form of value for the enterprise, maybe in the form of the representative's ability to connect the dots between calls, actually detect patterns in customer issues, and possess the motivation and know-how to properly inform product development (or pricing, or channel strategy, mergers and acquisitions (M&A), or any other critical business activity)?

Figure 1.2 summarizes the potential productivity gains attributable to strategic onboarding for those new hires who stay with the organization.

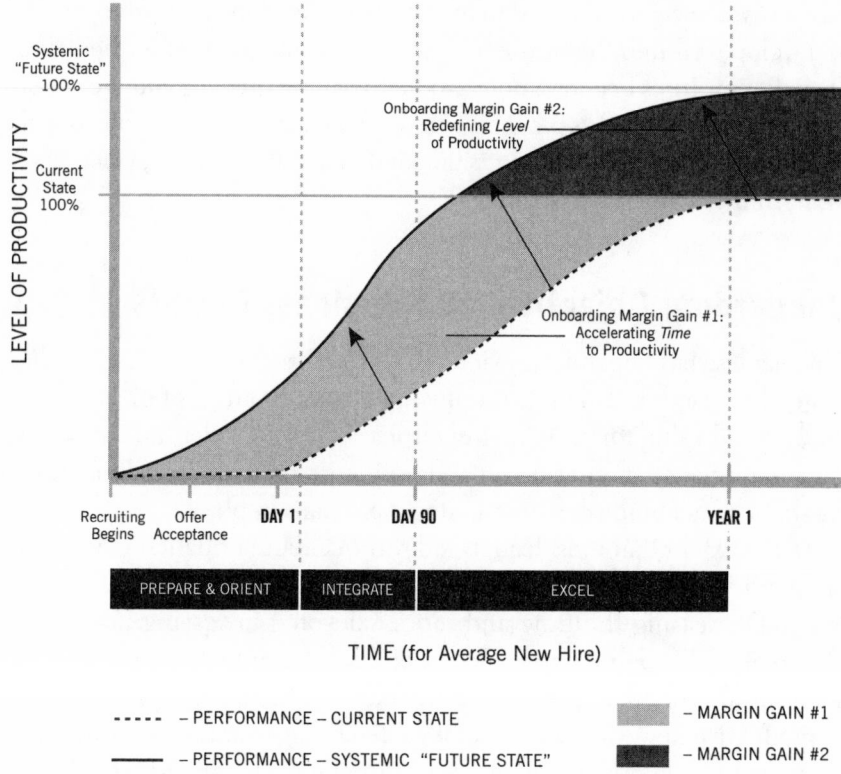

Figure 1.2 The Onboarding Margin

The top curve represents the level of competency a typical firm could expect to see in new hires over time thanks to a more effective program. The bottom curve represents the existing progress of productivity performance over time. As the graph shows, new hires operating under a more effective program would get a jump start on their jobs, reaching maximum productivity—what the organization would define as 100%—some time between day ninety and the one-year mark, well before employees at the firm might currently reach maximum productivity (see Figure 1.2).

The area of the graph represented by the darker gray area is the entirely new value firms may hope to create by readying and equipping new hires to operate on a new level of redefined expectations. As the graph shows, this new value can be realized in the course of Year One and will continue to develop well into the future as employees come to excel in their jobs. Overall, new hires become more productive more quickly, and they operate at that higher level as part of the new steady state. This, combined with the gains attributable to lower attrition and better attrition mix, yields what we term the *Onboarding Margin.*™

Onboarding Objectives and Business Results

This exercise has hopefully provided you a rough sense of how much value more effective onboarding can unlock. To explore further how onboarding can add value for particular enterprises, let's consider the many specific performance improvements and business results individual managers can hope to accomplish with a strategic program in place.

To the extent that most leaders today think about enhancing new hire onboarding, they usually have at least the following business result in mind: Decreasing the time and money devoted to serving new hires. Companies do spend a fair amount of direct spend on onboarding (in addition to indirect spend, which includes all the costs associated with unproductive new hires), much of it wasted because of their insufficiently organized and poorly designed efforts. An effective onboarding program can address this basic requirement and help cut waste in a number of ways. For instance, many companies have employees fill out paper-based forms, which in turn means the company needs extensive administrative departments to collect, organize, and collate the data. By standardizing and having employees read and complete forms online *before their start dates*, you can drive cost savings and compliance while also creating a potentially more interesting first day (as time is freed up to tackle far more engaging experiences). New hire training programs offer another example. Currently, many programs are unable to address new hires' needs in a number of areas. Lacking standardized information, hiring managers are left to improvise their own solutions to integrate the new hire. A more effective onboarding program avoids the duplication of efforts, saving time and money and avoiding needless frustration for the new hire and his or her manager.

To help drive efficiencies, minimize waste, and allow for better new hire experiences, many companies invest in software to administer the process. What most leaders don't realize is that minimizing this Day One and early entry waste is actually the least that strategic onboarding can deliver. Minimizing Day One waste is a decent opportunity. In fact, sometimes it's helpful to make greater efficiency as the primary objective when getting a program off the ground. By delivering results there, you'll have momentum and have an easier time getting buy-in for subsequent investments.

Yet managers and executives shouldn't make the mistake of limiting the idea of onboarding to a piece of software or the single business result of minimizing waste. These cost savings are largely a one-off savings opportunity, and they exclude the far greater upside. Table 1.1 lists bigger ways in which strategic onboarding will help a firm improve performance. It also lists specific business impacts—including minimized waste—that firms can expect to see as a result of achieving their improvement objectives.

As Table 1.1 suggests, a solid onboarding program can deliver much more than simply reducing administrative cost. Some of the objectives listed here (e.g., attrition) are easier to quantify in their business impact than others (e.g., improvement of the employment brand). It's also important to realize that no single strategic program, no matter how well conceived, can hope to deliver on every single objective; in fact, many companies go wrong precisely when they attempt to tackle every objective

Table 1.1 Outcomes from Strategic Onboarding

Improvement Objectives	Business Impact
• Knowledge Transfer	• Attrition
• Engagement Levels	• Time to Productivity
• Employment Brand	• Level of Productivity
• Automation	• Ability to Meet Emerging Talent Needs
• Consistency of (Positive) Experience	• Competitive Position
• Organizational Transformation (business and /or cultural)	• Recruiting Cost
	• Labor Cost
• Accountability—Roles and Responsibilities	• Onboarding Administration Cost
• *Other: unique to your organization and circumstances (as determined by your diagnostic)*	• *Other: unique to your organization and circumstances (as determined by your diagnostic)*

at once. As discussed later, the key is to assess which objectives will have the biggest impact to your company and then devise a customized program focused on delivering on those objectives.

Let's run through the onboarding improvement objectives and explain how strategic onboarding can make a big difference:

- *Knowledge transfer.* Today a lot of enterprise value is derived from the knowledge of existing employees. Firms widely recognize employee know-how as a company asset, even if it doesn't appear on the balance sheet. Many companies have invested a lot in trying to distill employee know-how into a formal knowledge management system. When an employee transfers out of a position or leaves the company altogether, knowledge loss always occurs. New hires represent a great and unique opportunity to transfer the most important knowledge of the enterprise to the future workforce and future leaders. This issue is even more pronounced given that a large number of experienced Baby Boomer employees will soon retire. Strategic onboarding helps by offering mentor and apprentice programs, and developing and engineering the significant relationships that new hires require to learn from veteran employees, thus creating an effective knowledge transfer program.

- *Engagement levels.* Employee engagement[2] is critical for any labor-dependent business. In fact, engagement affects several of the business impacts on the right side of Table 1.1 — most notably time to productivity, level of productivity, level of attrition, and attrition mix. High performers and "high prospects" who are not sufficiently engaged operate at mediocre levels and soon begin a job search. Ironically, low performers (or low prospects) also maintain mediocre output levels, but unfortunately they are more likely to stay on the job. Both of these are terrible outcomes for the organization. A study of professional services firms found that offices with engaged workers were over 40% more productive.[3] Other studies have found that engaged workers are more customer-focused and profitable, and less likely to leave their employer. As shown later in this book, strategic onboarding fosters engagement by helping new hires get excited about their work, their career prospects, and the enterprise's mission.

- *Employment brand.* All companies have employment brands in the minds of current and prospective employees, recruiters, and career counselors. Sometimes these brands are more pronounced and positive, as in the case of firms who win "best place to work" awards. If you've engineered a system that produces more positive experiences more often, the message will get out. A firm's reputation will improve, making future prospects easier to identify and cheaper to recruit. Moreover, you will attract the kinds of new hires that your firm desires; that is, those attracted by the specific cultural and performance values your brand conveys. Negative experiences produce the opposite result by eroding the firm's employment brand through negative word of mouth.

- *Automation and standardization.* We estimate that 80% or more of medium and large businesses have onboarding processes that are tedious and paper based, require multiple steps of manual administration, are deployed across the enterprise in inconsistent ways, lead to haphazard and wasteful outcomes, inefficiently deploy resources challenging new hire readiness, and create frustrating experiences for new hires and hiring managers. Software can make this a more pleasant and lower-cost experience for everyone involved.

- *Consistency of experience.* Many companies with existing, piecemeal programs possess pockets of excellence around onboarding, whether in specific functional areas, specific locations, or other organizational units. A strategic approach determines and applies best practices across every part of the enterprise that brings in new hires. It helps firms avoid the bitterness that arises when some employees enter smoothly, while others have less positive experiences. In Columbia, South Carolina, The Sisters of Charity Providence Hospitals, has vastly improved its onboarding by standardizing its orientation program.

Retention rates for new nurses rose from 78.2% in 2005 to 86.1% in 2007, whereas the retention rate for new graduates rose from 60 to 94%.[4]

- *Accountability—roles and responsibility.* Too many onboarding systems flounder because stakeholders do not know what role they have in the system, they are not provided sufficient guidance and support, and nobody is holding them accountable for fulfilling their responsibilities. Strategic onboarding programs perform better because clear delineation of roles and accountability for performance is baked in. Systems are established to provide support at the right moments, using the right tools.

- *Organizational transformation (business and/or cultural).* One of the most exciting and strategic long-term business results an onboarding program can provide involves organizational transformation. Given the high rate of employee-based renewal, a fantastic opportunity exists to transform a business by enlisting new hires in a mission of change—either business change (e.g., entering a new channel or a new business) or a cultural change (e.g., a new way of behaving). New hires need to know that their firm is enlisting them as change agents; otherwise, they'll think that company veterans have bought into the change, although in many instances they have not. New hires also need to understand the organizational benefits of change and why change presents both a challenge and a thrilling journey for them. When a strategic onboarding program properly mobilizes new hires as a force for change, the impact on a firm's bottom line can be profound—certainly far more significant than the one-off cost savings that many firms now mistake as onboarding's basic benefit.

- *Other/unique to organizations and circumstances.* All firms are unique. Because a strategic program design includes a comprehensive diagnostic phase (detailed in Chapter 8), your company will have a chance to discover improvement objectives that are unique to you and that comprise big opportunities for the organization.

Knowledge Transfer: The Case of Reliance Industries, Nagothane Manufacturing Division (India)

To hasten the learning speed of new engineers at its chemical plants, Nagothane trained fifty-one mentors and embedded them with younger engineers for periods as long as nine months. The firm matched mentors and protégés based on the compatibility of their respective training and learning styles. Employees noted their progress on an online portal monitored by senior executives. The result: Time-to-readiness has plummeted from a year to six months. Nagothane also supports a separate online learning portal on which employees can report lessons learned as a result of their experiences. On one occasion, knowledge shared on this $60,000 portal allowed the company to avoid a plant shutdown, saving it $4.3 million.

Source: ASTD 2008 BEST Award. *T+D*, October 2008.

Now that we've looked at some key improvement objectives for effective onboarding programs, let's briefly consider some of the business impacts firms can see when these objectives are realized. Figure 1.2 has already evoked the kinds of substantial productivity gains strategic onboarding can bring. Productivity is critical—and we'll spend more time exploring it in a minute—but there is a lot more to achieve. With a strategic program in place, firms find themselves better able to meet human capital demands to realize their business plan. Attrition improves (in both level and mix). Labor and recruiting costs also diminish, as do onboarding administration costs. Of course, business impacts don't correspond one-to-one with the program objectives; many objectives, once attained, can lead to several positive business outcomes, and business outcomes can in turn arise out of the attainment of many of the program objectives listed on the above Table 1.1.

Onboarding and Enhanced Productivity: A Closer Look

Although well-designed onboarding programs have many components and objectives, optimal programs have one leading goal in mind: to maximize the productivity of an organization's employees. In this way they contribute to an organization's bottom line. Improving output per employee maximizes the revenues created by or operating costs reduced by each employee, while minimizing the cost of employing these value-creating strategies. This section provides a framework for analyzing productivity and understanding the impact onboarding can have.

Onboarding drives productivity by serving as a multiplier of the key variables that contribute to employee output. Let's first define these variables and describe how they come together to yield output. We developed the following expression to describe employee output—or New Hire Contribution—as a function of four primary elements:

$$\text{New Hire Contribution} = \text{Capability} + \text{Context} + \text{Connectedness} + \text{Drive}$$

Capability is a combination of an individual's intelligence and skills, including the capacity to develop and improve on these traits. *Context* is an individual's understanding of his or her organization, business, industry, etc., based on an accurate education and experience base. *Connectedness* represents an individual's internal and external relationships to the organization that are relevant to the business, function, and role of the new hire. Finally *Drive*, in simple terms, is the employee's level of pursuit of excellence.

Let's examine *Capability* a little more closely. Although individuals are born with a level of innate intelligence and have valuable natural or developed skills, there is substantial room to develop both of these traits through continued development and encouragement. The capacity to develop know-how and skill, therefore, may be just as important, if not more, than an individual's innate level of both traits.

Context is the variable that may be most often taken for granted, but it is crucial to bringing together the other three in a way that drives significant New Hire Contribution. Understanding the organization means much more than knowing who runs it and what it does. It is a deeper comprehension or mastery of the organization's mission and goals, the strategy that has been set to get there, the competitive and regulatory landscape, the customers and their needs, the resources available, the business model the firm employs to execute on the strategy, and the firm's culture and way of doing business and driving change. When employees truly understand the organization, they can act most fully as agents of the organization's mission and not simply complete tasks assigned to them. With the right Context, employees can step up beyond their defined role, title, age, and experience level to add more value to an organization than originally expected or planned. The period early in an employee's life cycle with a given organization can be more significant, but the chance for success radically decreases without sufficient context. The key is to provide context that will allow the employee to use his or her capabilities, connections, and drive to deliver the very best possible results.

Experiential understanding includes all of the contextual knowledge gained during a lifetime in and out of the profession. The more an individual understands about the realm in which the organization operates, whether in a certain market, industry, region, and so on, the more value that individual can add to the organization. This is not to say that experiential understanding is necessarily measured in years of life or work experience. We gain experiences and worldly knowledge through research, specialized learning experiences, or, in the modern age, through being a curious individual with an Internet connection.

Our *Connectedness* in the business environment affects our ability to get things done more quickly and to a higher standard. The personal and professional relationships we have provide us with leverage under certain circumstances, such as when we are looking for a job. According to the US Bureau of Labor Statistics, about 70% of jobs are found though networking.[5] The more connected we are (in terms of both number and quality), the better the job search outcomes will be. The same applies in professional endeavors. When a situation arises, a new task is assigned or an unfamiliar request is made, a new hire who has many connections (and understands the relative value and area of subject matter expertise) can reach to his or her network to get perspective and assistance rather than working from scratch to determine the optimal solution. Strategic onboarding can increase the number and quality of connections both within and beyond the organization.

Drive is the combination of ambition, entrepreneurialism, and attachment to the enterprise. Ambition provides the energy for an individual to pursue excellence in everything he or she does. Entrepreneurialism provides the grittiness, the willingness to sacrifice and push and the necessary creativity to create efficient and effective answers. Attachment represents the degree to which the individual cares and is motivated to perform for the organization's benefit. The greater that each of these factors is for a given new hire, the greater the net new hire contribution over the short, medium, and long terms.

These four variables—Capability, Context, Connectedness, and Drive— together influence the result of the New Hire Contribution (NHC) or productivity. As the preceding equation indicates, we can think of adding up an individual's unique blend of Capability, Context, Connectedness, and Drive to arrive at his or her potential New Hire Contribution. Conceptually it would even be possible to score an individual in each of these variables on a scale of, let's say, 1 to 10, and come out with an overall NHC "score." In this case, a maximum score of 40 (10 + 10 + 10 + 10) would represent the super employee, one who could add the maximum potential value to a given organization. We should note that our equation for New Hire Contribution purposely excludes the issue of resources (e.g., size of team, budget, tools, etc.) made available to an employee. For the purpose of discussing managing new hire potential in the context of onboarding, we treat all things as equal with regard to level of resources.

Mathematically, the lowest possible score would be a 4 using this scale. However, most recruiting organizations screen for individuals who have a minimum level of capability and drive (let's hope so anyway). Thus, even the most inexperienced of new hires for a moderate position would join the organization with, for discussion sake, an NHC of "10" (4 each for capability and drive, and 1 each for context and connection). Our expectation is that once the individual starts work, the organization can influence all four of these factors to raise the NHC.

Take another example. Perhaps your organization hires an individual with a couple of years of experience in the industry who meets Recruiting's minimal requirements for capability and drive as discussed. Because the individual comes from the industry, it is reasonable to expect that he or she has some Context and Connectedness (i.e., contacts) that may be valuable in the new position. Together, this may warrant a score of 4 in all four categories, yielding an overall NHC of 16. This represents a 60% increase in new hire contribution from the "base case" inexperienced employee discussed previously. Whether or not the "perfect" NHC score exists (or you have had the great pleasure of working with a new hire who achieves one) is beyond the point of this text, but you can play with this model and think about your existing employees and the candidates in your recruiting pipeline and see how their differences in capability, context, connectedness, and drive result in different NHC scores.

We've discussed New Hire Contribution, but how exactly can your onboarding program impact it? Chapter 2 shows that a strategically designed program encompasses a multitude of *elements*, including engagement and networking, effective training modules for teaching culture and strategy, mentoring programs, early career development programs, and much more. Each of the onboarding program elements acts as a contributing force for at least one, if not several or all, of the four factors that make up NHC. We refer to the combined effects of the onboarding elements together as the Onboarding Multiplier. The equation that follows summarizes these effects.

The Onboarding Margin New Hire Contribution =
(Onboarding Multiplier) × (Capability +
Context + Connectedness + Drive)

The elements of an onboarding program, represented in the Onboarding Multiplier, therefore, enhance the core variables of New Hire Contribution. Onboarding elements can in fact significantly affect the score an individual would receive in each of the four NHC variables by providing stronger opportunities to develop in each of those areas when compared with a run of the mill or nonexistent onboarding program. Let's take a look at how the different elements of an onboarding program can affect the NHC. A strategically designed mentoring program that engages new hires from Day One or earlier can pump up all four NHC variables: Capability (mentors often provide informal training and skill development); Context (mentors help ramp up new hires to the organization's culture, mission, business model, and strategy); Connectedness (mentors often provide networking opportunities to new hires by offering to arrange meetings with individuals within their own network); and Drive (mentors can assist new hires in identifying stretch roles and other opportunities to drive motivation). Formalized networking events, however, may affect on three variables: through networking with more tenured employees a new hire gains more context to the organization's mission and strategy; networking clearly impacts one's connectedness; and one may argue that networking can have a positive impact on drive, if a new hire engages with individuals that get him or her more excited about career prospects. As all onboarding elements have varying degrees of impact on the overall NHC, a well-designed diagnostic (as discussed in Chapter 8) will identify for you which elements will ultimately have the highest impact.

Employing basic algebra, what we have now is a way to describe the effect that onboarding programs can have on NHC. Taking together the onboarding elements referenced above, we can speak of a single "onboarding multiplier."

A successful onboarding program adds value by multiplying the Onboarding Multiplier by the four key variables a new hire brings to the organization. It must be acknowledged that at least some of the employee output variables would develop naturally over time even in the absence of high-quality onboarding. For example, an individual's contextual knowledge will increase as he or she spends more time at the organization regardless of any formal onboarding program. However, a strategically designed onboarding program will begin to act as a multiplier or accelerator that greatly improves the outcome.

Let's assign the Onboarding Multiplier a "standard" value of 1. This is the value of a run of the mill onboarding program. Each element of the Onboarding Multiplier, therefore, also has a standard value of one. The better an onboarding program is designed, the greater the value those multiples can achieve. Is it possible to take an average mentoring program and turn it from a 1 into a 50? Probably not. But even a 20% increase in quality (in other words, a multiplier of 1.2), can substantially affect an individual worker's output because of the multiplying effect of the Onboarding Multiplier.

The Onboarding Multiplier does not always impact *positively* on an individual's NHC variables or the overall employee output ranking itself. Poorly designed onboarding programs (or well-designed programs executed poorly) can *detract* from an individual's capability, drive, connectedness, or context and in turn *decrease* the individual's overall New Hire Contribution. Imagine that a new hire is immediately placed on a long-term and unique project with few other colleagues and no initiatives or programs in place to engage the individual. It would be very difficult for this new hire to develop a connection to, and engagement with, the firm he or she has just joined. This would undoubtedly result in a decrease in connectedness and possibly in drive, leading to an overall reduction in output. If you value the productivity of your new hires, it's that much more critical to examine your onboarding practices through a strategic and strategic lens to avoid negative results.

Remaking the New Hire Employer–Employee Compact

So far we have made a business case for strategic onboarding by focusing on the direct benefits an onboarding program provides to the enterprise. Yet onboarding offers employees concrete benefits as well. When we look at it from an employee's perspective, we realize that a solid program holds the potential to fundamentally remake the compact between employees and their organizations. This compact, the mutual agreement between employer and employee, has already changed in recent years—and not necessarily for the better. Employees are now asked to work harder, smarter, longer hours and give up cherished long-term benefits. The promise of "lifetime employment" has also been shattered. Employees today are far less loyal. As one study has shown, younger workers will change jobs an average of ten times before they turn forty.[6] Onboarding allows you to remake the compact between employer and employee in a way that makes employees more fulfilled and that allows firms to realize increased engagement, retention, and productivity. We believe that onboarding presents an exciting opportunity for a firm to think differently and make an explicit promise and then deliver more value to the new hire beyond a resume line item and a paycheck.

Onboarding benefits employees in the first instance by giving them the tools they need to succeed and grow into more fulfilling careers. When effectively onboarded, employees gain new skills better and faster, securing their job and job prospect, moving up the ladder, and growing financially at a quicker clip. Doors open as employees' skills improve and relationships develop, both inside and outside the firm. Employees are able to move more quickly from positions that don't necessarily excite them to ones that do. If new hires enter a top company in the finance department because of their accounting degrees, onboarding might help them gain confidence that this company will offer a better chance of navigating toward their true aspiration of, say, running a part of the company. It allows them to become aware of the skills they need to develop, provides the network connections they need, communicates an understanding of the overall organization and how it makes money—all this allowing them to make the right choices to take themselves where they want to and have the capability to go.

Beyond providing skills, Strategic Onboarding helps employees by inspiring them and giving them the appropriate sense that they are performing meaningful work. Most workers today want more than a paycheck. They want to be happy at work, realize a great future, and feel connected to something bigger. Onboarding's strategic piece helps new hires connect their own work with the organization's larger objectives. If you define your job as a customer service representative in terms of how many calls you take, it can only be so interesting. By contrast, if the CEO gets you excited to be part of an organization whose mission it is to help customers and drive profits, then your job has meaning above and beyond its purely functional elements. You are not just another worker in the factory building; you are the agent of the brand. You become more satisfied with this entry position, and your engagement improves right out of the gate. And if you continue to receive experiences that reinforce the vision and your future, you are far more inclined to stay at the job and work more productively.

We crossed paths with a recent ivy-league finance graduate who, thanks to a poor economy, was working retail for a top fashion brand. She had a job on Madison Avenue, but she was unhappy as a floor salesperson. This woman said she couldn't imagine ever entering the corporate side from her current position as a clerk in the retail division. She was looking for a better job of any kind. From our perspective, this woman held the potential to become a classic success story—the smart employee who starts on the retail floor and works her way up. Unfortunately, she couldn't conceive of how her current job folding shirts and straightening the dressing room could ever lead to a fulfilling career with the company. Many customers that she interfaced with were demanding and obnoxious, and nothing about the job stimulated her intellectually. If delivered correctly, onboarding could engage this woman, open her eyes to career paths within the company, and get her excited about the role she plays on the front line delivering the brand to consumers. As part of a strategic program, management could inspire her by connecting her work to the larger mission. It could stimulate her to deliver a superior experience by showing her profiles of people who entered this company at the same very level and today hold senior executive positions in every core function of the enterprise. Would she fully buy in? We can't tell you for sure, but we can tell you that some numbers of her peers would, and that the outcome would be tremendous for the company.

Let's look at a contrasting example—that of Apple's retail division. The tech support personnel at Apple's retail stores—called "Geniuses"—offer a highly differentiated and (and some say) superior customer experience in support of Apple's brand and products. Geniuses seem to know almost everything about the products and associated problems, and they patiently and enthusiastically help resolve customer problems, on occasion even going the extra mile and fixing items for free. It is largely seen as a contrast in expectations (both of consumers as well as business students) given the general perception that a tech guru is not likely to be the same kind of person who may hold excellent interpersonal skills and make wise business decisions in real time when interfacing with customers. How do the Geniuses get so good? Exceptional onboarding. From conversations with individual Geniuses, we learned that prospective Geniuses who have proven their technical prowess must first make the grade by working at an Apple store for a month out on the retail floor to get a feel for consumer interaction. Prospective Geniuses are then flown to Apple's headquarters for a full month of training, all expenses paid. The first two weeks involve intense classroom work, followed by a week of self-study and a week of testing. Upon their return, Geniuses are made to shadow other Geniuses and establish formal relationships with mentors before being allowed to proceed with their jobs. It's a huge investment for retail, but it produces employees who are unusually passionate about their jobs, expressive of Apple's brand, and appreciative of Apple's investment in their success.

The Needs of a New Hire

Let's take a more methodical look at employee needs and the ability of strategic onboarding to meet those needs. The psychologist Abraham Maslow described in his 1943 paper, A *Theory of Human Motivation,* a hierarchy of human needs (Figure 1.3), starting from base physiological needs and extending upward through safety, love/belonging, esteem, and full self-actualization. The overarching premise of the model is that individuals start at the bottom and really only pay attention to the next level of needs (higher up the pyramid) once they satisfy the ones on the current level. Maslow's hierarchy helps guide our thinking about employees. Corresponding to bottom-level physiological needs are the employee's need for financial resources in the form of compensation—the paycheck that allows us to eat, live with a roof over our heads, and achieve a lifestyle that increases our chances of attracting a mate. Of course, this is the need that recruiting, not onboarding, fulfills for a new hire. Thanks to a firm's recruiting function, employees have their most basic physical requirements met; they're able to survive. But this is where Recruiting's ability to fill employees' needs ends.

Once employees enjoy a steady income, they naturally become concerned with keeping it—an imperative that corresponds to "safety" or security on Maslow's hierarchy of needs. New hires need to feel reassured that their livelihood will remain intact, the company will remain healthy, their function won't be outsourced, and they possess the basic skills required to remain in the organization. New hires also need to feel like they understand the firm's culture well enough so that they won't make any career-limiting gaffes, like ordering a drink at a business lunch (or not

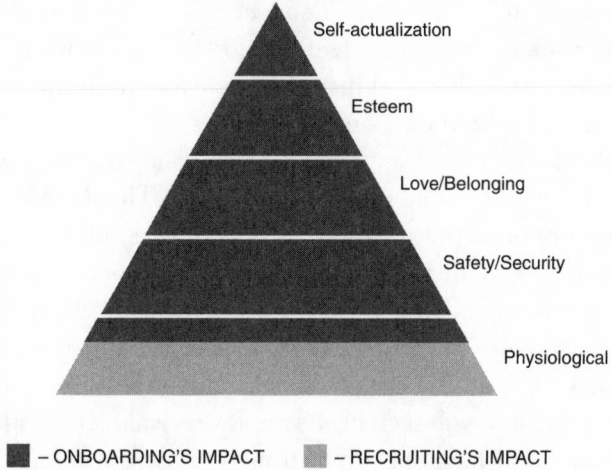

Figure 1.3 labels (top to bottom): Self-actualization, Esteem, Love/Belonging, Safety/Security, Physiological

▓ – ONBOARDING'S IMPACT   ▒ – RECRUITING'S IMPACT

Figure 1.3 Potential of Recruiting and Onboarding to Satisfy Maslow's Hierarchy of Needs

ordering a drink), or advocating an idea too stridently. As will be seen in subsequent chapters, onboarding gives employees the skills, knowledge, personal relationships, and cultural awareness to achieve a level of security in an organization.

Onboarding also provides employees with a sense of "fitting in" at work, corresponding to what Maslow sees as the third-level human need for love and belonging. Onboarding's interpersonal network development element gives employees a head start in making friends and allies within a firm. Onboarding also helps employees build relationships by giving them the skills they need to do their jobs well. When employees perform sooner and at a higher level than their bosses and peers expected—when they stay longer than the average employee and take the company's mission as their own—their colleagues, bosses, and the company as a whole take notice and begin to "love" them. It may sound strange to speak about love in the context of managing human capital in an organization, but *every* executive we speak with quickly speaks about the junior employees they have worked with over the years with whom they just "loved" because of their strengths as an employee. Some hiring managers claim—tongue in cheek—that finding an employee you love in this context is as hard or harder than finding romantic love. In a workplace setting, "love" translates into an ability to have open, frank conversations with bosses and peers, among other things. New hires feel comfortable to say what they really think, and as a result, they find themselves pleasantly affirmed, validated, and appreciated for their own unique qualities.

Such validation leads directly to a next level called esteem—self-esteem, achievement, respect of others, respect by others. Thanks to relationships built because of onboarding, and thanks, too, to employees' abilities to function both at higher levels and as authentic members of a community, new hires are positioned to feel great. If we give people more tools to succeed better early on—if they understand the culture, have the requisite skills, and have a chance to impress others—their sense of self-worth (and therefore satisfaction) will skyrocket. Employees will feel proud to work at their firms and will likely become strong evangelists for corporate and employment brands.

Onboarding's components that teach strategy also play an important role here. To the extent that companies can change employees' perceptions of their jobs from a functional description to one that contains a sense of mission that "I am excited to be part of this," companies will dramatically enhance employee self-esteem. The recruiting process already does try to inspire new hires, but onboarding must reinforce this idea, in ways both large and small, during the first year and beyond. Think, for instance, how uninspiring it is to arrive at a new job only to spend the first day or two filling out forms, completing compliance materials, and taking care of other boring administrative tasks. New hires in this situation take nothing away from that first day that helps them regard the company as the best in the world. These new hires will not feel especially great about themselves ("We are what we do."), which in turn will affect engagement levels, and ultimately, job performance. With a dynamic strategy in place, we can craft the new hire's initial entry into the firm to be far more inspirational, leading to higher productivity from Day One, or even earlier.

Once employees feel high self-esteem, they are in a position to satisfy the highest-level need, self-actualization. Strategic onboarding helps further nourish self-actualization in part by providing early career support that maps out fulfilling, enriching careers as well as tools to help get new hires on their way. Onboarding's strategic immersion and development components again prove helpful, too. As new hires become more connected to what an organization does and its broader mission, they develop a feeling of purpose and direction. They start to equate their own personal success with that of the organization, creating a positive dynamic that benefits all parties to the employment compact.

It's interesting: Many companies today are guilty not so much of ignoring employees' needs for self-actualization, but rather of overpromising and underdelivering against those needs. Recruiting machines at large corporations often hype up the sales pitch for these firms, enticing new hires with visions of meaningful, satisfying work that later prove too good to be true. A service company's recruiting video, for instance, may excessively glamorize lower-level service positions, making the teller position look like mission control in a space shuttle and the customer service position like Mother Teresa. (Yes, videos like this do exist.) This company has probably delivered on the lower four levels of employee need, but the job is still a job, and there's a great chance that new hires will come away disillusioned from this video. Other companies make similar promises and deliver far less to employees than this company does. At these firms, employees quickly become cynical and unhappy.

Companies with powerful and positive consumer brands need to be especially aware and vigilant on this point (delivering against expectations), because many new employees arrive at their employer only to discover that the consumer brand is at odds with the firm's employment and operating brand. Apple's consumer brand is suffused with user friendliness, for instance, whereas Apple's headquarters and development culture is known to be quite intense. To assure the best, most fulfilling workplace experience for new hires, and maximize productivity gains for the firm, the recruiting engine and ultimately hiring managers need to convey realistic information about the job, the firm's culture, and the extent to which employees can hope to realize self-actualization as they define it.

Even the best onboarding program will rarely assist the new hire in achieving self-actualization during the first year on the job. But new hires will be on quicker paths to self-actualization, and more importantly, they'll come to believe in the course of the first year that their new employer can deliver far up the Maslow pyramid. As a result, employees will be more inclined to feel that the firm is the place for them over the short and the long term, leading them to *give* more of themselves. Managers seeking to affect organizational change thus need to figure out how to help people chart a path toward the achievement of their overall needs. To help an organization move toward success, managers must articulate *customized* paths toward employee self-fulfillment that take into account the unique strategies, visions, and organizational capacities that individual firms adopt.

Summing Up

Onboarding today remains relatively new, little known, and underappreciated. To help encourage firms to make the investment, this chapter has sought to convince organizational leaders and operational managers that onboarding is well worth a company's time, energy, and dollars. It has been argued that such programs can deliver astonishing value in an area of the business where none was thought to exist. Onboarding isn't just about delivering efficiencies in a traditional orientation process; rather, by going well beyond orientation and striving to meet new hires' needs throughout the entire first year of their tenure, strategic onboarding can deliver clear improvements across a variety of metrics. These improvements add up, measurably affecting firms where it counts—the bottom line.

That's not to say that onboarding will improve your company's retention or other metrics by 50% or 60%. Rather, the gains to expect are in the neighborhood of two to six percentage points, say from 10% to 8% or 4%. Yet these gains wind up giving firms a perceptible boost in financial measures such as revenue, cost, net income, or market capitalization—as detailed in an analysis in this chapter's appendix. They place onboarding on par with lean manufacturing, innovation, focus on core competencies, outsourcing and other progressive disciplines that over the past 20 years have helped companies run better, compete, and create new value. Just as these disciplines have boosted broader economic performance, so too might onboarding. Also consider its prospective importance given that today we are competing on the back of human capital, not manufacturing capital.

In some ways, it makes more sense for firms to invest in onboarding going forward than it does in these other value-creating disciplines.

Proficiency at innovation has proved lucrative for many firms, but it's awfully hard to become the next Apple. With onboarding, you don't need a lot of new technology. Simply roll up your sleeves and become more thoughtful about the way your firm incorporates its new talent, and you can help your firm uncover vast stores of previously hidden value.

Given all that onboarding has to offer, here is a final argument for the leader who's still dubious about changing the way his or her firm incorporates new hires: The competition probably is not yet doing onboarding well, so an opportunity exists to create competitive advantage. Firms that act early will hold a unique weapon in the battle for high-potential labor. Prospects are always more inclined to work at a firm that's regarded as a superior place to build a career, and a strong onboarding program will stimulate that impression by helping new hires build better careers. Firms that hasten to embrace strategic programs will also realize earlier productivity gains, generating profits that they can in turn reinvest to assure even greater value-creation going forward.

We've just added up the great value strategic onboarding can deliver, but we have yet to explore exactly what strategic onboarding entails and how the various elements working together can help deliver the Onboarding Margin. This is the work of the next chapter. If you opened this book thinking state-of-the-art onboarding is just a standard orientation made better, perhaps by a new software program, cleaning up an administrative mess, or a few extra hours or days of initial training, then you are in for a pleasant surprise.

Appendix: An Economic Analysis of the Onboarding Margin

We wanted to test widely the economic impact the Onboarding Margin might have on various companies if onboarding was adopted successfully. We created a model based on a conservative set of assumptions, testing across a wide set of companies to measure impact on attrition, productivity, profitability, and ultimately total shareholder return—in the form of market capitalization. Ours is not a perfect analysis, but it displays—albeit directionally—what is at stake for operating entities.

We started with six industries and representative companies from each (relying on publically traded companies for ease of access to necessary data), as follows:

- Aerospace & Defense: Boeing, Lockheed Martin, Honeywell International, Northrop Grumman
- Energy & Utilities: Exxon Mobil, Chevron, Constellation Energy, Halliburton
- Financial Services: Bank of America Corporation, Citigroup, Franklin Resources, Goldman Sachs
- Healthcare: UnitedHealth Group, WellPoint, McKesson, Medtronic, Johnson & Johnson
- Technology & Telecom: Cisco Systems, Google, IBM, AT&T
- Consumer Packaged Goods: PepsiCo, Kraft Foods, Procter & Gamble, Coca-Cola

These companies were all selected for their size and representative nature by someone outside of our Organization Development and Onboarding practice; that way, we could ensure a lack of bias with regard to any knowledge of these companies' current state of onboarding. All of these companies were treated equally with regard to the assumptions about potential impact, irrespective of any knowledge that we had on the current state of their onboarding efforts. The objective was to build and test a broadly applicable model, not to pass judgment on the performance or impact of any particular company.

Onboarding Margin: Attrition Effects

Our next step was to determine the hypothetical impact suboptimal onboarding might be having today on the overall economic performance of the businesses. We started with the current cost of attrition. To calculate the cost of total attrition for an organization, we applied some common numbers by industry for average attrition levels. Aerospace and Defense, 12%; Energy and Utilities, 15%; Financial Services, 15%; Healthcare, 12%; Technology and Telecom, 15%; Consumer Packaged Goods, 10%. Next we determined the total number of individuals leaving each benchmark company a year. Given the current economic condition at the time of the analysis, we assumed 0% net company growth in revenue and head count. Consequently, we assumed that the number of employees entering a company in a given year was equal to the number of employees leaving. Next we needed to determine the average cost for a new employee at each company. To do so, we started with the median salary per company. We used external research databases of salaries to find median salary for employees at different levels. Once salaries for each level within a benchmarked company were determined, we removed positions and salaries that were outliers so to avoid skewing results. The median salary by industry was as follows:

- Aerospace & Defense: $75,016
- Energy & Utilities: $81,047
- Financial Services: $75,744
- Healthcare: $69,644
- Technology & Telecom: $80,368
- Consumer Packaged Goods & Retail: $53,410

Although average salary rates can help determine the cost of a new employee, it was necessary to include a factor for recruiting costs. This factor includes HR costs of looking for new employees, temporary replacement fees, headhunters, paying a leaving employee for remaining vacation days, etc. Although many sources cite 1.4 times salary cost as a figure for employee replacement, we applied a more conservative factor of 0.75 times salary per employee.

With these inputs, the following calculation was performed to arrive at the annual cost for the benchmark companies within an industry: (# of employees that attrit) × (average salary) × (recruiting costs factor of 0.75). These numbers were then applied against a ratio for each industry to reflect the fact that the benchmark companies only reflected a percentage of the actual sectors being examined. Once applied to the larger and complete industry as represented by all of the companies in the industries, the total annual cost of attrition—purely for replacement cost purposes—was as follows:

- Aerospace & Defense: $5.8B
- Energy & Utilities: $3.1B
- Financial Services: $90.7B
- Healthcare: $11.3B

- Technology & Telecom: $7.3B
- Consumer Packaged Goods & Retail: $2.8B

These are pretty astonishing numbers. Yet we were not finished. Although these figures reflect current attrition rates, we wondered what could happen if onboarding could reasonably help attrition. How much would industries actually save?

To quantify the potential savings of a robust Onboarding program, we assumed that attrition rates would drop to current industry best-in-class standards. Note that we were not pushing the envelope far here. We were not asking for attrition levels to redefine themselves in any seismic way; rather, we were assuming a scenario in which best in class results became the norm. Based on secondary research, we assumed the following best-in-class attrition rates for the following industries:

- Aerospace & Defense: 10% (vs. 12% previously)
- Energy & Utilities: 10% (vs. 15% previously)
- Financial Services: 10% (vs. 15% previously)
- Healthcare: 9% (vs. 12% previously)
- Technology & Telecom: 10% (vs. 15% previously)
- Consumer Packaged Goods & Retail: 8% (vs. 10% previously)

Applying these new best-in-class attrition rates to the same cost of attrition calculations preformed for current attrition rates, we determined that the cost of attrition with a robust Onboarding program would offer significant cost savings. By industry, the cost savings potential was as follows:

- Aerospace & Defense: $973M (total cost of $4.7B vs. $5.8B previously)
- Energy & Utilities: $1.0B (total cost of $2.1B vs. $3.1B previously)
- Financial Services: $30B (total cost of $60.5 vs. $90.7B previously)
- Healthcare: $2.8B (total cost of $8.4B vs. $11.3B previously)
- Technology & Telecom: $2.4B (total cost of $4.9B vs. $7.3B previously)
- Consumer Packaged Goods & Retail: $568M (total cost of $2.3B vs. $2.8B previously)

The next thing we looked at was attrition mix—regrettable versus non-regrettable, because as we have discussed, not all attrition is created equal. Although the potential cost savings for lowering general attrition rates through onboarding is compelling, the figure is just that—very general. With this in mind, we set out to determine the cost of "regrettable" and "non-regrettable" attrition under current and best-in-class attrition models. Under current attrition rates, we assumed that 65% of attrition was regrettable (we were sorry to see them leave), and 35% was non-regrettable (we were happy to see them leave). Under this model, the breakdown of regrettable vs. non-regrettable attrition under *current* conditions was the following:

- Aerospace & Defense: $3.8B regrettable vs. $2B non-regrettable
- Energy & Utilities: $2B regrettable vs. $1.1B non-regrettable
- Financial Services: $59B regrettable vs. $31.8B non-regrettable
- Healthcare: $7.3B regrettable vs. $3.9B non-regrettable
- Technology & Telecom: $4.7 regrettable vs. $2.5B non-regrettable
- Consumer Packaged Goods & Retail: $1.8B regrettable vs. $1B non-regrettable

Having broken down current cost of attrition by regrettable and non-regrettable rates, the next step was to find how these costs would be impacted under a best-in-class attrition mix scenario. We assumed that attrition would shift from a 35% non-regrettable/65% regrettable ratio under the "current model" to a 65% non-regrettable/35% regrettable ratio under a best-in-class model. The results are shown in Table 1.2.

Table 1.2 Cost Savings Attributable to Favorable Attrition Mix

Industry	Current State Cost of Regrettable Attrition	Best-in-Class Cost of Regrettable Attrition	Potential Regrettable Cost Savings
A&D Industry	$3.8B	$1.7B	$2.1B
Energy & Utilities Industry	$2B	$718M	$1.3B
Financial Services Industry	$59B	$21.2B	$37.8B
Healthcare Industry	$7.3B	$3B	$4.3B
Tech & Telecom Industry	$4.7B	$1.7B	$3B
CPG & Retail Industry	$1.8B	$794M	$1.05B

Onboarding Margin: Productivity Effects

Now we wanted to move on to the productivity opportunity. We assumed that 90% of new hires were retained into their second year. Additionally, based on extensive secondary research, we found it reasonable to assume that 25% of retained employees were operating at an average of 50% optimal productivity levels. Although other sources suggest that a far larger percentage of retained new hires operate at lower productivity rates, we selected a lower percentage to arrive at a more conservative calculation. Then we assumed that the remaining 75% of second-year new hires were operating at the maximum productivity level (100%). Again, the idea that this many (75%) new hires are operating at 100% productivity in year two appears conservative by all accounts from our experience or feedback.

Now comes the thoughtful but tricky part. Because the objective of every employee is to help produce company profit, we took the profit of each benchmark company and calculated the contribution to profit for the average employee (using total head count). Then we calculated the prospective impact of each of the retained second-year employees (25% of the 90%) who were operating at less than 100% productivity, *and imagined what would happen if they had actually been operating at 100% productivity.* This bump added to the current net profit of a company yields the potential net profit bump. When applied to at the industry level, the net profit increase potential is significant (Table 1.3).

Table 1.3 Profit Potential Attributable to Higher Productivity Levels

Industry	Current Industry Net Profit	Industry Net Profit Potential w/100% "Productive" Employees	Industry NP Increase Potential (Delta)
A&D Industry	$15.4B	$15.6B	$210M
Energy & Utilities Industry	$80.6B	$82.0B	$1.4B
Financial Services Industry	$88.6B	$90.1B	$1.5B
Healthcare Industry	$49.2B	$49.8B	$673M
Tech & Telecom Industry	$40.7B	$41.4B	$698M
CPG & Retail Industry	$36.5B	$39.9B	$415M

Onboarding Margin: Combined Effects of Attrition and Productivity

To make this analysis even more fun, we looked to see what these combined numbers (attrition impact and productivity impact) would yield to investors in terms of market value (as measured by market capitalization). We applied traditional industry-specific stock price to earnings ratios (P/E) ratios as compiled by NYU's Stern Business School as follows: Aerospace and Defense 14.6; Energy and Utilities 24.51; Financial Services 13.08; Healthcare 28.36; Technology and Telecom 33.32; and Consumer Packaged Goods 23.50. Based on these historical P/E ratios, the impact to average stock price gain was as follows:

- Aerospace & Defense: +15% or +$34B in additional market cap for the sector
- Energy & Utilities: +3% or +$65B in additional market cap for the sector
- Financial Services: +44% or +$514B in additional market cap for the sector
- Healthcare: +22% or $278B in additional market cap for the sector
- Technology & Telecom: +23% or $280B in additional market cap for the sector
- Consumer Packaged Goods & Retail: +4% or $34B in additional market cap for the sector

Recognizing that we did not have a perfect sample by any means and that the analysis was applied to a given year (and that profit changes year to year for a whole host of reasons), we simplified further and determined an average prospective impact of 19% (the simple average of the prospective six rates of stock price improvements noted). Just to be on the safe side, we cut this answer in half, bringing us down to ~9%. Then we did the same again—knocking this number in half, bringing it down to 4.5%. We asked respected HR leaders from large corporations what would happen to their career if they took an action that resulted in their company's total value going up by 4.5%. (Don't forget, these market caps are really large numbers.) Each and every person offered the same response: A *wonderfully big smile.*

Cautionary Comments

- Please note that the calculations for a given industry are not numbers with which you should run to your colleagues. We feel far more comfortable talking about the average impact across industries than we do speaking about impact for a given industry—given all of the year-to-year variables at play.

- Our analysis on market cap excluded the impact of improvement in time to productivity (Gain 1) and raising the overall average level of productivity (Gain 2) of your new hires, which is a huge part of the Onboarding Margin! Why did we exclude these two very large factors? Because the numbers were getting big enough without it, and we simply felt far more comfortable making a smaller claim.

- This entire analysis was done not with precision in mind, but rather to determine with directional accuracy whether or not the Onboarding Margin was worthy of our, and your, attention. We think the results speak for themselves.

Notes

1. In modeling total industry impact, we treated the sum of the benchmark companies' net profits as a percentage of the total net profit of an industry (*Sources:* Yahoo Finance Industry Browser and NYU's Stern Business School data). As a result, the benchmarks' net profit was a percentage of total industry net profit:

- Aerospace & Defense: 64%
- Energy & Utilities: 62%
- Financial Services: 5%
- Healthcare: 18%
- Technology & Telecom: 87%
- Consumer Packaged Goods & Retail: 75%

This percentage was applied as a ratio to the sum of all model inputs for benchmark companies in a given industry to provide total industry calculations. All subsequent industry inputs/figures are based on this ratio and reflect the modeled total industry figures.

2. We used 2008 for all company data in the analysis.

2

THE STATE OF THE ART: ESSENTIALS OF STRATEGIC ONBOARDING

Fact: Every new hire in your organization is onboarded. This is true regardless of whether or not your organization has any formal strategy or program for doing so. As a series of on-the-job experiences interpreted separately by the hiring manager and the new hire, the process includes formal events as well as the far more numerous everyday experiences that take place from the moment of offer acceptance through, say, the end of the first year. In the mind of the new hire, onboarding also includes all non-experiences that the new hire may have expected but that never actually occurred or were disappointing. All of these experiences—and non-experiences—shape new hires' perception of employment and thus influence their engagement and ultimately their long-term interest in the position and the company.

Everyone is onboarded, but not all new hires are onboarded particularly well. Not all of them are integrated in a deliberate, consistent way that creates optimal value for a firm while providing more value for new hires. Very few companies have a system in place that provides the majority of new hires an optimal onboarding experience that lasts for the entire first year, is truly strategic in design and impact, and significantly redefines the employer-employee compact to both parties' advantage.

The inadequacy of most existing onboarding efforts was brought home to us recently when we spoke at an onboarding conference. Standing before a hotel ballroom of 150 senior and eager HR leaders representing some of the world's premier companies, we asked our audience, "How many of your companies' currently have onboarding programs at your company?" Hands shot up across the room. "Now, how many of you have programs that span more than two weeks?" Half of the hands lowered. "More than three months?" Only a few hands remained raised. We decided to investigate further. In a post-conference poll of our onboarding community of 3,800 corporate HR managers, only 15% had programs in place that spanned more than two weeks. On this basis alone, it became clear that many premier companies have orientation programs, but few actually have effective, full-fledged onboarding programs.

To understand just how primitive and ineffectual the process continues to be at a vast majority of companies, and how much companies could accomplish with strategic programs, it is helpful to establish just what the state-of-the-art looks like. This chapter describes essential characteristics of an ideal, leading edge onboarding program. We refrain from describing a single representative program, since again, no onboarding programs as yet deliver the full value described in Chapter 1. Rather, we offer our vision of a strategic program that knits together actual onboarding design characteristics that we have uncovered at progressive companies across industries. These characteristics are not specific practices, but rather broader "best principles" that apply to all organizations irrespective of their industry, competitive situation, and strategic objectives. Comprehension of these best principles provides companies the guidance required to begin developing a customized, state-of-the-art program appropriate to their own unique circumstances and business objectives.

A Brief History and the Weakened Compact

Appreciating the cutting edge in any discipline requires a firm knowledge of what has already passed into existence. We begin by briefly examining a summary of the recent history of the employer-employee compact in the United States and the associated efforts to manage and integrate new hires over time.

At most United States companies during the 19th century, employees were treated as contractors, paid simple wages, and hired and fired at will. Orientation for a new hire was informal, with managers showing the new employees around, explaining policies, giving them a sense of what to expect in their job, and providing task instruction as required. For the most part, labor was considered a simple factory cost, and it was usually viewed as secondary to the cost of raw materials and equipment.

In response to strikes and other worker unrest, many companies at the turn of the 20th century adopted the paternalistic practices of "welfare capitalism." These practices included providing medical care, pensions, paid vacations, profit sharing, and employee representation. Manufacturers in rural areas often functioned as "company towns" with inexpensive housing, schools, and even parks and churches. Managers found the resulting gains in employee retention, morale, and efficiency well worth the expense of these programs. With industries having expanded faster than public infrastructure could keep up, and so many workers having left supportive family structures to travel to factories, the practices also met practical needs.

Welfare capitalism declined in the 1930s, partly because 1920s prosperity had gradually improved social infrastructure enough to make many of its practices less necessary, but mostly because of the New Deal. The Roosevelt administration saw the paternalistic practices of welfare capitalism as undermining the dignity of workers and preventing them from negotiating freely. The administration suspected that many companies by the 1930s employed paternalistic practices to discourage workers from joining unions; in fact, the administration called them "feudal and repugnant to American principles." Labor unions, unlike company-sponsored employee representation plans, offered workers the promise of an independent voice at the same level as management, providing far greater dignity. By protecting unions and widening the scope of collective bargaining, New Deal legislation sparked a rapid increase in pensions, health insurance, and paid vacations. Unions bargained for pensions, insurance, and other benefits that might be called paternalistic, but no way as much as company-owned houses, churches, schools, playgrounds, and clinics.

In the tight labor markets of World War II, high income taxes for both companies and individuals spurred many companies to expand benefit programs in lieu of wage increases. Supply and demand for labor, more than employer concerns about efficiency or safety, were probably the leading motivation in all of this "human capital" investment.

It was also during this period that new employees at many large companies started to experience something approximating present-day orientation. Instead of reporting immediately to their supervisors, entrants first went through a filter of personnel departments. Clerks recorded their admission, collected vital information, and explained basic employment policies and benefits. Unions often added their own, separate process for welcoming new employees.

Growing prosperity during 1950s and 1960s made companies worry more about the cost of labor disruptions from strikes than the added cost of the benefits. Big labor, big business, and big government, having united so well to win the war, now worked together to provide for their "organization men." As companies adopted a growing array of benefit programs in the 1950s and 1960s, orientation became an ordeal of filling out paperwork and choosing among an array of options. New employment laws only added to the focus on compliance. And as behavioral scientists called attention to the talent inherent even in rank-and-file workers, companies in the late 1960s started developing broad-based training programs. With the introduction of these training programs and their spread to the bulk of the workforce, many companies experimented with assessment centers that tried to match the skills of new entrants with company needs, but unfortunately these rarely went beyond the superficial.

During this same period, companies started paying special attention to their managerial and professional talent. Even before the war, companies had developed special career tracks and benefit programs for these skilled employees, who were increasingly segregated from other employees by education. By the 1960s, with the growing prestige of management science, companies built up extensive hierarchies of these employees by offering elaborate developmental paths. Succession planning, mentoring, stretch assignments for high potentials, and even 360-degree feedback all became more common at larger companies. But the special "management tracks" set up at many big companies often saw their budgets and breadth challenged and cut, partly because of pressure from union leaders, who condemned management tracks as elitist. Because of inconsistent investment, orientation for many management employees rarely went beyond a brief, rigid, and highly generic encounter. High-quality, formal development programs were often the exception.

Both of these kinds of programs, general employment benefits and career tracks for managers, declined during the 1980s and early 1990s. Deregulation, global trade, financial innovation, and reductions in shipping costs made markets more competitive, squeezing corporate profits. Unions weakened, while income tax rates fell. Shareholder activists derided companies as cautious, bloated empires operated for the glory of the management.

In response to such environmental conditions, companies either eliminated some of the most meaningful benefits and programs or, as in switching from defined benefit to defined contribution pensions, greatly weakened them. The federal government made these defined contribution plans tax deductible and even encouraged the decline of defined benefit pensions by making it easier for plans to be portable (e.g., rollovers into 401K retirement assets). The elimination of the guaranteed pension and the portability provisions of the retirement fund ran parallel with the growing propensity of employees to jump from company to company, with little regard for loyalty.

Changes in business practices had also undermined the employer and employee compact. Expanding markets, intensifying competition, and the spread of management ideas (thanks to MBA programs) were making companies more and more similar. Firm-specific knowledge mattered less than it once did. Although management never attained anything like the trappings of a true profession, companies were increasingly comfortable getting needed talent from outside hires. Meanwhile, the same trends that made business more competitive also made it less certain. Companies had a harder time predicting their needs for managers, and with no small irony they were reluctant to spend a great deal of money to develop talent that might jump to competitors.

As companies resorted to hiring into management from the outside, it became easier for employees at other firms to jump ship. This in turn made companies even less concerned about keeping talented employees for the long term, furthering the trend away from career development. Employees were encouraged to manage their own careers, yet they weren't provided the information and tools required to do so.

Whereas big government, business, and labor had triumphed in World War II, it struggled in Vietnam and Watergate. A wave of corporate downsizing during the period led to a new skepticism about the virtues of size and stability. Companies now sought to appear "lean and mean." And a new generation of employees developed who was less inclined to trust institutions.

After the long boom of the late 1990s, with their managerial fat skimmed away, companies suddenly faced a shortage of skilled managers—what some commentators dubbed a "war for talent." Corporate profits strengthened, and HR departments received new attention. With a great deal of the growing HR budget now going toward recruiting costs, commentators argued that a company's future competitiveness would depend not on technology or other material resources, but on the skills of its employees. Many observers and commentators called on employees to see themselves as free agents, with no expectations from a company beyond what a contractor would seek.

Present Day Orientation and Onboarding

If you had polled human resource consultants and specialists during the early 2000s, you would have found that many companies still saw orientation as mere paperwork. Firms typically spent only a day or two, and they did almost nothing to explain even their basic operations and culture. Most companies were now putting their employees through at least some kind of job training as part of quality improvements, computerization, or a change program. Yet training usually had little to do with getting employees started or establishing a career path. A 2000 survey by the American Society for Training and Development suggested that companies spent less than 10% of their training budget on orientation.

Since 2000, onboarding has become widely recognized as an emerging discipline within HR circles. The word evokes a practice that goes beyond the traditional orientation, yet precisely what it means has remained elusive. Onboarding seems to have its roots in certain pioneering steps taken at a few companies beginning in the mid 1990s. Corporate downsizing of both people as well as benefits had weakened employee loyalty, and the media was warning of a "war" for the most talented employees. In response to executive concerns about turnover, HR and operating managers at the most progressive firms now envisioned a timeline of support, not a one- or two-day affair.

One onboarding pioneer was the Ford Motor Company. The firm implemented a "boot camp" that emphasized teamwork and networking as much as employee satisfaction. All salaried workers started with a multi-week program of experiential learning and team building, trying to solve real business problems under tight deadlines. The intense program aimed to build relationships that lasted long after the boot camp.

Reflecting this new approach, a number of companies moved traditional, administratively focused orientation work to the days before an employee started. Cisco's "Fast Start" program, developed in 1998, put the standard paperwork online and asked employees to fill it out before the first day. The work also included reading a variety of documents on the company's operations, strategy, and culture. The company's IT department aimed to have new employees' computer, software configurations, and phone ready by the time they showed up for Day One. Aiming to free recruits from the bureaucracy that often dampened enthusiasm and energy, Cisco put its new employees through two days of training and then had them work closely with their managers over two weeks to set personal goals (a rudimentary version of what we'll address in Chapter 5, "Personal Progress and Prospect: Early Career Support"). Each employee also received a peer sponsor or "buddy."

At Cisco, orientation now had a much larger purpose than administration and compliance; it aimed to have talent hit the ground running almost immediately while making that talent feel connected to the organization. In recent years, a growing number of companies have jumped on the onboarding bandwagon with precisely this goal in mind. Yet as we've seen, Cisco remains one of the few companies to have implemented a program that extends past the few days or week traditionally devoted to orientation. Some of the more progressive large firms have implemented program content that improves upon traditional orientation, such as incorporating social networking programs or activities designed to introduce new hires to the organizational culture. Yet we've found that even these firms have not rolled out programs that fully embrace a more elaborate strategic approach.

Among firms that have embraced the onboarding moniker, the limitations of many present-day programs have become all too clear. Because most programs are so short, information is presented so quickly that new hires feel overwhelmed, as if they are drinking out of a fire hose. Many report "tuning out." And most new hires never even bother to read the lengthy binders that are passed out in an attempt to cover the material that didn't fit into the classroom time. As much as 90% of the content is typically delivered so early that the new hire hardly has the context required to understand and internalize it in a meaningful way, as depicted in Figure 2.1.

Ninety percent of the material shared in these introduction sessions is usually not reinforced at a later date. Also, the information delivered tends to target the lowest common denominator; it applies to all new hires, with limited customization for specific new hire groups (defined by level of experience, line of business, function, role, location, etc.). Without context and well-considered reinforcement, and when limited to the lowest common denominator, the content organized and delivered has modest

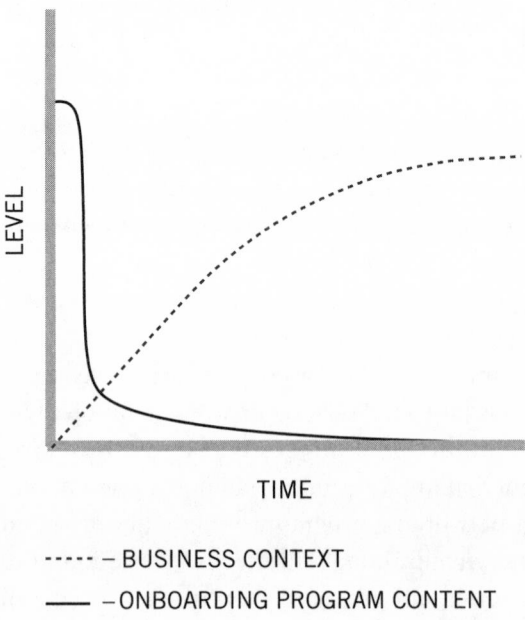

----- – BUSINESS CONTEXT

—— – ONBOARDING PROGRAM CONTENT

Figure 2.1 Early Content Delivery

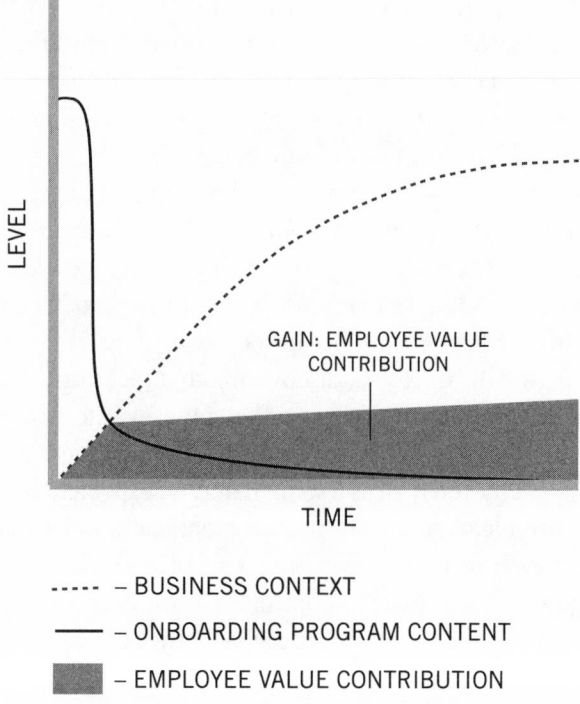

LEVEL

GAIN: EMPLOYEE VALUE
CONTRIBUTION

TIME

- - - - - – BUSINESS CONTEXT

——— – ONBOARDING PROGRAM CONTENT

▓▓▓ – EMPLOYEE VALUE CONTRIBUTION

Figure 2.2 Value Contribution from Early Content Delivery

impact over time, as noted through the employee value contribution depicted in Figure 2.2.

Because companies over the last few years have focused on optimizing the administration of onboarding programs, they have failed to update and expand their programs in ways that could capture significant new value. Companies today may sign up new hires for benefits more efficiently and with greater compliance, and in a fewer number of cases they might have computers and other tools ready for Week One, but they have not provided new hires with the knowledge, skills, encouragement, and other resources they need to excel at their jobs.

We should remember a simple but relevant fact. Although employment can be fulfilling and a great experience, it still remains work at its heart, and work is hard. It inevitably includes challenges, frustrations, disappointment, and some disillusionment. It is hardly ever simply and entirely wonderful. Neither HR nor an onboarding program can remake this reality, nor should it try to or claim to do so. Yet we can do two things: (1) help new hires become far better prepared and conditioned to overcome these downsides themselves; and (2) excite new hires so that they feel motivated to address their challenges enthusiastically.

For an example of how a traditional onboarding program can come up short, consider the story of one new hire at one of NASA's research centers. In recent years, this research center brought in new managers and executives only to lose more than they hoped because of cultural clashes. One recent hire, a former military officer, was unusually organized and punctual. Imagine his unease at discovering that meetings at the research center often did not start on time, and that a loose, academic atmosphere of experimentation, discovery, and spirited debate reigned. The new hire thought he had achieved a lot as a soldier, and he expected that his accomplishments would lead people at his new organization to accept his opinions without much resistance. Yet NASA scientists had different notions of credibility; they were used to coming up with decisions consensually through discussion, proofs, and peer review rather than yielding to someone simply on the basis of his or her rank or past experience. Because the new hire knew little of the research center's organizational culture, and nobody bothered to orient him to it as part of a formal program, he found it hard to adapt, and he wound up leaving the organization in short order. Although this outcome represents a failure in the recruiting function (which hadn't vetted for it well enough), strategic onboarding can overcome such failures with great success.

Cluing a new hire into an organizational culture's unwritten rules would comprise a step forward for many firms, but it would not be enough by any stretch. The most fundamental problem with existing programs is their non-strategic nature. At most organizations, the HR or Learning and Development department owns onboarding. They deliver the content, but this content is not connected to the business units and therefore is not aligned with actual activity or expressive of actual strategy. Onboarding also does not have buy-in from diverse stakeholders, so participation is half-hearted or worse. We have seen cases in which operating personnel have openly ridiculed content and participation. A new hire starts, and the new hire's manager, not understanding the broader importance or workings of onboarding, or after seeing weak content being delivered, pulls the new hire out of the orientation program to "get them going on the job."

Most large organizations maintain dozens of micro-onboarding programs distributed across business units, functions, geographies, and even small teams. These offer little consistency of experience and rarely leverage best practices across programs. This approach is not only inefficient, but also ineffective. Although many leading onboarding programs choose the "state" versus "federal" model, in which most delivery and some design of the program occurs outside of corporate, a holistic approach requires at least some consistency in structure, branding, and experience. By applying a common platform, all business areas share in the ideas of their peers, and the organization can feel confident that all new hires are benefiting equally from a common onboarding standard.

The Scope of Strategic Onboarding

Inspired by these shortcomings and the more progressive approaches we have seen unfolding at our clients, we have developed a framework for a state-of-the-art strategic program that integrates new hires into any organization, large or small, in any industry. In essence, we think firms should seek to shape the varied experiences new hires have upon entering, just as winning brand marketers try to convey a 360-degree experience across multiple touch-points.

An organization will never be able to control all of the experiences a new hire has, nor should it try. Rather, we seek to help new hires assimilate into company culture and workplace reality as fast as possible and with upmost enthusiasm. If there is too much hand-holding, white glove service, or other forms of support during initial orientation or, worse, throughout the course of the entire first year, post-orientation will present an abrupt and unpleasant shock as new hires begin to encounter the organization's unfiltered reality. The real opportunity lies in engineering the right kinds of experiences from offer acceptance through Year One—experiences that will allow new hires to acclimate to company culture, understand opportunities and expectations, master the firm's strategy, build valuable relationships and skills, create new value for the enterprise, and begin to develop their careers within the firm.

To understand just how comprehensive onboarding content might be, it helps to think of the many "firsts" new hires experience that materially affect how they view their new organizations. New hires integrate into the firm through their experience of their first customer visit, that first time they get pushback from a customer, learn that the commission schedule was more complicated and less remunerative than they had initially expected, complete an expense report (and find the system more painful than at their last job), have a question about benefits, and quite significantly, receive informal and/or formal performance reviews. Onboarding includes that first stretch assignment, that first time they are working without direct oversight, the first meeting, and that first time they have access to confidential information; and the list goes on and on.

Companies can enhance some of these first experiences; others they cannot. Some of these firsts involve HR processes, whereas the far greater majority constitutes normal business processes. Resources are limited, so companies must prioritize which of these experiences are most worth shaping. But they need to recognize what is happening to the new hire as they experience these firsts—all of the impressions, intake and opinions formed)—and they need to address these firsts so that the experiences become educational and carry moderate risk.

Consider this: What if your boss personally hand delivered your first paycheck with a letter saying how happy he or she was to have you? On the other hand, what if you got that first paycheck with too much money deducted for health insurance (you signed up for the individual plan, but in error had deductions taken out for a family plan), and the next pay period the mistake was not fixed, even though you brought it to the payroll department's attention? Clearly these experiences matter. To do onboarding right, we need to figure out the business processes and experiences to which a new hire is exposed, determine which have an impact on success or failure, distinguish which of these it makes sense to try to influence and which the new hire or hiring manager alone can more efficiently address, and then design an approach for exercising that influence. We need to be highly selective and very smart.

For a sense of how a more experiential approach to onboarding works, consider the practice of delivering performance reviews. Virtually all firms regularly review employees, yet most do not deliver reviews to new hires in structured ways that help new hires assimilate. A firm that embraced a strategic approach to onboarding would adjust the standard review form and review process. The firm would give instructions to a hiring manager specifically for use with a new hire, offering different versions for different new hire segments such as experienced new hires versus new college graduates. This progressive firm might also include in the review meeting the original recruiting manager who had been there at the very front end when original expectations were established to see how things are progressing and be able to provide additional support. Perhaps this firm might even tie the recruiting manager's bonus to the retention rates of the new hires placed, rather than only to positions filled in the quarter.

The instructions disseminated by this firm would direct reviewers to perform certain actions, such as discussing whether the new hire's actual experiences met with expectations, reviewing whether and how any training taken has supported the new hire's work performance, discussing ideas for how the manager might support the new hire, reviewing the company/ unit's strategy, and comparing the work culture here with the new hire's previous employer's culture. Additionally, this firm would make sure that other reviewers have background information regarding this specific employee's prior experience, accomplishments, concerns, and aspirations. With this information incorporated into the discussion, each of the individuals providing the review will be in a position to speak directly to the new hire's specific aspirations. The instructions might mandate that reviewers discuss the consequences, purposes, and process of the review so that new hires understand the meaning of any negative feedback they are receiving and can track their progress. All of this would help new hires remain engaged while simultaneously shortening the amount of time they require to improve their performance. Both parties win.

Although many of these ideas are incorporated in some world-class performance review systems, the key is to customize this standard and existing tool so as to address new hires' needs. New hires, after all, represent a very expensive investment, and this first year is the year in which most of the investment risk exists. If we can reduce this risk, we radically improve the organization's overall and downstream performance with its human capital, as new hires matriculate into tenured employees.

The Four Pillars of the Onboarding Margin

Starting from the new hire's point of view might make onboarding management and design seem hopelessly complex. How do we begin to wrap our heads around a new hire's many experiences? Through our work with leading corporations as well as smaller as well as public organizations, we've identified four interrelated content areas that prove essential to helping a new hire fit into an organization. These content areas comprise an analytic framework for shaping the primary new hire experiences, drawing from patterns we've seen in successful onboarding programs as well as what is needed to fill consistent gaps or failings.

Beyond the common administrative tasks that today's onboarding programs typically perform, such as enrolling the new hire in benefits programs and giving the new hire tools like a phone or a computer, state-of-the-art strategic programs should shape new hire experiences by providing support in mastering organizational culture and performance values; help in development of an interpersonal network; early career support; and strategy immersion and direction. Let's briefly consider these four areas in turn.

Cultural mastery

The first area, cultural mastery, is clearly relevant to a new hire's experience. Many organizations or entities that accept new entrants do something to introduce the culture. To become a US citizen, you need to study the nation's history because existing citizens want you to know, appreciate, and believe in the nation's values. Likewise, colleges have orientations, religions have coming-of-age rituals, and sports teams have training camps that build team spirit even as they whip new players into shape. Initiation processes have survived and thrived for one reason—they work.

It's ironic that in the business environment, an environment that exists purely for the purpose of performance, we have hardly invested in cultural initiation. Formalized orientation programs present some high-level cultural information, and most managers recognize that their organizations do in fact possess unique cultures. But most companies do not equip managers with tools they need to capture, distill, and ultimately help acculturate the new hire. Nor do they talk clearly and directly enough about its performance values—the unspoken habits of thought and behavior built into the firm's definition of successful performance. After an initial employment period, many firms assume that cultural initiation is something that happens naturally and a bit mysteriously as a result of a normal process of socialization. Later on, colleagues in the company will comment upon whether a new hire "gets it"—and express frustration when they don't. Surely we do become acculturated slowly on our own, but firms would improve engagement, time to productivity, and retention significantly if they provided a stronger platform for these new entrants to "get it."

Interpersonal network development

The second area in which firms can help integrate new hires and improve the experience of joining the organization is with Interpersonal Network Development. To succeed in any work environment, new employees need to forge strong and productive connections with others. This is not necessarily about having fun at work and developing friendships, but rather about networking so as to fit in better, gain perspective, create access to knowledge and other relevant resources, accelerate time to productivity, take productivity to the next level, and develop accelerated, more fulfilling careers. It's also about developing relationships beyond the workplace—having an easier time finding a place to live, becoming more at home in new neighborhoods, and building professional connections for significant others.

By expanding onboarding to include socialization, firms add significant value. But it is neither acculturation nor socialization that offers the greatest yield. The next two areas of intervention in the assimilation process— strategy immersion and direction and early career support—drive the biggest gains and create the most competitive advantage. We call these two pillars the "power levers" that raise the level of productivity and nurture more passionate and longer-term commitment to the enterprise. If you speak to companies that leverage company alumni successfully, you find that alumni who continue to create value for the enterprise are those who best understand the enterprise. They are the ones who developed sincere affection for it and experienced significant career development while at the company. Investment in these two areas will help re-write to both parties' advantage the employer-employee compact—with a return far greater than the investment.

Early career support

Early career support excites new hires by appealing to their own interest. Most people seek to build steady and advancing careers—at least the people we want working for us. When people accept new jobs, they evaluate the prospects that their new job and new organization will push them further down the road to success. By helping new hires develop their own skills and job prospects, and giving them reason to believe that the enterprise they chose can deliver career advancement faster than other employment options could, you will motivate individuals to perform and stay with your company. This additional value is something that employees calculate. In fact, new hires worth their salt assess how their skill and career advancement prospect compares with personal aspiration on Day One, and they never stop measuring. Given the weakening of the traditional compact, improving the career development opportunities available to new hires is the number one way to define an improved compact and positively differentiate a firm's employment brand.

Strategy immersion and direction

The final area that an effective program should cover—strategy immersion and direction—appeals to new hires not merely by making them more effective, but by helping them feel that their thinking is taken seriously and giving them a stronger sense of purpose. The enterprise (not just a single representative) needs to hold significant conversations with new hires about the organization's overall direction and scope—what the firm does, why it is doing it, and where it is headed. You need to establish early on that these conversations are two-way; firms need to indoctrinate new hires into the strategy and its full context, and they also need to solicit new hires' observations, ideas, and commentary.

Strategy discussions should go beyond the abstract level and connect to the individual's business area and role. This way, new hires will understand how their daily work affects the company's success. We aren't only talking about engaging with high-level new hires on this topic; it is extremely beneficial to do strategic orientation with front-line employees.

Think about it: What do you think the strongest and most insightful new hires do if they do are not able to find an audience for their thoughts and ideas? They go elsewhere. Over time, the enterprise ends up with the wrong retention mix (as outlined in Chapter 1) and a low return on investment. High prospect new hires exist in all points of entry—every function, level, and division—regardless of pedigree. Your job is to engage them before they decide to disengage. The great news is that the bar here is low. The great majority of companies are hardly attending to this low investment/high return opportunity.

Now we aren't saying that every new hire needs to receive strategy immersion the same way. It can and should be tailored appropriately to the major new hire groups (e.g., executive hires, front-line employees, young recruits, etc.). Orienting all new hires on the strategy allows them to perform their jobs more creatively and passionately, because they now understand the larger picture. With strategic thinking a vital skill in today's knowledge economy, strategic orientation also equips the new hire to succeed personally.

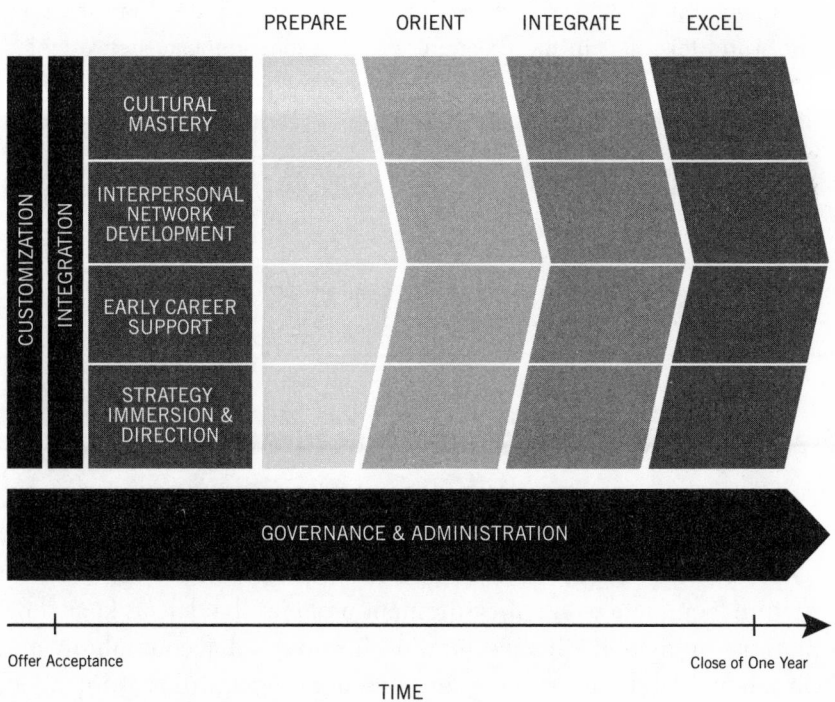

Figure 2.3 Onboarding Margin: A Systemic Model

These four content areas (Figure 2.3) do not, in themselves, reflect new thinking about social, organizational, and business systems. Thought leaders have written weighty tomes on subjects such as competitive strategy and corporate culture, and we are not advocating that firms redefine these areas. What is new is our melding of these important topics in which firms currently engage employees into a strategic approach to onboarding new hires. It is that simple. It is the power of what these four content areas can do together when applied and customized to the new hire investment and integrated into the fiber of the company that pushes the envelope and the return.

Spotlight: Shell

The executive onboarding workshops at the energy company Shell, held at the 6-month point of a new hire's tenure, wraps all four onboarding pillars into one exciting onboarding program element. External hires from around the world take part in the program, allowing for significant networking opportunities and the building of strong work relationships (interpersonal network development). Workshop participants learn about the company's "global challenges and long-term agenda" (strategy orientation) and "leadership behavior" (cultural mastery). They sign pledges relating to personal development plans (early career support).

Source: Anna Munn et al. *Executive Onboarding: How to Settle in a New Hire.* *ceoforum.com.au.*

Necessary Resources and Structures

Beyond tackling these four pillars, companies must put the same quality structures in place that any significant organizational initiative requires to succeed. An effective onboarding program requires a defined governance structure, complete with a measurement program that lets us know how things are going and what we should improve, and accountability and instructional guides for making sure that the program runs as intended. Your lean manufacturing system has this. Your quality systems have it. Your sales processes have it. A program that distinguishes world-class companies requires an administrative system to coordinate the roles that critical stakeholders play in the onboarding process. If a program is truly systemic, reaching organically across an enterprise, administration and governance become the invisible threads that tie everything together. Their presence is also what gives onboarding the unified look, feel, and utility of a significant strategic initiative within the firm.

At the United States Marine Corps, onboarding is taken very seriously. The organization prides itself on bringing in their very best people to develop new cadets, and then hold this staff accountable for it. By contrast, most businesses come up woefully short. How big is your recruiting department? Five or ten people? Two hundred? Now, how big is your onboarding department? Probably zero, or a number close to it. We put people in recruiting because we understand the competitive nature of finding talent and the importance of filling open positions, but we do not apply anything near this level of resource to ensuring that our investments succeed. This has to change.

Giving onboarding the status of a key strategic initiative means demanding results and putting the resources and processes in place required to obtain them. Individual managers today are held accountable for productivity in areas in which we can measure it. We need to start holding managers' feet to the fire for additional metrics such as attrition, whether on a quarterly or annual basis. Our polls show that very few front-line leaders or executives have goals, let alone being held accountable for attrition of new hires. We need to build this accountability into people's job descriptions and individual processes. And we need the proper support systems in place to help our managers achieve their goals.

Let's take an example. If managers at a large corporate law firm finish a case, by our standards they need to close out the project by sitting down with new hires and discussing various onboarding topics. These post-engagement consultations should not take place indiscriminately or informally; rather, managers should receive guidelines about new hires' needs and how to have these conversations. At our consulting firm, managers receive reminders as a matter of course upon completion of an engagement that they have to do a performance review for new hires. It is all built into our system: Triggers, a template, an instructional guide or framework for doing the onboarding task properly, presented on a just-in-time basis. Would you expect anything less of any other process that contributed to a high-yield initiative, such as lean manufacturing?

Branding your program

To make onboarding recognizable as a strategic initiative, and to sharpen its impact, firms should take care to brand it for new hires and existing employees. The brand is more than just an easy name that you give it; it is the reputation that you earn. Is your onboarding brand going to be about self-service and self-reliance? Or should it emphasize the support provided by the company? As part of the process of designing an onboarding program, managers should go through a branding exercise (and not simply a naming exercise) with representative stakeholders, considering what they want to achieve and making sure the onboarding program content delivers on that. Branding should also reflect what firms learn in the diagnostic phase of creating an onboarding program.

Developing a brand identity package (the program's name, logo, tagline, and supporting graphics) will serve your program well, not least by providing you with a platform to summarize and communicate the intended new experience. Creating a brand gives you a chance to take the necessary piece parts of onboarding scattered throughout the organization and define them as a unified, well considered experience. It provides a high-level map for new hires and employees responsible for delivering parts of the program. By branding your program, you are also making an explicit commitment to your new hires, thus establishing and in most cases raising expectations. As with any other branding effort, you must design and execute on your onboarding program to ensure that the brand promised conforms to what you actually deliver. If not, you have only managed to create a community of "buyers" (employees who bought into your promise) who now feel passionate about how much they have been let down. At too many companies, the recruiting process dangerously inflates the value of the employer-employee compact in the course of selling the employment brand, leading to many poor onboarding outcomes as realities fall short of expectations.

Program branding is also great because it can deliver some easy wins. Most firms today have existing processes that have never been tied to onboarding but help in new hire integration. An onboarding designer can carve out new value at very little expense just by identifying these programs and putting them under a common umbrella. Your firm likely has training programs in place that are available to all employees. By assessing these, identifying which are most relevant for new hires and/or specific new hire segments, and integrating them into a branded onboarding program, you create value for new hires—and by extension, the firm. You are granting new hires better access to existing resources in one place, as one system. You are also creating value by helping current employees see the deeper strategic connection between these existing programs, in turn leading them to become more enthusiastic participants.

Diverse participants

If onboarding affects the experiences of new hires across the four pillars, and we give it pride of place as a key strategic initiative, whom exactly should we hold accountable for its success? Our answer: Nearly everyone. In a state-of-the-art strategic approach, onboarding ceases to be solely HR's responsibility. Rather, everyone in the organization understands that they have some responsibility for integrating new hires properly.

A systemic approach will identify all the business processes that affect the new hire so they can be coordinated to produce one tailored experience. To get laptops to all new hires on Day One, you have to work with IT. To ensure a great first assignment for the new hire, you need to work with hiring managers. To capture an understanding of product strategy you need to work with Product Management within the Marketing function. Facilities management will have roles. Each of these and many other departments and participants in these departments need to know that they will bear specific responsibilities for new hires' successful integration, as determined by certain agreed-upon metrics.

Mid and upper level leaders have critical roles to play and formal responsibility to shoulder, up to and including the CEO. Top brass needs to convey the importance of new hire integration to the organization.

Leaders also should contribute across the four pillars, helping unveil the nuance of the culture in community discussions, partaking in social events, holding career development workshops in which they offer their own inspirational success stories, and most importantly, providing new hires with specific direction and challenge—letting new hires know what the firm expects from them. Management bears responsibility for setting specific policies and structures, ensuring that a new hire's reporting structure and team is well positioned to help the new hire achieve early wins. Although it may sound outlandish, imagine the impression that new hires would have if they received a riveting message from each member of your company's board of directors expressing thanks for joining the team and building excitement for the mission at hand. These do not need to be personalized, but they do need to be regularly updated to reflect the current posture of the enterprise. In truth, engaging the board in this most critical investment is far from outlandish, because new hires represent nothing less than the company's future.

As far as cultural mastery of onboarding is concerned, mid-level managers should evaluate whether they themselves live up to the expression of culture that the organizational leader is communicating. If the organization is in the midst of cultural change, mid-level managers need to help new hires navigate between the old and developing culture, since both matter during this transition period, and the newest members of the tribe are most inclined to misunderstand the character of the change. Middle management should hold periodic roundtable discussions with new hires that report beneath them to see how they are navigating the culture. Because hiring managers interface directly with new hires, they represent the front line of cultural practices. As part of a systemic approach to onboarding, managers need to have periodic pointed conversations about the culture with new hires, starting at the very beginning, and at a minimum during interim and annual reviews. The greatest contribution managers can make involves providing real-time lessons. With some coaching, managers can learn to make the most of teaching or mentoring opportunities as they arise.

Rather than failing because of design flaws, many programs fail because of the lack of clear role assignments for those responsible for delivering the onboarding experience. Those responsible for program delivery must understand their responsibilities, expectations, measures of success, and the broader impact of their contribution. Without a clear direction, your program will prove disorganized at best and dysfunctional at worst. High performance programs clearly specify the identities of all onboarding program delivery participants as well as their specific roles and tasks. They then provide them with the materials and tools necessary to succeed. Overall, successful onboarding resembles a manufacturing line in which everyone knows their clear role, does their job, and produces a great product item after item.

Spotlight: Bank of America

Today, more organizations offer systemic, integrated onboarding programs for executive hires than for front-line or lower-level hires. It is a practical place to start if a company has limited resources. Bank of America onboards its new executive hires in a process that lasts between 12 and 18 months. Executives gain strategic insight into specific businesses and customers, learn Bank of America's unwritten cultural rules as well as performance values for people in leadership roles, and develop an understanding of social networks and stakeholders at the company. The company assumes that successful onboarding goes beyond hiring managers and includes "the fullest possible spectrum of stakeholders." Individual executives receive peer coaches as well as senior advisors, they are placed into a cohort group with other new hires, and they meet with the CEO, the executive team, and "other executives previously hired into the Bank from outside." HR generalists and leadership development specialists also participate in the new executive hire's onboarding process. Overall results: Among the almost 200 executives recruited externally by Bank of America between 2001 and 2006, only 12% were ultimately terminated—much lower than the 40% turnover rate experienced with executive hires at some large corporations. As we argue in this book, it's time to take a systemic approach and extend it as much as possible to the entire population of new hires.

Source: Jay A. Conver and Brian Fishel. Accelerating Leadership Performance at the Top: Lessons from the Bank of America's Executive On-Boarding Process. Human Resource Management Review, 17 (2007), 442–454.

Adequate time length

Given just how many meaningful firsts new hires experience, state-of-the-art onboarding requires more than just the usual few days or week afforded to standard orientation. Strong onboarding programs start at Offer Acceptance (the point when employees mentally commit to trying to make the most of the selected opportunity), and continue all the way through the span of the entire year of employment or a complete business cycle, *whichever is longer for your business.* The content of the onboarding program is then distributed throughout the entire period, as noted in Figure 2.4—no more drinking out of the firehouse in this model.

Processes of strategic education, personal network development, cultural assimilation, and anticipatory career development take time when done correctly, and many of the most important first experiences do not take place until a full year has transpired. We also recommend programs of this length for another reason. Research has shown that more than 25% of new hires make the decision to leave their new company three to 12 months after joining.

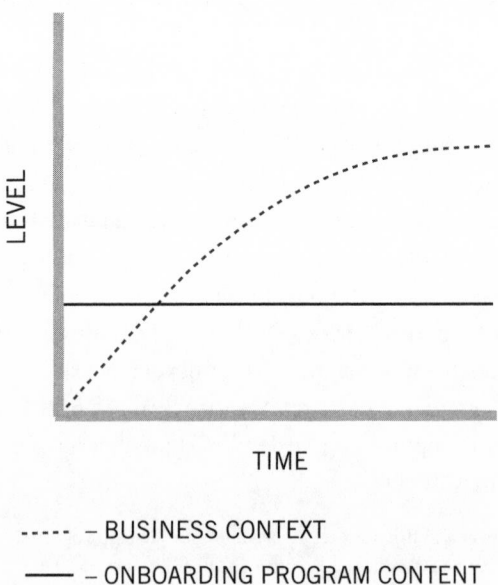

TIME

----- – BUSINESS CONTEXT

—— – ONBOARDING PROGRAM CONTENT

Figure 2.4 Distributed Content Delivery

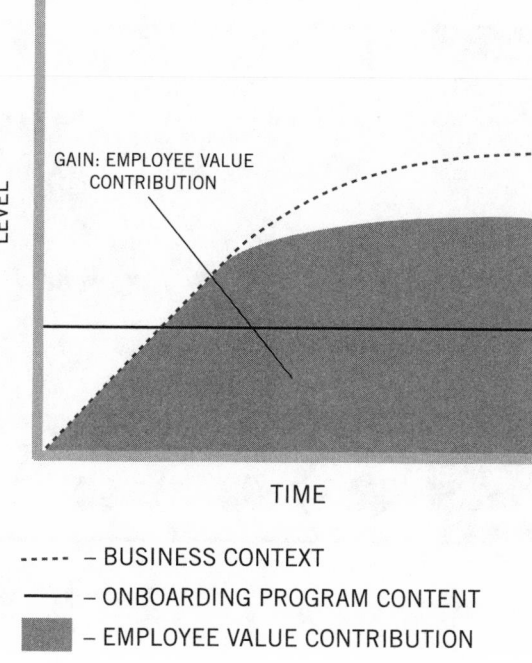

Figure 2.5 Value Contribution from Distributed Content Delivery

You cannot just dump large quantities of information on new hires all at once and hope they will assimilate it in anything approximating a useful way. The helpfulness of reinforcing and repeating information means that in general the longer an onboarding program can last, the better. As shown in Figure 2.5, pacing the content delivery out as the new hire gains more context can help the new hire contribute greater value as represented by the shaded area under the curve.

Four phases

Based on our experience working with clients, we believe that a state-of-the-art onboarding program should roll out progressively over the first year in four phases. We call these phases Prepare, Orient, Integrate, and Excel. Figure 2.6 shows our recommendation for how the content delivery associated with each pillar should be distributed across the four phases.

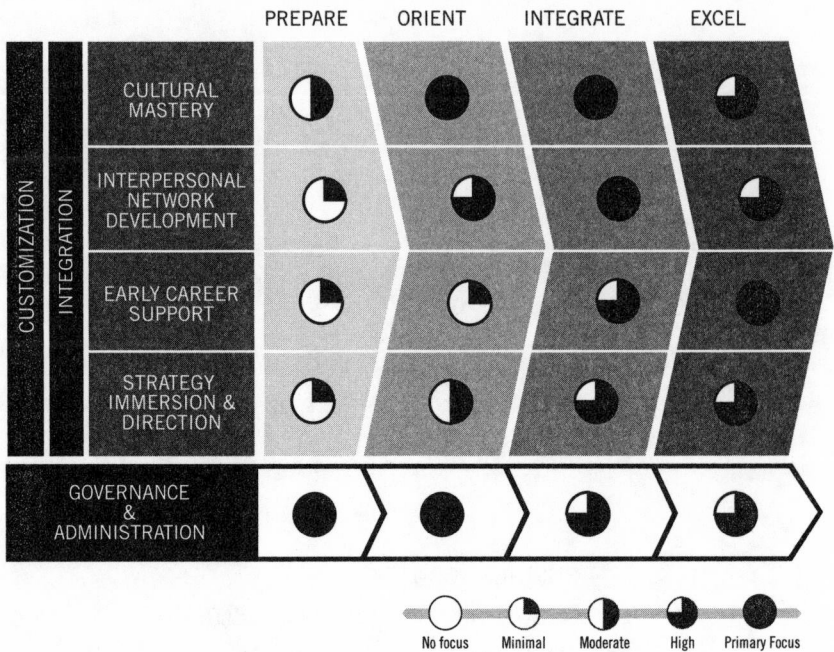

Figure 2.6 Activity Matrix for Realizing the Onboarding Margin

During the Prepare phase, new hires receive pre-Day One support to establish personal connections with co-workers, complete administrative paperwork and self-educate on their new role. By front-loading many of the administrative tasks before Day One, program designers can use what used to be the orientation period as an opportunity to dig in and engage new hires with exciting content, such as strategic perspective on the mission at hand, information about the company culture, and directed interactions to begin establishing a personal network.

During the Integrate and Excel phases, new hires receive regular mentoring support, feedback from hiring managers and cohorts, socialization opportunities, strategic education, and career planning advice. This design aims to provide consistent, continuous guidance on the activities and developmental areas most relevant to the new hire at key points throughout the year. These areas and the program's focus shift over time, as represented in the preceding graphic (Figure 2.6). New hires should feel as

---

SPOTLIGHT: Wipro

At Bangalore, India–based IT services firm Wipro Technologies, new college hires undergo a three-week training program before their start dates and while still attending school. New hires hit the ground running, and the company builds stronger relationships with the schools attended by new hires.

Source: ASTD 2008 BEST Award. *T+D*, October 2008.

---

if they are in a larger development program, and the program itself should feel distinguished. It should rise above the actual work and diffuse a broader sense of vision and purpose. And it should be honest (more on this point shortly).

Approaching onboarding in terms of the four phases helps us understand more clearly how onboarding can enhance a company's productivity. Initiating the Prepare phase at the moment of offer acceptance gives companies more lead time to get people productive; in the case of some new hires, months can go by between the time an offer is accepted and the first day of work—time that can be used to handle administrative tasks, begin networking and career path exploration, generate enthusiasm for the job, and build contextual knowledge. By proceeding through a more engaging, thoughtful introduction to the firm during the Orient phase, and by providing resources for new hires to become more familiar with the business during the Integrate phase, the firm brings more new hires up to full productivity faster than they could using a standard orientation program. The Excel phase then solidifies the integration process, bumping up new hires' performance (and achieving the Onboarding Margin). This allows the firm to carve out new value while affirming that the new hires' choice to join the company was a wise one. By distributing the content throughout the first year, and deferring largest content distribution to later phases, the onboarding program will maximize the value the new hire can contribute to the firm by the end of Year One, as depicted in Figure 2.7.

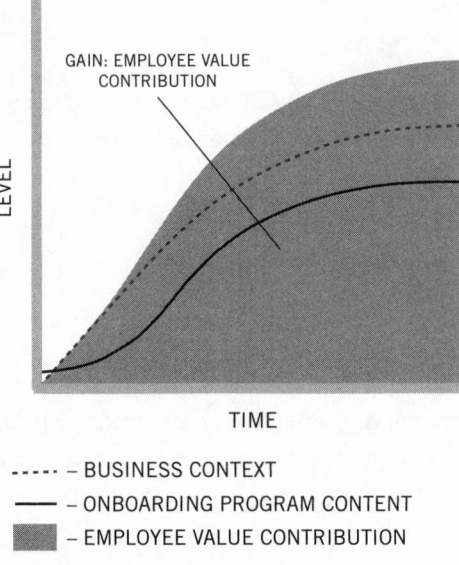

Figure 2.7 Value Contribution from Deferred Content Delivery

Customized Program Designs

So far we have unveiled a vision of a strategic program, assuming that new hires undergo common experiences and companies can benefit by attempting to shape those experiences in a consistent way. This is not to say that companies should take a completely standardized, one-size-fits-all approach to onboarding. Just as marketers segment consumers into meaningful groups and then tailor products, services, and communications specific to each segment, designers of an effective onboarding program need to target those new hire groups that will provide the greatest impact. Organizations should determine which elements would assist all new employees and which require customization to maximize relevance and value. This approach allows for common experiences across all new hire segments, enforcing a consistent onboarding brand, while still allowing for unique features relevant to each constituency.

We expect different things out of a senior leader than a staff member; thus, the onboarding experience of each should differ. Employees in the field and those who sit in corporate offices experience drastically different cultures and environments. Does it make sense to integrate new hires the same way in both places? A strategically designed onboarding program will balance the features and content that should be consistent across all new hire segments with customized features and content so as to yield the most value for the new hire. Other parameters of new hire segmentation include generations, geography, traditional employment categories (exempt, non-exempt, union, non-union, expatriates, etc.), business unit assignment, functional assignment, role assignment, degree of prior industry and function experience, diversity categories (ethnicity and gender), skill sets, and interest areas, among others.

This is a long list, and you are not going to win by seeking to cover them all. In most companies limited resources won't allow such coverage. As part of the diagnostic process that kicks off the design of any onboarding program, designers need to identify strategic priorities and determine which of these unique populations will move the needle and achieve the desired business results.

Onboarding Case Study: John Deere

Although we know of no single company that has adopted all the features of the ideal onboarding program, some innovative onboarding initiatives in recent years go a long way toward realizing the vision we have outlined thus far. One example is the program implemented for executive new hires at John Deere, the world's largest manufacturer of farm and forestry equipment and a major player in construction equipment as well. For years, all John Deere hires went through a fairly standard online orientation process. Before they arrived, new hires received information on their work location, where to park, training to complete within their first year, and a map of the company's sites. They received roadmaps with year-long calendar of milestones, and they participated in a two-day orientation process featuring large-group informational meetings.

In 2007, HR implemented a new, enhanced onboarding program for executive hires. The company was concerned that the wave of Baby Boomer retirements would leave the organization short of leaders. All that experience could not be replaced by new college grads, so the company would have to start hiring more mid-career people. It is expensive to do searches to get these people, and Deere prided itself on low turnover of employees. So the company knew it would have to provide special support to these newcomers. Instead of simply making itself available when a VP called for help in getting a new manager up to speed, HR knew it would have to take the initiative. The department wanted to design a "bulletproof" process to ensure that every new leader got the training and networking needed to be effective early on. At the same time, outside research into orientation showed that HR-only processes did not pack as much punch for employee engagement; managers needed to be involved, too.

John Deere wound up creating an executive onboarding process that addressed their concerns about retention. Every week, members of HR run reports to scope out all the senior-manager level job offers accepted. For each new hire, HR schedules a half-hour meeting with the hiring manager a few days before the start date. The meeting is especially important for managers who have not hired under the new approach, but everybody receives it. The HR manager informs the hiring manager about what the newcomer will go through, emphasizing the manager's responsibility to jump start the new hire's networking. The HR manager has the hiring manager compile a customized list of stakeholders for the newcomer to meet: senior leaders, peers outside the division, direct reports, even outside suppliers and key customers. HR might suggest certain people to include, but the list must come from the manager; this is not just HR going through the org chart.

HR then encourages the manager to send a group email to all of these stakeholders, typically 20 to 30 people, asking them to set up a one-on-one meeting. To help move this process forward, HR even prepares a generic email that needs insertion of only a little detail about the person's background; but the manager is free to write what he or she likes. All the manager has to do is populate the group email with addresses (all of which are hidden to the recipient) and send it out.

This has typically been enough to get the networking going. Since the hiring manager is usually pretty senior in the organization, his or her requests carry weight. And in any case, most stakeholders are eager to do their own networking with this new leader in the company. HR has not had to push the process.

Another big part of executive onboarding is a series of 17 weekly, one-on-one, half-hour meetings on key topics. Some sessions cover John Deere's performance management process, whereas others cover finance and accounting and corporate citizenship. A complete list of the areas covered is noted in the following sidebar. A key objective of this part of John Deere's onboarding process is not only introducing the new hires to the functional leads, but also to help them understand how these functions support the new hire's business area. Although it may not be information that the new hire immediately employs, the new hire now knows who the point person is once a need arises. The new hire also begins an immersion program into company strategy through a finance session, and by virtue of what is learned from each of the functional leads.

John Deere's Executive Onboarding Process

- Performance Management, Career Development, and Open Mentoring
- Succession Planning, Leadership Education, and Coaching
- John Deere Learning, Staffing, and Recruiting
- Corporate Compliance
- Public Relations and Crisis Management
- Compensation
- Benefits
- Legal
- Finance
- Team Enrichment
- Environmental Sustainability, Product Safety, and Standards
- John Deere Lean 6 Sigma/Quality
- Engineering Product Development
- John Deere Credit
- Corporate Citizenship
- Executive Onboarding Follow-up

HR keeps a list of people from throughout headquarters able to present on all of these topics, and they rotate assignments so the same person isn't on the hook for most of them. As Mindy Moye, Ph.D., Manager of Employee Engagement, found, the key to making all of this work is to avoid burdening anyone. Fortunately, she's gotten a lot of cooperation: "Directors and Managers want to connect with these new leaders as well. The original meeting schedule was a good deal shorter, but people from various areas actually approached me and said they wanted their areas to be on the list." These training sessions run through four months, at the end of which the executive should be fully informed and have established his or her basic network. Additionally, because these individuals are the leaders of their respective functional areas—vice presidents and directors—the new hire can quickly see the commitment John Deere has to his or her success and key relationships are formed early.

Other program elements comprise the company's regular performance management process. Hiring managers become involved with the newcomers pretty quickly in order for them to enter their goals into the system within the first six to eight weeks of employment. The company emphasizes measuring people according to the goals they've set, but coaching is also important, so HR strongly recommends that hiring managers help set up newcomers with a mentor. Sometimes, the global talent manager steps in to help make an appropriate match.

At the end of the four-month onboarding process, HR interviews every newcomer for feedback. Many of these managers have had experience joining two or more companies, and they are often quite impressed with the extent of John Deere's approach. Hiring managers also seem to appreciate the effort; they say they wish the company had the process when they started. Besides the positive feedback, evidence suggests that attrition is declining. The internal response has been so positive that John Deere has started a slimmed-down version of the program for internal promotions into leadership positions. To date, this entails a shorter set of sessions with a slightly different focus for the internal transitioning leaders. The company has not set up the networking component, assuming that internal people already developed pretty good networks.

Summing Up

This chapter has presented a vision of what an ideal state-of-the-art onboarding program might look like. Forged as a composite of design principles we have seen during the course of our work with leading firms, our framework seeks to design a superior experience for new hires as they pursue the inherently difficult task of transitioning into an unfamiliar organization. People navigate these transitions on their own, yet if we can engineer a new hire experience much in the way consumer marketing seeks to design a complete brand experience, the transition can happen more rapidly and successfully, thus unlocking hidden value. At this point, we are hoping that you, too, see it as quite strategic.

As we have discussed, the primary features of a state-of-the-art onboarding program include coverage of four pillars, a year-long/complete business cycle time span, the provision of resources and a structure befitting a key strategic initiative, and customization of the program in line with the firm's strategic objectives. On an even more fundamental level, we've suggested that successful onboarding reflects "design thinking," an approach that encompasses both observational research and deep empathy with key participants in the onboarding process, especially the new hire and the hiring manager.

The next five chapters expand in some detail on the four pillars, as well as on the structural support required to deliver them. Before we dig in, we'd like to spend just a moment thinking about a picture of human nature that can inform your onboarding program. Human resource professionals talk a lot about "hiring for fit." Hiring for fit is important, but we have learned that by and large people are quite adaptable. They have a strong survival instinct, and many also have a strong ambition to thrive when given the right conditions. When it comes to personality, interests, and potential, a large majority of people can potentially "fit in" with most organizations. Different cultures do exist, but just as tourists can get around pretty well with some simple navigational aids, so too can most new hires. What people share in common far exceeds the differences that divide them. Likewise, the potential for adaptation is greater than the uniqueness that exists among organizations.

Our objective is to push the percentage of those who make it even higher and to push higher the contribution level of those individuals. Invest in creating an environment that stimulates rapid adaptation and direction and the organization will benefit. Worry slightly less about hiring for fit (it is really hard to do anyway), and worry slightly more about providing the conditions and stimulus for the newly arrived to thrive.

Resources

Stuart Brandes. *American Welfare Capitalism, 1880–1940*. Chicago: University of Chicago Press, 1976.

Neil J. Mitchell. *The Generous Corporation: A Political Analysis of Corporate Power*. New Haven, CT: Yale University Press, 1989.

Peter Cappelli. *Talent on Demand: Managing Talent in an Age of Uncertainty*. Boston: Harvard Business Press, 2008.

Part Two

THE NEW, NEW HIRE COMPACT

3

TEACHING CULTURE SO THAT OUR NEW HIRES "GET IT"

Jessica was excited to overhaul the distribution processes at her new employer, Luccia Semiconductor.[1] Jessica's previous role as a senior logistics manager for one of the technology sector's foremost supply chain innovators made her a highly touted recruit, and she was eager to showcase her skills. In her first four months at Luccia, Jessica had toured manufacturing and distribution facilities on three continents, dissected historical performance measures, and developed a series of process-change recommendations that were sure to impress. Her business case was airtight: She could save the company millions each quarter and cut distribution time by 30%.

Standing before her boss and a small group of supply chain VPs, Jessica confidently launched into her first presentation, which laid out her finely tuned process-improvement proposal. Five minutes in, she reached a slide that was sure to inspire the group to take action: A graph that quantified the wasteful spending plaguing the distribution function. It was at this point that something surprising happened. Jessica had just begun her detailed description of the group's inefficiencies when her boss's supervisor, the Logistics Vice President, Frederick Joseph, interrupted. "Jessica, let me help get us refocused. Thanks for raising this issue, but we have a full agenda today, and I think it would be a far better use of time for the whole group if you and I discussed your ideas later."

Confused, Jessica sheepishly sat back down at the board table. Her boss pulled her aside after the meeting to discuss what had happened. "Fred has been with the company for 15 years. He practically built the logistics function from the ground up. Your presentation was spot on, but it called his management skills into question in front of the other VPs. That's why he cut you off."

Jessica was upset. She wasn't boorish or untactful. In fact, she had long been noticed as someone who knew how to get along with others and collaborate productively. At a post-crisis meeting with her mentor, Jessica learned that she had misread her new organization's culture. At her old company, the culture encouraged constructive debate, regardless of level or stature, and nobody felt like fingers were being pointed—it was the norm. The mantra *"best idea wins"* was plastered on the wall of every conference room of the manufacturing operations headquarters and at each facility. Jessica had mistakenly assumed that this same culture prevailed at Luccia. She had never even considered the possibility that the two organizations would possess such different cultures. Unfortunately, nobody had coached her about this. Now she had gotten an abrupt and disturbing wake-up call.

Jessica's experience is hardly unique. For most new hires, understanding a new company's culture is a difficult, nuanced, and gradual process. It's also mystifying, since so much of the company culture remains under the radar. New hires learn about the culture through osmosis over the course of numerous interactions with other employees. Gaffes and miscues are the norm, leading to frustration and sub-par performance. Often a company's professed culture taught during the initial orientation program doesn't reflect realities on the ground so much as the culture desired by management (unlike Jessica's previous employer, where the mantra was the culture). In other cases, companies do not spend much time at all orienting new hires to the culture, either formally or informally. This omission amounts to a huge error made by some of the greatest organizations. With adequate instruction, the manager can help prevent these gaffes in the first place, or at the very least, apply damage control for the new hire and turn the gaffe into a helpful learning experience. The sooner new hires understand the organization's unwritten rules, the more risk we can take out of the system for them, and the more quickly they can make an impact and feel gratified by their contribution.

This chapter makes the case for teaching culture, and it offers instruction for how to do it effectively and systemically. We do not wish to stifle individuality or foster group-think (we abhor the word *acculturate*), but merely provide hires with proper insights so that they can make informed judgments about how to conduct themselves (*acclimate* works better for us). Firms seeking to improve retention, productivity, and other metrics as well as those seeking to transform their cultures and operating norms should work to convey an honest and deep understanding of culture to new hires. But what exactly does that mean? We offer best-in-class principles for transferring unspoken company norms to new hires in efficient and meaningful ways. Instruction from the CEO, structured mentoring encounters, simulated work experiences, hiring manager interventions, cohort support groups, wikis on the company intranet site, and many other tools can all serve to introduce new hires to reigning values, language, and practices. What is most important is that firms take time to understand the unspoken ways that business gets done in their organizations and implement a systemic approach for teaching it. Doing so improves the learning curve and helps reduce the painful outcomes for those who "don't get it."

Corporate and Organizational Cultures

Before we can appreciate the need to immerse new hires more fully in culture, we first need to consider what culture is ... and is not. United States Supreme Court Justice Potter Stewart famously noted in a 1964 censorship case that "pornography is hard to define," but "I know it when I see it." The same can be said about culture. Sociologists and anthropologists have spilled much ink setting forth competing theories about what culture is. Business scholars have applied these theories, offering an important distinction between organizational culture and corporate culture. Roughly speaking, corporate culture is comprised of the values and traditions that derive from the mission and vision set by a company's leaders and make the firm unique in the eyes of management, employees, and the marketplace. Organizational culture includes corporate culture but is broader, also reflecting how people in any organization actually think and behave, perhaps unconsciously.

When managers refer to *culture,* they often talk more narrowly about consciously articulated corporate culture. Many firms take pride in their heritage and spend a fair amount of energy communicating their history to new hires. Yet heritage and an articulated sense of corporate culture aren't always as relevant operationally as leaders might think. No matter how aware one becomes of their organization's corporate heritage, they are still operating in the complexity and the dynamism of *the here and now.* If you compare your corporate heritage with how your organization actually functions, you will find you have two different animals. Corporate cultural elements that have allowed for success in the past, or that correspond to an idealistic sense of what sets your organization apart, are likely not to help your employees succeed right now or help your organization perform at its best.

In speaking of culture, then, we refer to the broader organizational culture that arises out of how people actually come together to get work done (and in the case of dysfunctional cultures, avoid getting work done). We especially like MIT Professor Edgar Schein's notion of organizational culture:

> A pattern of shared basic assumptions that the group learned as it solved its problems of external adaptation and internal integration, that has worked well enough to be considered valid and, therefore, to be taught to new members as the correct way you perceive, think, and feel in relation to those problems.

By this definition, a unifying culture emerges naturally over time in the course of the organization's actual functioning. It is a "set of assumptions" about the world that are tried and true and are passed on to new members as established norms. Because organizational culture also includes within it the formally articulated corporate culture, we also need to consider the stated values that people working together maintain. Finally, we need to consider observable artifacts—the language, symbols, style, and behaviors—that shape workplace experience.

When we think more closely about Schein's definition of organizational culture, we begin to see how treacherous culture can be and why new hires often get caught up in cultural snafus. Members of an organization might consider the common assumptions of a culture to be "valid," and they might impart them to new members. But even some company veterans may not necessarily be aware of these assumptions, let alone the skills necessary to distill and communicate them. They thus fall back on unconsciously communicating social norms in the course of attending to regular business. In the absence of explicit instruction, new hires do not learn about culture as efficiently or unambiguously as they otherwise might. Meanwhile, new hires have trouble teaching themselves because of something we coined the *Irony of Norms*. The Irony of Norms says that social norms by their very definition remain invisible, and only violations of the norm stick out and actually get noticed, not the norms themselves. Because new hires tend to depart from the norm, it is (ironically) their behavior, and not the organization's, that runs the greatest risk of sticking out. Therefore, new hires find themselves dog-paddling through the new culture, not sure where to go, making their way as best they can.

Many companies convey shared values as part of their mission statement and in the course of delivering performance reviews or mentoring. Yet in general, the discussion stays at a high level, the firm communicating hazy, feel-good values (e.g., "we value diversity"). Language like this attempts to present a sharp corporate culture, yet it does not do much to convey the realities of organizational culture. New hires are left to glean organizational norms from dress or ethical codes, expense reimbursement rules, and other policies. This is an inefficient and frustrating way to learn. An organization's attitude about technology adoption, for instance, often is not directly communicated; instead, it comes through in the way a new hire is given information, the devices he or she is given, rules provided around the use of technology, or the absence of these things.

Performance Values

Schein's definition also helps us because it suggests why culture is inherently relevant, even vital for both new hires and organizations. Specific elements of organizational culture emerge and are passed on because "they've worked well" over time. These elements amount to unspoken assumptions about which problem-solving approaches have allowed the firm to adapt to external conditions and thus will likely do so in the future. In the context of an employee's experience, these elements take on life as

Table 3.1 Organizational Performance Values

Performance Value Categories	Examples
1. Personal manner—*what we consider acceptable, what we believe represents excellence, and under what conditions we expect it*	• Some organizations instinctively value *progressiveness and innovation* as opposed to *exercising caution and reducing risk.* • Some organizations are *friendly and patient,* and others are *anxious and have a low tolerance for over-analysis.* • Some organizations *are fast-paced and dynamic,* whereas others *are low-key, understated, and steady.*
2. Productivity and Work Pace—*what we expect in output, as well as how hard we expect the engine to run*	• Some organizations tend to valorize *perfectionism,* whereas others emphasize getting the work out *efficiently* and moving on. • Some organizations are *biased toward speed,* whereas others are more *deliberate and process driven.*
3. Priorities—*what matters most to us (and what matters next, and so on)*	• Some organizations place *profit as the primary* objective, whereas others highlight a *portfolio of objectives.* • Some organizations *listen very closely to customers;* others are so good at *influencing customers* that they listen more to internal functional strengths and their supply chain. • Some are *more focused on cost,* and some are more *focused on revenue.*
4. Interaction—*how we interface with one another*	• Some organizations are *highly competitive* and even cutthroat, whereas others naturally tend to be more *supportive or nurturing.* • Some organizations tend to be more *forgiving* when mistakes are made, whereas others tend to be *uncompromising.*
5. Process—*how we process standard work and opportunities*	• Some organizations are *disciplined* in their processes, whereas others tend to be *fluid.* • Some organizations exhibit a strongly *hierarchical* mindset, whereas at others the spirit is more *democratic.* • Some organizations drive change via *creating consensus,* whereas others drive change through *top-down directives.* • Some organizations make decisions based on *hard facts,* whereas others make decisions *by instinct and gut feel.* • Some organizations *leverage external resources* regularly, whereas others have a far greater "*not invented here*" attitude. • Some organizations *develop from within,* whereas others *hire for the task at hand.*
6. Response—*how we respond to actions and surprises*	• Some organizations are *great learning entities,* whereas others are highly *resistant to learning lessons.* • Some are more *proactive and pioneering,* whereas some are more *reactive and fast (or slow) followers.* • *Some organizations call all hands meetings when competitive news of merit develops,* whereas others hardly give it a mention *and maintain a quiet steady hand* (or remain blind and dumb).

unwritten *performance values*, i.e., things that the organization believes make for a great employee. Organizations judge an employee's performance and prospects according to how well he or she embodies accepted performance values. One company might posses a culture that features vigorous open debate as a performance value, whereas another might value quiet consensus building behind the scenes. At both firms, this dimension of culture helps determine whether an individual's job performance comes across as strong or weak. Clearly everyone benefits if new hires understand exactly what these performance values are.

In thinking about performance values, we can break them down into the six categories outlined in Table 3.1 on the previous page.

Our clients offer a number of common responses when we show them Table 3.1. They note that our list of sample performance values is far from complete. Many times organizations do not line up at the extreme end for any given performance value, but hover in a murky territory in between. Performance values are constantly shifting and evolving. And certain attributes are far easier to discern in some organizations than others. Clients also point out that many of the performance values we discuss are subject to interpretation. One new hire might conclude after a discussion with his boss that the company is "hierarchical," "slow," and "political," whereas another might just as reasonably conclude that the company is "careful" and "has strong processes" and "checks and balances." Finally, clients remark that no organization is comprehensively any *one* thing as it relates to distilling culture. Although an attribute may largely describe an organization, some parts of the organization might diverge from the norm. What may hold true for one work group may not apply to the larger division, nor the whole business unit or corporation.

The New Hire's Perspective

Often, cultural norms at companies are inherently elusive, ill-communicated, or implicitly transmitted; and these cultural norms directly inform judgments about performance. It's safe to say that new hires face quite a challenge indeed. Let's imagine the trepidation a new hire must feel when he or she first comes onboard. In fact, there is no need to imagine it— we've all been there. We have all been thrust into a new environment that is much different from what we are used to but in ways we can only partially grasp. Lacking deliberate instruction in a firm's implicit code or language, we're left floundering on our own, coming up with a fuzzy sense of the rules from what little data we have.

Learning the lingo

Workplace slang offers a great example. Each workplace and industry has its own unique vocabulary that has developed over time and through shared experience. When you start at Procter & Gamble, you need to figure out what acronyms like SMOT (Second Moment of Truth; i.e., the moment when a customer uses and judges their product), GBU (Global Business Unit), or XFS (Cross Functional Solutions) mean (a full 34% of Procter & Gamble's search activity on internal corporate networks are for acronyms).[2] FedEx Office's workers need to understand what the firm's "purple promise" is (shorthand for the firm's commitment "to make every customer experience outstanding"). Army clients we've worked with use slang that is quite funny at first to outsiders, asking questions like, "Who is the belly button (i.e., the person in charge) on the issue?" or "What does it look like from your foxhole?" At Accenture, employees track billable hours by "entering it into ARTES," whereas at Booz Allen Hamilton it's "entering my TOL." At all organizations, being able to "speak the language" builds confidence and shows that you are a part of the firm—an insider.

We hear so many reports of new hires struggling to learn the lingo. Some companies provide dictionaries, but nine out of ten times we find that the dictionary simply provides technical definitions (e.g., spelling out the acronyms). They hardly ever instruct new hires as to the deeper meaning, origins, and evolution of key words, nor do they provide an explanation for why they remain so central. By failing to help new hires understand vocabulary to the fullest, you are missing a huge opportunity to fill in the blanks and teach what really makes the organization tick. In the case of the professional service firms we have noted, the language used to reference the time entry systems speaks directly to the firms' core business model and how they drive profitability. By bringing forward these definitions, the company can meaningfully discuss the business model and supporting management structure that contributes to the company's success.

Major issues the new hire faces

New hires might hope that the few days or week of orientation help them wrap their heads around slang and the many other informal elements of company culture, but it doesn't usually work that way. In the ensuing days and weeks, they are left to fend for themselves in negotiating a number of daily questions big and small. Some of the major things they are anxiously trying to figure out include:

- *Informal ways colleagues make decisions:* What gives people "permission" to decide on an issue? Is it their ability to muster facts? Is it the boss' approval? The inherent authority that comes with their job? A combination?

- *Communication styles:* Does the hire's new workplace like the one-page memo? The PowerPoint deck? Three bullets? Casual conversations in the hall? Do people like to gain information on a need-to-know basis, or is an open communication more efficient and therefore desirable? And again, the language: What do casual words and phrases really mean?

- *Idea advocacy:* Does the organization prefer a structured or formal process for bringing forward ideas—e.g., using templates and a defined process and forums—or does a culture of open brainstorming reign? Do ideas need vetting before expression in an open forum, or do colleagues feel comfortable with a new hire just bringing something up?

- *Who's who:* Who is important to company decision making? Who do I need to impress? With whom do I need to develop a good working relationship so as to successfully partner on work assignments? How do the leaders' styles differ?

- *Dispute moderation:* Some organizations designate people and processes to address and formally moderate disputes when they arise, whereas others encourage colleagues to moderate disputes themselves. What's the rule here?

- *Managing up:* Is the hire's new culture hell-bent on micro-managing? Does he or she have to keep superiors constantly updated on progress? Is there a consistent standard, or are there certain scenarios in which superiors require a higher communication standard? Is the weekly or monthly check-in sufficient? And how does the new hire keep people informed? Through water-cooler chats? A formal scheduled meeting? An online template? Or emails on an exception-only basis?

- *Appropriate conduct:* What is the right time, place, and means to do *anything*?

Negotiating these issues—and again, this is only a partial list—takes time and energy, detracting from new hires' ability to become effective at their jobs as quickly as they would otherwise, and reducing their engagement. It's an intimidating process for new hires, since they are trying to impress their new colleagues, yet they sense that these colleagues are already evaluating them on the basis of norms that are puzzling and only partially revealed. Think of how frustrating, let alone unproductive, the following situation would be:

> At your last job you had grown accustomed to the standard of approaching business challenges by examining first and foremost what the competition was doing, how they respond to customer needs, and how they might respond to your firm's actions. In contrast, your new company has an internal focus, but no one took the time to highlight this fact for you. Being conditioned for eight years at your prior firm, you are probably thinking and taking actions that are not in concert with your colleagues and your reporting manager. You seem not to make any headway in your job, and for a while at least, you are not sure why. You think you're doing everything right, and then your manager informs you that in this first 6 months he found that your thinking is "frustratingly off." If you decide to go against the grain, you won't even necessarily know how to do that well; you will be clueless about which battles to fight, how to fight them, and whom to choose as your allies and enemies.

Leaders in your new culture might negotiate decisions casually over lunch rather than during a formal meeting. Choosing one over the other can make all the difference, and when you get it wrong early in your tenure with new employers, it is not fun for you or them.

Other factors and situations can render new hires' frustration especially pronounced. If you're already experienced with other cultures or are new to an industry you come in with ingrained habits and attitudes that might conflict strongly with your new organizational culture. In the early 1980s, John Sculley transitioned from President of PepsiCo to CEO of Apple Computer. Scully had grown famous in his old job for being a "marketing guy," the executive who had successfully introduced the "Pepsi Challenge" and won share from Coca-Cola, a challenge deemed similar to Apple's need to win share from Wintel (Microsoft Windows- and Intel-based personal computers). Upon entry to Apple, Sculley needed acclimation into at least three distinct and new cultures—that of the personal computer industry, Apple, and finally the Silicon Valley tech community. Think about how challenging it must have been for an accomplished leader familiar with Pepsi's process and data-driven culture to encounter the entrepreneurial, personality-driven world of Silicon Valley for the first time. In fact, it was too challenging. As *Wired* magazine summarized the shift, "the suave East Coast marketing executive ... took for himself the mantle of Apple's visionary leader. Nearly everyone pretended not to notice how badly it fit."[3]

If new hires do not enter a firm with ingrained habits, sometimes they come brimming with positive and potentially unrealistic expectations about the culture, only to become disappointed when these expectations don't pan out. Such disappointment often occurs when the organizational culture a new hire enters breaks from a well-known consumer brand associated with the company. A high-end luxury company, for instance, might convey in its advertisements the very epitome of sophistication, elegance, and extravagance. Show up at its corporate headquarters as a new hire, and you might discover evidence of a very different internal culture and associated performance values. The office furniture is dated, employees come dressed casually, and mid-level employees operate in a bit of a frenzy. In short, everything about the place seems unrefined and decidedly inelegant. If you came to work thinking that every day would be "special," you would be in for a rude awakening.

In this case (involving a real-life company, by the way), important aspects of the organizational culture are at least immediately visible. Organizations such as IDEO, Nike, Best Buy, Bloomberg, and The White House possess visually unique work environments that create an impression of the culture. The vast majority of workplaces, however, are visually every bit as generic as that portrayed in the television show *The Office*. Consider how much more puzzling these workplaces are for new hires. Even if you don't come in primed for a certain culture, you still find that your most important sense—vision—offers little help in deciphering the world of work you've just entered. As a designer of your company's onboarding system (or a hiring manager), you need to consider whether your new hires are entering with false impressions of your brand that have been affected by the consumer brand or other influencing factors, such as significant moments in a company's history that have developed into nearly mythical status.

New hires notice contradictions

Entering hires also have their new company's often-unrealistic portrayal of its organizational culture with which to contend. To the extent that companies talk about organizational culture with new hires, they often make matters worse by downplaying negative aspects of the culture or even outright ignoring them in the course of presenting what is really their aspiration for the culture. As consultants, we walk into the most admired companies, those that make fantastic products that have changed the world and created immense wealth, and we find that the people who work for these companies—including their leaders—commonly lament about "how screwed up we are." We hear this all the time. New hires are especially primed to discover the flaws in culture, because they're put into vulnerable positions that encourage defensive reactions on their part. When management comes along with lofty and ultimately quite meaningless rhetoric about how noble the firm is, they create an unpleasant experience of cognitive dissonance. New hires are told the firm values innovation, yet upon offering a suggestion they are informed in a condescending tone that "we don't do it that way." They were told the firm values collaboration, yet they have just sat through a meeting in which two functional managers squabbled over who owned a certain process.

Left unresolved, as is so often the case, such contradictions can cause new hires to become increasingly cynical and distanced from firms they initially might have been quite excited about joining. It gets worse from there. New hires are smart, sensitive people who commiserate with other new hires. They wallow together in complaints and negativity. Instead of the excessively positive image of the organizational culture the firm intended, new hires feed on the frustrations of those around them, discovering more and more about the culture they had not noticed and do not like. Imagine what this does for the firm's energy level, productivity, and talent retention.

This is what new hires often experience when they encounter unspoken norms in a new organizational culture. It is not a pretty picture—not for the new hire, and certainly not for the firm. Yet the large majority of managers take a defeatist stance and do nothing. They assume that acclimating to new organizational cultures is difficult by definition. They think that new hires and companies alike need to buck up; that companies just have to accept a period of lower productivity as new hires get up to speed, as well as tolerate a certain amount of attrition. However, this just isn't true. Although no onboarding program can give new hires a perfect and instant sense of familiarity and ease, an effective program can and should make the acclimation process much easier. What if we put systems in place to communicate unspoken norms to hires? What if we engage in an ongoing, progressive dialogue about organizational cultures, revealing them honestly, flaws and all? What if we exposed hires over time to the nitty-gritty of our performance values, offering explanations about why they exist and advice for how to perform in line with these values? Mark our words: When these initiatives are implemented, performance rises.

New Hires and Onboarding as a Lever to Drive Change

If nurturing happier, more productive, more engaged, and more committed new hires is not reason enough to include cultural education in a strategic onboarding program, consider this: Structured cultural education can also play an important role in helping an organization support new strategic initiatives.

Transformational strategies do not exist in vacuums. Executing them properly means addressing organizations' daily functioning and experience, and specifically, helping our workforces to develop new skills, processes, and habits. A wonderful illustration of this appeared in the classic Christmas movie *Miracle on 34th Street*, which portrays the competition between two retail stores, Macy's and Gimbels. A Santa Claus hired by Macy's for the holiday season delights customers by referring them to other stores when Macy's own merchandise doesn't fit their needs. In a lesson to any modern-day retailer who seeks to become more customer-centric, Macy's starts to infuse the practice of referring customers to the competition throughout its workforce, and in response so does Gimbels. Employees deliberately cultivate new skills and capacities, such as an awareness of customer needs and desires and extensive knowledge about the offers available at other stores. Contrary to Hollywood depictions of it, the transformation of employee behavior in real life does not always happen right away. But of great import for the conception of your onboarding initiative — unlike veteran employees, new hires actually represent an easier group of employees to adapt to the new company direction and can be a great lever to drive organizational transformation.

If true organizational transformation reaches deep into the daily life of a workplace, it is not enough for firms to take a one-off or haphazard approach to cultural change. In a recent *Harvard Business Review* article entitled "Leading Change: Why Transformation Efforts Fail," noted management thinker John Kotter cited eight common errors, including "not anchoring changes in the corporation's culture."[4] As Kotter relates, the firm must make repeated efforts to "show people how the new approaches, behaviors, and attitudes have helped improve performance." Doing this might involve taking time out at every meeting to assess why performance was improving or running articles in a company newspaper linking performance and cultural change. At Home Depot, cultural change in the early 2000s actually went well beyond these techniques, including the establishment of five-day learning sessions for almost 2,000 district and store managers at the retail chain. The firm has also institutionalized the new culture by offering ongoing training programs, including its Future Leaders Program.[5]

Given that the average large organization renews as much as 30% of its workforce in three years (12% attrition gets you there pretty quick), formally enrolling new hires in the organization's change efforts can prove an immense help in getting the job done. To understand what enrolling new hires in change might mean, just think of General Electric. For a 15 + -year period, the company's entire operating strategy centered on a six-sigma initiative to drive continuous improvement, elimination of waste, and quarter-to-quarter earnings improvement. By the late 1990s, the culture found itself in a difficult position when six-sigma began delivering diminishing returns. The company became more and more reliant on a single operating unit — GE Finance — to deliver enterprise-wide financial returns, which itself began to stress. In 2000, with the appointment of CEO Jeff Immelt, the company began to remake itself as an innovation leader. Instead of finding marginal gains from existing businesses, GE would need to discover new customer needs and enter emerging industries. You can imagine the degree to which a behemoth like GE, formerly so focused on operational excellence, needed to transform its culture to meet this new leadership mandate. Given the length of time this transformation would take, GE clearly had an opportunity to capitalize on turnover in its workforce to bring in personnel who would prove even more amenable to embrace the new culture than existing employees, who were conditioned to the old culture.

How Robert W. Baird Does It

The Milwaukee-based financial services firm of Robert W. Baird & Co., Inc. has made great strides in leveraging the onboarding of new associates to drive change. In the case of its Private Wealth Management business division, Baird has used new hires as a key lever in driving a cultural as well as business model change.

Baird's Private Wealth Management (PWM) business division serves the financial needs of individuals, families, executives and businesses through 70 branch offices across the United States. Until 2002, Baird served their high net worth clients much like other investment firms, with individual Financial Advisors bringing forth investment solutions to meet their client needs. In 2002, Baird shifted toward a team-based approach, whereby Financial Advisors with complementary strengths work together to best address the myriad financial issues of higher net worth families and individuals.

In recent years, many financial services firms have begun to support the formation and development of financial advisor teams, but few firms provide the solid foundation and framework for teaming like Baird does. While a team approach is strongly encouraged by Baird's Executive Management Team, veteran Financial Advisors are not required to join or form teams. However, the organization does require new, non-veteran Financial Advisors to join or form a team before their hire process can be completed. This is a very unique approach in the industry, but one that boasts big payoffs as Baird's non-veteran Financial Advisors success rate after five years is 65% versus industry standards of 15%.

The process for onboarding new, non-veteran Financial Advisors (titled Financial Advisor Associates or FAA until graduation) is a long and rigorous process. Each FAA is required to complete $5\frac{1}{2}$ months of training, pairing products and services education with professional development at the team level. Phase I of the four-phase program focuses on Series 7, Series 66, and Life & Insurance licensing. Phase II includes 33 curriculum modules to ensure each FAA has a broad and deep understanding of the solutions offered and supported by Baird. Phase III is a two-week phase during which all FAAs are required to participate in training at Milwaukee headquarters. In addition to participating in roles plays, case studies, and technology demonstrations, team members are also required to join their FAAs for a two-day instrumental business planning workshop. The final phase of the program, Phase IV, requires each FAA to present their team's formal, comprehensive business plan to a panel of representatives from Sales Management, Talent & Development, business coaches and veteran Financial Advisors. This presentation establishes the FAAs role on their newly established team and brings them to the final component of onboarding—graduation with CEO & President Paul Purcell.

Throughout the new hire onboarding and teaming processes, Branch Managers who oversee Baird's PWM branches, play critical roles. They are responsible for the profitability of the branch network and are thereby incentivized to do what they can to coach their new teams and advisors. The entire process is supported by a team of specialists in Human Capital, Products & Services, Compliance, Legal Services, Marketing & Communications and many more areas of Baird's Corporate Resource Groups. By involving key stakeholders from across the organization, this approach is intended to enhance the likelihood of new advisor and new team successes. Evidenced by their success rate of new associates being about four times greater than the industry average, it looks like the PWM division of Baird is achieving its goal.

The enrollment of new associates into the team structure at the onset of onboarding has been a key contributor to helping to institutionalize the team-based approach as part of Baird's culture and successful business model.

Getting Started: The Cultural Audit

We have examined how important it is for firms to include cultural conversations as part of strategic onboarding programs. Now it is time to discuss how to do it. Before firms can begin to develop a formal way of engaging new hires on the topic of organizational culture, management first needs to become aware of its organizational culture. We advise that managers begin by reaching across silos and performing a formal *cultural audit*. This exercise entails a cataloguing and analysis of all aspects of culture—the unconscious assumptions, the stated corporate values, and dominant behaviors, practices, and symbols. The exercise also includes the identification of perceptions about the culture, including any dominant myths that employees might have. If you are embarking on an onboarding redesign effort, the cultural audit will be conducted as one element of the diagnostic effort in your initiative (which is discussed in detail in Chapter 8). However, as a short preview, consider the Cultural Audit activities listed in Table 3.2. Depending on the depth of understanding of the current state that you begin with and the level of resources that will be dedicated to conducting the audit, you may incorporate some mix of these activities, but not necessarily all of them.

An audit can prove especially valuable if it uncovers practices that lead to identification of undesirable perceptions or rumors about the culture. At one of the firms with which we work, a perception had quietly taken hold that golf was a vital part of the organizational culture, especially at the top echelons. Certain executives, including a number of women, felt left out, since they weren't especially enamored with golf. They even came to believe that their lack of enthusiasm toward golf would impede their careers, as they simply felt sidelined in too many conversations. In fact, this perception was overblown. Senior managers of this company had many other interests besides golf, and the last three big promotions had

Table 3.2 Cultural Audit Key Activities

• Conduct data-gathering activities	• Employee surveys
	• Employee focus groups
	• Targeted interviews with business leaders
• Catalogue key aspects of culture—organizational and corporate	• Perceptions
	• Stated corporate values
	• Dominant behaviors, practices, and symbols
	• Unconscious assumptions
• Analyze the results—identify consistency and differences between…	• Corporate culture and organizational cultures
	• Company heritage and current strategies
	• Perceived culture and actual
	• Stated culture/values and the ones that reflect aspirations for culture

gone to individuals who had never stepped foot on a golf course. By uncovering such misconceptions, a cultural audit enables the onboarding designer to either dispel them or instruct the new hires how to negotiate a cultural terrain that might cause them discomfort—before resentments arise, productivity falls, and people leave.

Cultural audits also provide an opportunity to discover any discord between a firm's visual culture and its organizational culture. At Nike's corporate headquarters, managers want employees to think like its consumers, so a visual culture of athletic performance reigns. The buildings are constructed as shrines to athletes, employees walk about in casual athletic clothing, and the campus includes a great number of specialized running tracks and athletic fields. If Nike's deeper organizational culture is one of severe competition resembling athletic performance— if the best answer wins and we don't attend to the losing ideas except to learn lessons from them—then the physical culture and organizational culture align. But if not, then some employees are going to feel confused. A cultural audit would alert Nike to the need to educate new hires as to the differences between the layers of culture they would encounter if this discord existed.

Finally, cultural audits are helpful because they afford managers a chance to discover any disconnect between the firm's stated corporate culture and the strategies they are attempting to implement. Heritage and tradition are vitally important to sustain, yet a firm's stated values cannot remain stagnant over time; survival requires at least some evolution and adaptation. Senior leadership needs to question whether implicit, unspoken norms should change to meet strategic imperatives. We suggest that senior leaders evaluate and update the cultural audit together on an annual basis, analyzing what kind of cultural change the company must pursue to support the strategy as well as how the firm can use new hires to drive cultural change. Middle managers should also participate in these yearly "cultural summits," as they are typically the ones in an organization who translate strategy to boots-on-the-ground action.

You may have your own personal opinions as to which performance values organizations should emphasize to sustain a healthy culture. In the context of onboarding, however, judging specific performance values misses the point and actually causes managers to fall into a trap. In trying to communicate culture, many managers use the exercise as an opportunity to try to change their company's culture for the better. Clearly, improving culture is commendable and most certainly part of a manager's role. Yet as we've suggested, managers err when they fail to distinguish performance value aspirations from real ones currently in operation. Both the real and ideal can be communicated, so long as they are distinguished from one another. Otherwise we are only setting new hires up for confusion and poor performance.

Framing Messages about Culture

Once designers understand what their organizational cultures are about, the next step in developing a strong cultural component to onboarding is framing an appropriate educational message. Perhaps the most important principle to follow is a simple one: *Honesty*. Do not take a sales or advertising approach in communicating culture to employees. Speak openly about the "true culture" so employees can get a sense of what their actual experience will be on the job or can validate what they have experienced of the culture so far. Firms should even strive to point out existing shortcomings in the culture, the reasons these shortcomings exist, and the efforts the organization is making to bring about change.

One company that does a great job of presenting an apparently honest portrait of its own culture is Netflix. Posted on the company's web site is a 128-page PowerPoint presentation on company culture in which the CEO and founder Reed Hastings himself introduces the firm's culture in an open, honest, and engaging way. The presentation opens by observing that "lots of companies have nice sounding values statements," including Enron, whose stated values of "integrity, communication, respect, and excellence" were engraved in marble in the main lobby. However, given Enron's demise, these words "had little to do with the real values of the organization." The presentation then lays out in clear language Netflix's nine values: Judgment, Communication, Impact, Curiosity, Innovation, Courage, Passion, Honesty, and Selflessness.

Here is where some firms might stop, but Netflix's presentation does not. After describing the nine corporate values, Netflix's CEO goes on to outline seven other "aspects of our culture," some of which—"high performance, freedom and responsibility, context not control, highly aligned, loosely coupled"—are essentially performance values. Under "high performance," for instance, the CEO outlines Netflix's assumption that every employee will be a "star" in his or her position, or *they won't work here* (how is that for frank talk?). As part of this performance value, the firm promotes honest assessments of performance, counseling new hires to collect frank feedback: "To avoid surprises, you should periodically ask your manager: 'If I told you I were leaving, how hard would you work to change my mind to stay at Netflix?'" The CEO also goes on to explain his business rationale for valuing all-star performance above things like hard work or loyalty, arguing that in creative work such as that performed by Netflix's workers, high-performing colleagues are "ten times more effective than the average employee—a far greater spread than in procedural work." High performance workers have an especially big impact, which is why the firm is "so manic on high performance."

We are not endorsing Netflix's opinions or values per se. What is more important is how clearly Netflix communicates what it expects from new hires. The Netflix example suggests a few "best principles" of onboarding *messaging* as it relates to culture. To achieve maximum impact, designers of an onboarding program should not merely communicate the unvarnished truth about their cultures and firm performance values; there is more. To this end, we have our own list of ten best principles. These should serve as guidelines as you begin to design your onboarding program and its inherent message. Here are our first four best principles:

Best Principle #1: Use simple language that new hires can understand.

Best Principle #2: Go beyond lofty rhetoric to provide specific examples of how the performance values might play out in everyday life.

Best Principle #3: Make some effort to explain the business rationale behind the values.

Best Principle #4: Express the culture in passionate terms while also invoking the authority of company leadership.

Truth in Advertising: Apple

The carefully designed welcome box Apple gives to all new hires before their start dates contains a short, clear, and inspirational statement of what the firm values and doesn't value in the performance of new hires. It is so effective that we'll let it speak for itself:

"There's work and there's your life's work. The kind of work that has your fingerprints all over it. The kind of work that you'd never compromise on. That you'd sacrifice a weekend for. You can do that kind of work at Apple. People don't come here to play it safe. They come here to swim in the deep end. They want their work to add up to something. Something Big. Something that couldn't happen anywhere else."

This statement is a very big motivator. Does it excite the workforce and affect the Onboarding Margin? You bet it does!

To provide further evidence of this point, our capture of this story was not from Apple. Rather it was from a new hire who proudly posted photographs and verbatims of his welcome kit on his personal blog. He was so moved by this message that he wanted to share with his community. His blog received great comments of endorsement from friends and admirers. His new employer had already begun (even before Day One) to move this new hire up Maslow's Hierarchy of Needs pyramid (see Chapter 1).

The key, ultimately, is to take new hires beyond the veneer of established and unspoken norms in a way that does not dumb down the organizational culture or evade its full complexity. We cannot just say that our company is forgiving or unforgiving. Organizations are uneven, so of course they will be forgiving in some ways and unforgiving in others. For instance, our firm might want to convey that the accounts payable is unforgiving in its rules for out-of-pocket expense reimbursements, but that if a manager took on a risky initiative and it didn't work out, we'd be very forgiving. By using simple language, going out of their way to identify areas of distinction, and citing specific examples, as the Netflix presentation does, well-designed onboarding programs can give new hires a deeper experience of this complexity without eliciting confusion. As for the third principle, new hires will not only understand a cultural norm, but also assimilate and believe in its wisdom if they can understand an underlying rationale for its existence. When Netflix's CEO provides productivity data about work, he isn't just teaching organizational values, he's going out of his way to explain the wisdom of the values. That is how you get buy-in.

In advising specificity, we emphasize that firms need to be smart. You cannot dump everything about an organizational culture on new hires all at once, which is another reason why programs should unfold over an entire year after a new hire comes onboard. Just as important, the onboarding designer has to figure out which elements of culture are important to understand, and which ones new hires can figure out on their own. It might not be as important to teach new hires about expense reimbursements in detail, since they will learn it naturally and it is quite honestly not all that significant. Yet it would be important to explain to new hires how people in the organizational culture are used to receiving criticism or negative feedback. In designing a cultural component to onboarding, managers need to identify and prioritize the mission critical components of culture. Let's ask ourselves, if we really want to move the needle on our organization, what cultural knowledge will help us do that?

Here is an approach that we like to use when developing messaging for new hires. Instead of using phrases like "We're great because…," use phrases like "We're at our best when…." Telling people why we are great does little to acknowledge limits or weaknesses in our organizational cultures. Instead, it causes a skeptical workforce (we hire smart, inquisitive people after all, right?) to question the credibility of the statements. It also does nothing to challenge the new hires. The company is apparently already "great," and as a result is seemingly not striving to become anything else beyond what it already is. By contrast, "We're at our best when …" conveys that the company can achieve strong performance, but there are also times when the organizational culture does not work so well. It is a humbler and more realistic statement, and on that account, a more inspiring one. As a caveat to what we've been advising, companies *can be* inspirational, so long as they do not go too far. As part of this exercise, try creating some pairs of contrasting "We're great because …" and "We're at our best when" statements for your organization. Try to make the "We're at our best when …" list as specific and descriptive as possible. Here are some contrasting statements we've created for an aerospace and defense firm and a consumer electronics company.

Aerospace and Defense Company

"We're at our best when we *collaboratively* create a solution that addresses a well-defined, incredibly hard customer engineering problem."

vs.

"We're great because we collaborate across lines of business to solve hard customer problems."

"We're at our best when we're not limiting our solutions to things we do ourselves, but bringing in external partners to serve customer needs."

vs.

"We're great because we bring best of breed solutions to the market."

Consumer Electronics Company

"We are at our best when global management is having a two-way dialogue with local markets rather than dictating top-down."

vs.

"We're great because global leadership has a two-way dialogue with local markets."

"We're at our best when we understand the perspectives and realities of our partners' businesses."

vs.

"We're great because we don't impose the 'our way' on our partners."

As a final word of advice for designing acculturation messaging, we want to stress the importance of customizing to different segments of employees. New hires require slightly different support depending upon where they are in their careers, where they work in the business, etc. If you have a limited budget, we advise *spending more of the development and delivery budget on acclimating more experienced hires.* Although this may at first sound counterintuitive, our research has found that on a relative basis, acclimation tends to be far easier for more junior employees. Why? For starters, they typically enter as part of a group of new hires, and cohorts tend to support one another navigating the new culture. Second, junior employees tend to possess fewer cultural biases on account of their limited experience. Finally, junior employees are typically acutely aware of how foreign the work environment actually is (because of their lack of confidence); as a result, they apply more energy to observing and learning the culture—they prove to be more tuned into the activity. More experienced hires enter with habits formed at prior work environments with different cultural norms, and they are also more confident and often less self-aware. Senior hires are also watched more closely, expectations are higher, and people are less forgiving. Senior hires thus need messaging that speaks about the firm's organizational culture more sharply and comparatively. And they need support structures (e.g., mentors) to play a more important protective and advisory role.

Developing a world-class cultural component to an onboarding program requires not merely the right message, but a coherent, systemic approach to delivering that message. Earlier, we cautioned managers against the urge to take some generic "best practices" and apply that to their own firms. What worked for one firm might not work for another. Here again, we don't offer specific suggestions, but rather the second batch of "best principles" to help guide you in developing the right tactics for use in designing your own customized onboarding program.

Best Principle #5: Make it interactive.
Culture is vague and hard to distill. For new hires to assimilate it and make it their own, they need to engage with it personally and creatively. A number of mechanisms allow for a more interactive experience of culture. One-on-one mentoring is critical. Firms should solidify the mentoring that already takes place with the following measures: establishing best practices, deploying the mechanism widely, offering clear guidelines and discussion points—specific to the new hire experience—for mentors to follow, and offering opportunities to assess employees' cultural learning. Firms might also consider implementing a peer "buddy" program for new hires, teaming them with a slightly more experienced employee who possesses similar job responsibilities. This more experienced employee would serve as a

resource for the new hire, helping him or her understand what the more experienced employee wished he or she had known upon first starting with the company, and serving as a safe person to consult when the new hire wishes to understand the lay of the land. In both cases, the mentor and peer buddy needs to have this responsibility as a formal part of the job description, and performance against the task should be measured and factored into annual assessments. Another technique we like is the new hire summit: Bring back the new hire class or cohort together periodically over the first year, perhaps at the six-, eight-, and 12-month marks, for interactive workshops about the firm's unwritten rules (among other educational and directive content). New hires have a chance to reconnect and share their experiences, allowing for collective learning about the culture. Firms might also incorporate into the first week orientation a panel staffed by recent new hires that discusses what people wish they had known when they started.

Best Principle #6: Interactive technology is better.
Technology can make a difference. Wikis located on central intranet portals enable new hires (especially younger ones and those who work off-site) to distill unwritten cultural rules efficiently and collaboratively in a less formal environment. In this instance, new hires can post what they are seeing as the unwritten rules and other aspects of culture and performance as they experience them. The collective group then has rights to modify the cultural assessments, resulting in a community assessment of the culture, which in turn validates or dispels the perceptions that are being formed. If you deploy this kind of community approach to capturing culture, you need to give the community the same guidance that you would consider when outlining culture. Wikis, blogs (as long as they are interactive and anonymous), and related tools allow new hires to experience culture in a fun, less structured, and more authentic way without the constant circulation of an approved HR definition of culture.

General Mills provides streaming television content through its Champions TV channel, offering cultural programs, social announcements, and corporate information. The company also has an email-based daily newspaper that informs employees about upcoming events, group announcements, and relevant news about General Mills and the industry as a whole. As one new hire remarked, "Thanks to the newspaper I know what's going on at both the wider company as well as in the market as a whole, which is pretty cool. It makes me feel like I'm part of something bigger than my department." But be careful not to deploy a one-way communication system that comes off as corporate indoctrination and programming—employees today are too smart and too skeptical. Before you can blink an eye, they'll write you off as inauthentic and the message as irrelevant.

Best Principle #7: Reinforce the message and make context relevant.

Firms should use a variety of media, venues, and circumstances to reinforce the education. For instance, the firm could provide on-demand messages on the intranet, broadcasts played at the beginning of a training session, messages posted centrally within company buildings, and a one-on-one mentoring program that reinforces all of this correspondence. Repetition helps people assimilate the cultural knowledge better than a more intense, single blast of communication can. And this leads to a related point: Cultural discussions, like other components of an onboarding program, require a gradual approach.

At the front end, firms might focus new hires' attention via a more intensive, multi-day orientation. This should be followed during the year by other elements, such as the new hire summit and ongoing cultural mentoring. Hiring managers must also address their teams' own local subcultures and communicate them over time. Whenever a manager starts a new project, whenever he or she starts a "first," the manager needs to take some time to provide guidance around the culture and performance values. Hiring managers should also take care to step in when people are doing things wrong in relation to the culture. It is often helpful for a hiring manager to sit down early on with the new hire and investigate what his or her old culture was like. This conversation should be guided by a standard template and guidebook. Six months later, hiring managers can talk about the culture again, doing a "pulse check" now that the new hire has more context for understanding the culture. During the annual review, hiring managers can once more evaluate how well the employee has done in integrating into the culture. In essence, managers must really see this as part of their jobs, part of "managing" to get the greatest effectiveness out of their employees, rather than as a burden passed down from the onboarding team.

Best Principle #8: Brand your onboarding program—and brand it appropriately.
Outfitting the onboarding program with a unique brand sets the tone and distinguishes the corporate culture from an external brand identity. According to one executive we spoke with, branding new-hire programs does not only "improve the new employee's perception of the company, but it provides continuity from the heavily-branded recruiting process." Starwood, one of the world's largest hotel and leisure companies, offers its branded StarwoodONE intranet for use as a common ground for new hires. This portal connects employees across the firm's different brands, serving as a reference resource for all things Starwood. Starbucks pursues internal branding on the first day of a new hire's tenure by offering what is known as the "Starbucks Experience." The firm spends the first hour of this day in coffee education, allowing the new hire to taste a half-dozen or so different roasts, much as a sommelier would taste wine. Leveraging its unique brand, Starbucks ensures that a new hire feels he or she works for a unique and world-class employer with a clear and cohesive culture.

Sometimes a firm seeks to achieve absolute congruence between the organizational culture and a firm's external consumer brand. In this case, the company should be sure to permeate all onboarding materials with a look, feel, and messaging consistent with the brand. Apple provides a great example here. Masterful at conveying its brand values of simplicity and high-end experience to consumers, Apple also applies the same conceptual and design vocabulary to the welcome and employee orientation packets it offers new hires. Enthused with the trademark simplicity and intuitive nature of these materials, one new hire reported: "… any company that can give this much attention to detail just in their HR *paperwork* should be fun to work for. I am looking forward to this new adventure."[6] In Apple's case, the onboarding experience reflects the culture that the firm wants to maintain. It sets the standard for what management wants new hires to adopt on Day One.

Best Principle #9: Get everyone involved.
Other onboarding advisors recommend that employees receive the names and start date of new hires so they can extend a warm welcome. This is great, but it would help far more to alert surrounding veteran employees to the identity of the new hire's mentor. That way, veteran employees can

alert the mentor when, say, Allison makes a cultural misstep or, alternatively, is fitting especially well into the new culture. Perhaps the most important thing a company can do is involve senior leaders. Robert W. Baird & Co. holds a Professional Development Forum at which senior leaders moderate panel discussions and the CEO leads a question-and-answer session for new hires. In breakout sessions, new hires learn about communications skills and project management, topics that bear significantly on any company's performance values.[7] As we covered earlier, Baird also involves mentors, coaches, corporate HR, and the branch manager in each new hire's onboarding process. At Bank of America, the company goes so far as to involve direct reports in the onboarding process of their executive hires. Through a facilitated exercise by an onboarding coach, the executive's direct reports are polled and involved in providing feedback to the executive on his or her performance thus far with the team. They also share cultural norms and performance values that will be important for them all to work together effectively as a team.

A letter every quarter from the CEO would help reinforce messages about the company culture, as would the sort of presentation that Netflix's CEO created. If best-in-class onboarding is inherently systemic, it falls on the CEO to set the broader agenda for teaching the nuance of culture for new hires, acknowledge the adaptation required of new hires, and offer the organization's guidance. Division heads and functional leaders should be engaged in talking with new hires about their businesses and the cultures of their organizations. The new hire's manager also plays a critical role in this process, holding conversations regarding culture at performance review time and when starting a new assignment. Getting everyone involved requires that you make a compelling case that this issue is important, something that your diagnostic (see Chapter 8) can help surface properly.

Best Principle #10: Take it into the field.
Building on Best Principle #5, we emphasize that in-the-field experiences can provide a great opportunity for cultural learning; after all, acculturation naturally occurs here, even without the aid of formal onboarding. Starbucks encourages its corporate employees to work a retail counter shift on a volunteer basis during the holidays, ensuring that all new hires are in the field within their first year and learning the "Starbucks experience." The program is popular, inspiring near universal participation.

As a Starbucks' VP told us, "this kind of flow of communication among different segments is just what staying [culturally] small is about." The program's volunteer nature, and the fact that it is so well attended, itself conveys the company's performance value of being motivated to understand customers and the customer experience. Perhaps one of the most extensive in-the-field programs we know of is at an industrial manufacturing company that makes diverse products for various markets. The company invests in a 270-day immersion program for their senior hires. Throughout that period, and before taking on their actual duties, managers spend their time going from business unit to business unit, function to function, and meeting to meeting, soaking in literally dozens of businesses and the cultures that support them. By the time they take on their roles, new hires can operate at peak effectiveness relative to the organization's needs, since they possess deep knowledge of "company-think" an understanding of performance values, and strong social networks. This is an outstanding investment on the company's part. Even if your company can't afford the same commitment, the company's approach suggests what state of the art looks like, offering general principles that can inspire your own, less intensive program design.

Summing Up

Cultural acclimation is a vital component of a best-in-class onboarding program. To improve retention, productivity, and related goals, and to enlist new hires in cultural transformation, firms should pursue open, honest, authentic conversations about organizational culture with new hires. The point isn't to assure total conformity, but rather to raise awareness of cultural realities so that new hires can better navigate them. Program designers first need to take stock of their organizational culture via a cultural audit. With a sense of the culture in hand, managers should then frame and deliver messages that truthfully convey over time the subtleties and nuances of the culture. Overall, orienting new hires properly isn't a quick and dirty task; it requires thoughtful program design and the involvement of stakeholders across the organization. It's worth the effort, though. As top firms know, taking the time to talk about culture results in happier, better-adjusted employees who work effectively for the ends intended. Simply put, it surfaces and releases hidden value.

Table 3.3 Cultural Mastery Onboarding Elements—Sample Tactics

Onboarding Phase	Element	Sample Tactics	Application Advice
Prepare	• Pre-Day One self-education on company, culture, values, and strategy	• Video testimonials hosted on new hire portal • Flash-based video game on new hire portal • Interactive self-training modules on portal • Multimedia content saved on welcome flash drive • Mailed informational packets, including (opportunities to get involved with other employees such as volunteer opportunities)	• Ideal medium may be affected by the generational composition and technological savvy of your org's new hires • Web-based multimedia activities are often the most engaging mediums for Gens Y and X—especially if they are designed for true interactivity • Use of portal engages virtual workers similarly as on-site new hires • Messages need to be written in an authentic voice
	• Welcome Message	• Welcome message/phone call from hiring manager • Welcome message/phone call from mentor or peer advisor	• Makes new hires feel valued and connected before Day One • Should be a scheduled event to ensure that you catch the new hire at a good time to speak • Provides a forum for new hires to ask questions and receive input from experienced employees • Provide guidance to the callers to allow for a conversation and make it clear that they must follow-up and resolve any questions raised in the calls
Orient	• Introductions to company culture, ethics, and values	• Discovery learning map and interactive games • Video content with case studies from employees • Presentations and interactive workshops from leaders from across the organization • E-learning module • Outline discussions between the new hire and their managers and their mentors • Designed network activities with experienced employees	• Hours of PowerPoint presentation is a surefire way to provide a *disengaging* orientation experience • Programs should provide job simulations, games and multimedia learning activities that build excitement and promote interaction • Best when veteran employees are brought into the process—helps "make it real" and sends a great message • Provides new hires with an opportunity to begin forming relationships with, and learning from, more experienced employees
	• Introduction to unwritten rules	• Recent new hire discussion panel on "what I wished I knew when I started" • Experienced employee presentations on "secrets to success" • Module on company acronyms and buzzwords	• Activities should include insider perspectives from current employees • This should be a two-way conversation that allows new hires to hear unwritten rules, learn the company vernacular, and ask questions • Education needs to "peel back the onion," e.g., don't just teach the vocabulary, discuss the business reasons why these special words were created and live on

	• Introduction to the company's cultural strengths and weaknesses	• Incorporate into one on one mentor discussions (We are "at our best when" and we are "at our worst when") • Use a discussion topic during round table discussions hosted by experienced employees	• Acknowledge and let new hires know that the company has some weaknesses • Illustrate the points through real-life examples • Distinguish between the current culture and the one to which you aspire
Integrate	• Reinforce the company culture, ethics, and values	• Incorporate discussions with new hires during the regularly scheduled pulse checks • Brown bag discussions to share experiences on culture that new hires have experienced during their tenure • Initial new hire summit where new hires reconnect with their cohorts at the three-month mark (then repeated quarterly) • Provide an online forum for reinforcement of the culture and performance values via a virtual tool (e.g., a virtual summit, wiki pages)	• Continued emphasis on discussing culture, values, and norms provides new hires with opportunities to learn to navigate them • Mix of in person and virtual forums are key to keeping virtual workers as connected as other new hires and provides a more flexible means for any new hire to participate
	• Introduction to cultural norms of the industry, including customers and clients	• Include as a topic in hiring manager checklist to conduct through conversations with new hire	• Alerts new hire to norms of the industry in which the company participates, possibly even more important for experienced hires, as they may have biases from previous employment
Excel	• Reinforce the company culture, ethics, and values	• Subsequent new hire summits where new hires reconnect with their cohorts at the third to fourth quarters • Use of wiki continues throughout the first year • Check-in "call" from HR or onboarding leaders at 6-month mark • Capture from the new hires their independent ideas on the company culture (could be a group discussion, survey, a 1:1 conversation with the hiring manager and the new hire) • Hiring managers and/or mentors discuss culture and performance value experiences during assignments and in the annual assessment • As new hires "graduate" at the end of their first year, they become peer buddies for the next class of new hires	• Discussions should explore what the new hires have experienced, comparing and contrasting corporate culture to subcultures (e.g., teams, divisions) • Check-ins need to be more than perfunctory actions. They need to be conducted by individuals who care to create value in the discussions • Provides an opportunity for new hires to share their own successes, demonstrating progress toward individual development • Capture the feedback on how the organization received the new hire and helps inform any refresh efforts on the onboarding program

4

"CONNECTIONS THAT COUNT"—EMPOWERING EMPLOYEES BY NURTURING VALUABLE RELATIONSHIPS

An HR executive for a leading corporation headquartered in the northwest had a vexing problem. New campus hires (i.e., college recruits) were leaving corporate positions at a rate 30% greater than the industry average, and he could not figure out why. The company was a premier employer. It performed better than the industry average in its recruiting, was in an enviable competitive and financial position, was considered progressive, and had a youthful culture that rewarded innovation and creativity. In many regards, it was the ideal place to launch a career. Why, then, were so many campus hires leaving?

Culling through attrition data, our client found that 70% of exiting campus hires left at the 11-month mark. He investigated further, walking the halls and pulling aside several new hires to ask questions. How did they like working there? Were they enjoying their assignments? How was their work-life balance? He received glowing responses.

So what in the world was going on?

Over lunch, the executive shared this mystery with a 25-year-old team member. "You almost lost me after 11 months," the junior employee offered.

"As much as I liked my job, this town is cold, and I mean that in more than one way. Our winters are frigid, and it's tough to get to know people here. And collecting friends in college was easy; everyone was in the same position when they first arrived, and we all needed people to hang out with. When I came here, I was mixed in with a far more diverse group, both culturally and also where everyone was in their life (married with kids, divorcing, second career, nearing retirement, etc.), and at the end of the day everyone went their separate ways. It was exciting being here at first, but I spent a lot of winter nights alone in front of the TV, wishing I was back on the East Coast."

"Why 11 months though?" our client wondered.

"Simple," the team member replied. "I took my apartment lease two weeks before my start date, at 12 months my lease is up, and I need a few weeks to pack up and move."

"Aha," our client thought. After using a series of objective interviews and surveys to test the story's validity relative to many other hypotheses, our client realized he was on to something. The company was recruiting from West Coast and East Coast schools, given the specific talent it was seeking to attract, and it was importing people into a foreign, culturally different, and (some might argue) challenging environment. The "isolated feeling" responses collected in our client's research were astonishingly high. Taking other HR executives through the evidence and explaining the cost of attrition, our client proposed a series of socialization opportunities for new hires—experiences that would help new hires cement relationships early in their tenure. He hoped to replicate the intense and personal networking environment found at universities. Starting at Day One, new hires would engage in a series of activities with peer cohorts and more senior leadership interaction would make them feel more supported and connected. Our client also determined that it was not sufficient to help make connections within the company. The new hires needed a larger local network, so he proposed organizing new employee networking events in conjunction with other local-area companies. His ideas, he thought, were a slam-dunk.

To his surprise, eyebrows rose around the conference table and a barrage of questions from his colleagues ensued: "Shouldn't our recruits be personable enough to form relationships on their own? If not, are we hiring the right people? If we treat our campus hires like college students, won't it set the wrong tone? Is this really our business? Aren't we much better off using our budget on training?"

Fortunately, our client managed to win over this skeptical audience; the data were too compelling. As he pointed out, the company was wrong in regarding high attrition as a fixed reality. Although managers had written off Gen Y campus hires as self-indulgent "job-hoppers," the reality was more complex. Gen Y sought satisfying, meaningful work more intensely than earlier generations had, and they also were moving around the country more in pursuit of their careers, both of which left them more eager to forge strong bonds at work. An opportunity existed for the organization to win comfort and loyalty among new hires by helping them become more socially connected. Enabling new hires to nurture social networks better would add value for new hires, redefining the employment compact in ways they found relevant, while simultaneously benefiting the company. Our client turned out to be right. The investment he was proposing dramatically reduced employees' likelihood of leaving. It also did something unexpected: Connections created by the programs helped to enhance business performance.

State-of-the-art onboarding programs treat new hires not as a short-term resource but as a long-term asset, one with the potential to appreciate in value if nurtured with upfront and sustained investments. In the last chapter, we made a case for investing in cultural orientation. This chapter argues that investment in relationship building, at all levels of hire and for all generations of employees, is also critical if we are to achieve the Onboarding Margin.

Most executives accept that professional networking is a necessary and incredibly valuable business function, and companies have long supported networking in various forms. Since the popularization of the term in the 1980s, networking has thrived as a means of identifying new opportunities for sales professionals and business development executives and of strengthening professions and careers in general. In its early incarnation, networking took the form of socializing in informal groups (e.g., the golf course, barber shop, local charities, sidelines of children activities, etc.) and formalized associations (the local business association, formal networking clubs). More recently, online social networks like Facebook have become popular, with sites like LinkedIn focusing exclusively on business communities. Despite all of this interest, as well as significant scientific study of the nature and power of social networks in business contexts, most companies have not devoted significant attention and resources to drive relationship building. Moreover, management has neglected the special social needs of one group that requires support more than any other: New hires.

We commonly hear from management the idea that "relationships happen." Although this is true, empirical evidence also suggests that companies can stimulate relationship building, just like it can acculturation, and reap the rewards. The point is to facilitate, hasten, and optimize the process and in this way generate new value. New hires need to make the *right* connections, and they need to do so in a timely fashion—before they have a chance to pass judgment on their decisions to join their firms.

To better nurture relationship building, firms should go beyond the scattered half-measures currently in place and embrace structured social programs that start very early and unfold progressively over the first year of the new hire's tenure. These programs should embrace both professional and personal networking, help new hires build networks both inside and outside the firm, mobilize stakeholders throughout the firm, including senior leadership, and also include provisions to ensure that new hires' families are comfortable.

Imagine how much you could affect productivity and retention if your new hires were connected to all the right people sooner; better understood the backgrounds, roles, and expertise of those people; and if they and their families felt generally happier and better adjusted in their lives. As an added benefit, this relationship stimulus not only helps satisfy new hires' social needs; it also helps drive the acclimation and strategic orientation processes outlined in other chapters. Everything working together as one system—that is onboarding at its best.

Relationships and Networks: A Look at the Evidence

Five friends from the same college who moved to Washington, DC for their first jobs got together for Sunday brunch. All had been transitioning into their jobs over the past two to three months, so naturally the conversation settled on their first professional experiences. Of the five, three were already contemplating a job move. A fourth was seriously unhappy. Only one of the five reported still feeling satisfied with her job.

As the discussion continued, the four unhappy group members agreed that their social lives at work had proved disappointing, to say the least. After an initial week of training exercises with other new hires, these friends were mostly left alone in their cubicles with a stack of assignments. Co-workers were 10 or more years older, and it was sometimes difficult to enjoy a non-work-related conversation. The loneliness made work seem like a daily grind instead of something in which an employee could take pleasure and pride. When one of these recent graduates found her lunch missing from the shared refrigerator, she did not even know whom to talk to about it, much less feel comfortable raising the issue. This only led to a growing feeling of insecurity.

As we saw earlier, the psychologist Abraham Maslow listed social belonging within his hierarchy of basic human needs. It is recognized by social scientists and physiologists that when social needs go unsatisfied at work, people indeed become lonely, anxious, and depressed in their employment and at home. We also know that relationships can make you happier at work; hence, the very convention in many firms of holding "happy hours." Empirical research bears out the wisdom of happy hour. According to research performed by the Gallup organization, 30% of workers polled strongly agreed that they had a best friend in the workplace. Among this group, 56% reported being engaged workers, 33% reported being unengaged, and 11% reported being actively unengaged. Compare this with the 70% of workers who didn't strongly agree that they had a best friend at work: Only 8% of this group reported being engaged employees, 63% reported being not engaged, and 29% percent reported being actively disengaged. Relatedly, a separate study of workers at a California telecom company found that those who behave benevolently toward their fellow workers and receive favors in return are more productive than those who do not.[1] The title of the article presenting this research put it well, "Best Friends Are Good for Business."

Recognition of relationships' emotional benefits has motivated organizations to socialize new hires via welcome breakfasts, team building outings, and the like. Firms also provide social outlets in the form of softball leagues, affinity groups, and involvement in charity events. Yet as our five friends discovered, such scattered measures were hardly enough to help them nurture the healthy relationships they needed to feel healthy and happy at work. A skeptical manager might object that the burden of assuring a single new hire's emotional well-being is huge, and attending to the sense of belonging of a whole cohort cannot and should not rest on an organization's shoulders. That is undoubtedly true; however, firms could do much more to ensure happy workers, and it remains in their self-interest to do so.

The benefits of nurturing networks and strong social relationships among new hires go well beyond a happier, better-adjusted, more invigorated workforce. In the business world, progress depends upon connections and relationships. As people work in organizations, they form relationships that allow for work to get done, whether it is a traditional, rote task or the more challenging task of transforming processes at an organization. People realize a number of practical benefits by tapping into a network. They gain more information about and perspective on the challenges they face. They gain a chance to spread the word and get buy-in and feedback on their ideas—which in turn helps them build consensus and achieve results. Finally, they gain creative stimulation from exposure to the careers, success, and ideas of other individuals, leading to better job performance, more engagement, and stronger loyalty.

By enhancing the process by which new hires forge professional relationships, firms can help them work better on a daily basis. Knowing whom to approach for an answer allows you to address the issue quickly, minimizing problems or minor annoyances and frustrations. You know how to work the system, which as an ancillary benefit makes you feel happier and less frustrated. It also increases your self-esteem, confidence, achievement, self-respect, and value in the eyes of others—all of which taken together comprise *the second highest category on Maslow's hierarchy.*

Sometimes connections allow employees to recognize problems proactively and come up with solutions. An operations engineer on a factory line is tasked with making sure the machines keep running. She notices that a part keeps breaking, or she spots an opportunity for improvement that might be applied elsewhere in the company. Rather than keeping this information to herself, she passes it along to a member of her network within the firm, who uses it to make improvements. This can happen in the first month of employment, the first year, the third year, or of course, not at all. When they do happen, collaborative relationships can develop into full-fledged partnerships over time, delivering measurable results for companies. Gallup research has shown that "those who have one or more strong partnerships at work generate better customer scores, safety, retention, creativity, productivity, and profitability for their companies."[2]

We've noted that social networks have gotten a lot of press in recent years. Twenty years ago, we all were told to go out and network professionally as a business activity. More recently, Web 2.0 and social networking have become fashionable, whereas social scientists have established the power of networks by charting the social contagion of variables such as happiness, smoking, and obesity.[3] How strange it is, then, that firms have not evolved more strategic programs for helping new hires build their professional and personal networks. If anything, the potential payback from networking inside a firm should exceed that offered by online social networking generally. As many people are finding, a service like LinkedIn offers somewhat limited benefits, since the members of a person's network often don't feel enough of a sense of shared interest to come forth with valuable exchanges. Online connections are easy to make, and so networking online often devolves into an exercise in collecting contacts (i.e., it becomes "a volume game") rather than what it might be—a means to truly create personal and enterprise value. By contrast, people networking within a company have a much stronger shared interest. If social networks provide value in the broad environment, they should provide all that much more value within the bounded construct of a company.

The Connection Matrix

Companies should help new hires build better personal networks internally, but they should by no means stop there. Our research and work with clients has led us to identify two dimensions: internal vs. external and professional vs. personal, yielding four unique kinds of networks of use to new hires:

- Internal Professional Networks
- Internal Personal Networks
- External Personal Networks
- External Professional Networks

Let's examine these four kinds of networks one by one, as well as their relevance for new hires.

Internal professional networks

Internal professional networks are relationships a new hire develops within a firm that bears directly on his or her fulfillment of job functions. Members of these networks include peers, subordinates, and bosses, all the way up to a company's senior leadership. They include key support staff in other functions, such as marketing, HR, business development, or finance, or in the same function but across an organization's business units. If you are an engineer at a firm like Mitsubishi with many kinds of technical businesses, you might want to network with other engineers who work in different business units but perhaps on similar problems or with similar technologies (i.e., *Communities of Practice*), or who work for your business unit at different sites around the world.

There is significant long-term value to establishing a peer network. Peers typically serve as the new hires' colleagues as they progress simultaneously through the organization. Having a strong peer network and consciously developing it as a priority can make an enormous difference in establishing and expanding one's influence over the long run. Not having a peer network can limit not only the new hires' happiness and provide trusted and helpful perspective and support; it can also lead to not being "known" well enough later on, especially in cultures in which collaboration and a "one-company" culture is important.

We have already evoked some of the ways internal relationships can help new hires adjust to their jobs and work more productively. Here we observe that firms need to pay special attention to helping newly hired middle and senior management hires build internal networks. Unlike lower level hires, middle and senior manager hires have job descriptions that essentially revolve around connections with people. Whereas a customer service representative's primary job involves performing a particular task, members of a company in managerial positions perform by interacting with and influencing others. Today, when every initiative involves a "cross-functional" team, new hire managers rely even more on the right network and relationships, and these relationships become even more mission-critical the more you ascend—or the higher you enter—the corporate ladder.

If your company hires its managers externally, then the social component of a strategic program clearly merits attention. However, for those firms that promote largely from within, a social component is arguably even more vital to include for the few outsiders these firms do hire; after all, these individuals will find themselves all the more behind their peers in understanding whom in a firm to leverage for their needs, both with regard to business needs and cultural orientation.

In all firms, a more comprehensive approach to building internal networks will prove helpful in allowing new hires entry into the perceived (or real) exclusive networks that seem to prevail in many workplaces. We found in our work, some of these networks might seem exclusive not because members of the network are actively preventing new hires from gaining entry, but simply because nobody has taken time to open the door and invite new hires in. To assimilate new mid-level and senior hires, firms need to integrate them into informal groups that exist within firms, understanding that existing employees are often too busy or distracted to recognize the need to do so on their own. A strong social component to a systemic onboarding program can compensate for the thoughtlessness or obliviousness of individual managers and help new hires gain access to a seemingly "closed" group of friends and colleagues.

Internal personal networks

A second kind of network that companies should help new hires nurture is the internal personal network. These are friendly relationships new hires develop with other employees within a firm. Personal internal networks might include members of a new hire cohort, employees who sit near a new hire, friends new hires might make in the company cafeteria, and colleagues the new hire interacts with regularly in meetings. Such relationships do not necessarily serve a specific business function; rather, they are nurtured on account of the happiness people find in having a "best friend at work," and they are built upon perceived personal affinity; for instance, a shared view on topics such as sports, politics, or religion.

Most new hires are going to make friends eventually at work, especially in larger organizations, which contain many diverse personalities. There, though, the task becomes finding people. The sooner you can help new hires find their friends, the better. Younger workers often enter a firm with higher expectations about the social aspect of the work experience, given their recent experiences in college; it is critical to meet those expectations as fully as possible. Younger workers are also more likely to enter with preconceptions regarding excessive, cutthroat competition at work, depictions of which are popularized in movies and television. Fortunately, these negative and dysfunctional ideas can dissipate quickly as valued relations are formed and new hires begin to experience the benefits associated with support. For older and more seasoned new hires, onboarding allows a firm an opportunity to exceed expectations as the new hires achieve a sense of belonging sooner and more readily than they might have thought. For all new hires, these personal relationships assist with the process of cultural and strategic orientation.

External personal networks

A third kind of network, the external personal network, also factors prominently in assuring a new hire's job satisfaction. Personal external networks include an individual's broader network of friends and family, as well as those of their significant others and family members. Although people spend most of their waking hours at work, the personal relationships they develop outside the workplace can also affect their job performance, since happier new hires are more productive and less inclined to leave. This is an especially important component for recent college graduates and any new hire who moves to a new geographic location for his or her job.

A number of progressive companies are experimenting with innovative ways of helping new hires build new social relationships outside of work. Target realized that many of the hip young designers they recruited from design hotbeds on the East and West Coast were having trouble adjusting to life in Minneapolis, so they created a program designed to offer them more "big-city" cultural opportunities. Realizing that a minority of new hires were having special difficulties finding a place in that same city, General Mills linked up with other big employers and helped to foster a new hire group with that same ethnic background. As these examples suggest, it is important that firms customize their social network facilitation in line with their employee populations. Firms need to figure out who is moving to the area, determine their unique needs, and take steps to fill those needs.

Employees with kids and families, for instance, might require help with things like finding schools, religious institutions, cultural opportunities, and employment opportunities for spouses, whereas a younger set of new hires may not.

External professional networks

A final kind of network pivotal to a new hire's success is the external professional network. This network contains peers located outside of the workplace who nonetheless enhance a new hire's ability to get work done. These peers could be functionally related to the new hire (e.g., other quality control managers), members of the same industry, or competitors and business partners (e.g., suppliers, value adding channel participants, or customers). All are part of the organization's and new hire's *business ecosystem*, and as such all can help the new hire get more accomplished with less energy.

Business Ecosystems Managers sometimes underestimate just how vital an ecosystem can be to achieving goals; a big mistake. Many years ago, Microsoft had a sales force of only a hundred people, a size clearly inadequate to achieve the firm's ambitious goal of getting everybody to adopt Microsoft's enterprise software products. Taking stock of the challenge, Microsoft realized that a number of independent technology businesses out in the market possessed the knowledge and local relationships required to sell the firm's products. So Microsoft embraced a business model centered on "Value Added Resellers," educating these members of its ecosystem and tooling and empowering them to sell Microsoft's products on behalf of the company. This created extreme leverage for Microsoft, enabling performance exponentially higher than what would have been possible given the investment the company made in its personnel. This is just one example of development and exploitation of an ecosystem. Firms also rely on external networks when they get communities of third-party developers to add enhancements to platforms, or enlist customers to serve as evangelists for products or even act as product designers themselves. This general theme has been further popularized via attention to relatively new concepts such as "crowd sourcing."

Given how vital ecosystems have become, firms must do as much as possible to help individuals develop external contacts. For a scientist working at a company's R&D lab, this might mean going to a professional association meeting to cultivate leads that can serve as future knowledge sources. Firms should strive to get new hires out to professional communities bearing on the firm's business—and do it early. Forging these kinds of professional relationships will instill a sense of pride of organization, and it can also have the added benefit of helping individuals simultaneously build their own personal relationships, since professional colleagues frequently become treasured friends.

Activating Relationships

Working with any of these four network types, companies will build new value by helping new hires forge more and better relationships. Because organizations cannot know exactly when networking will prove helpful in bringing about a specific business result, they need to increase social exposures to increase the likelihood of positive outcomes. Best Buy has recognized this, going so far as to design their corporate headquarters to stimulate random social interaction among their employees. The design is built around a central hub that connects a series of terminal extensions leading to individual office corridors on numerous floors. This design forces people to pass through the central hub dozens of times throughout the week—creating unexpected meetings between colleagues that are believed by most to stimulate conversations between individuals who would otherwise have minimal cause for interaction.[4] Similarly, companies should design social components to their onboarding programs that maximize the chances that new hires will build relationships helpful to them and their employers. What follows is a list of best principles that some of the best-in-class firms we have worked with and studied have incorporated.

Best Principle #1: Encourage participation in affinity groups.
Affinity groups (e.g., running clubs, social action or charitable groups, outings clubs) bring together people from within and outside a firm who possess common interests. Many companies provide low-level funding to clubs to help sustain their activities. If your firm currently does not have affinity groups, this is an important area to explore; such groups provide even greater utility for new hires than for existing employees. Even small

to mid-sized firms can nurture affinity groups at an informal level, encouraging existing and new employees to form or sustain them on their own. Diverse stakeholders have a potential role to play in making connections between a new hire's interests and those of other people in the firm. At various times during a new hire's first year, the HR recruiter, hiring manager, mentor, and new hire buddy could sit down with the new hire, exploring his or her social interests, creating awareness of existing affinity groups and providing resources and encouragement to start new ones.

Affinity can also serve as an organizing principle in the design of mentoring or orientation programs, particularly as relates to diversity initiatives. Citigroup's Sponsor Family initiative integrates a diversity component into the firm's mentoring program, creating core "families" of employees based on their social or cultural background. These families meet with a different member of senior management each month, a practice that creates mentor linkages and provides senior management with insight into the extraordinary challenges faced by many minorities. New connections are forged between the senior leader and "family" members—connections that could bring future benefits. Mentoring relationships serve as important conduits for the transmission of social, cultural, and strategic knowledge and for the bonding that comes with sharing personal stories. The use of affinity groups to support networking can also help build external personal and professional relationships.

Best Principle #2: Leverage resources in the larger community.
To help new hires build social relations outside the workplace, companies can draw on resources that exist in the local communities of which they are a part. Recognizing that many of its hires were young and coming from distant areas—and mindful, too, of being a grow-from-within organization—Procter & Gamble leveraged the cultural resources of Cincinnati in creating a web site for new hires that describes the many cultural and social opportunities the city has to offer. The web site offers discussions of the city's nightlife, its geographic location relative to other cities, and its diverse neighborhoods in hopes of easing the transition for new hires moving in for the first time. The site also includes advice from recent new hires about how to get the most out of what the city has to offer.

As one employee quoted on the site suggests, "Have an open mind. No city is perfect. Set your priorities and find your happy balance. For me, bars, restaurants, or night life were the least important, so I decided to stay away from downtown or other relatively crowded neighborhoods. More important things were—grad school and work opportunities for my wife, cost of living (I didn't want to eat peanut butter and jelly sandwiches every day trying to own a house), commute time to work and back (no more than 25 minutes each way), "intellect" level of the city (are there good schools around, what kind of industries exist in the city), and cultural diversity." As this quote suggests, Procter & Gamble has become keenly aware of the broader needs of its new hires outside of work. The firm has drawn on the resources of Cincinnati, yet it has refrained from advertising the city, opting instead for the open and honest messaging advocated in the last chapter.

Another resource firms can look to when designing social components of their onboarding program is other firms. General Mills takes a lead in organizing and funding social events for new hires in collaboration with other companies in the same geographic location as their headquarters. The firm also funds corporate teams (e.g., softball, cycling groups, soccer) and encourages them to participate in community activities alongside groups from other firms. As our research has found, managers at General Mills believe this program has contributed to reducing turnover among new hires that have had difficulty relocating.

Best Principle #3: Build stakeholder maps.
To help new hires understand who should comprise their internal professional network, onboarding designers should catalogue key players, the value they provide to the enterprise, and the assistance they could render to new hires. At Johnson & Johnson Canada, an external onboarding coach collects business and organizational data, creating stakeholder relationship maps for new executive hires.[5] As Malcolm Gladwell, author of *The Tipping Point*, has discussed, mavens and connectors play a large role in popularizing social ideas. New hires likewise should know the identities of "mavens" within a firm who can answer questions based on institutional and historic knowledge. At our firm, we do not have a formal knowledge management—program, but everyone knows who the old-timers in the company are, and they can turn to these individuals to learn if we have ever worked on certain kinds of projects or with certain kinds of clients. "Connectors" might not have the institutional knowledge of

mavens, but their own extensive personal connections allow new hires to more quickly locate the resources they need to complete important tasks. New hires' managers should also create more individualized stakeholder maps to ensure that new hires understand who in the firm can best help them succeed in their roles. Managers should also instruct new hires to create their own maps over the course of the first year, drawing on the firm's strategy and the nature of their roles for guidance. That way, new hires can one day serve as connectors for future classes of new hires. As we'll discuss later, these maps can also serve as valuable tools for the teaching of strategy.

Best Principle #4: Make it interactive.
It is not enough to circulate lists of contacts or post information on the Internet; you have to make social relationship building, well, *social*. Mentoring and buddy programs offer an excellent beginning; not only can new hires gain the mentor or buddy as social contacts, but these individuals can take steps to help new hires engage with others (e.g., by arranging meetings with other employees or pointing new hires to other employees, leveraging existing opportunities for socialization). *Lunch and Learn* events with experienced employees allow new hires to interact up the organizational chart, developing contacts potentially useful not only for the performance of future work tasks but for future career development as well.

For their executive hires, John Deere pre-schedules meetings for the first three to four months with key functional heads throughout the organization. Bristol-Myers Squibb likewise organizes meetings between new hires and important colleagues, using HR and an outside consultant to monitor progress during Year One.[6] With such mechanisms in place, hires get to ask the point people any questions they might have, and they also become familiar with the stakeholders who make decisions. PepsiCo tries to make acculturation and strategic insight learning fun by having new executives participate in an informational "scavenger hunt"—an intricate, daily/ weekly challenge that executives handle by tracking down individuals who possess the right information. By participating, new hires establish a network across the company, and they learn the specific roles of network members. As a result, they can soon call on the right people to help with future real business problems.

Best Principle #5: Start very early, but do not end there.
Relationship building is an area in which firms can make progress before Day One—and the earlier the start, the greater the impact to the Onboarding Margin. Some firms offer social networking sites as a means of forging connections early on, presenting details on the backgrounds, interests, roles, responsibilities, reporting lines, and contact information of the firm's members. New hires can search and sort (by keyword or tag) and identify individuals with common interests or career paths. Virtual workers, a rapidly growing part of the workforce at many organizations, particularly benefit from early exposure to online relationship building.

As part of connections made during the recruiting process, firms can also begin to connect new hires to current employees or the rest of the incoming class of new hires. Even the smallest of firms can set up a virtual group at no cost using tools like LinkedIn or a Google group page so that all new hires can see each other's names, find out in which areas they are living, and gain information helpful to the moving process. We founded just such a virtual group at our firm, and as a result, at least a few of our new hires actually decided to live together, making this housing decision before their start date and creating a strong cohort support bond.

Universities such as UC Irvine and Dartmouth engage new students pre-matriculation using new-student extranet sites; firms can do the same with new hires, adopting tactics such as pre-start visits and relocation packets. On UC Irvine's extranet site, new students make friends before even setting foot on school grounds, using functions like chatting and note-posting to share knowledge and ask peers for advice or help. An IT consultant for the school told us that "having one central resource that does everything really helps orient new students. Plus, it hasn't required a lot of maintenance." For companies and colleges alike, pre-start visits and other social events included as part of the recruiting process allow potential new hires to "interview" the city and not just the company. This ensures that the organization acquires people amenable to the geography and that individuals are relocated more smoothly, so they are better able to hit the ground running on their first day.

Like other components of systemic and strategic onboarding, the nurturing of social relations is not a one-off event; rather, it must be continued progressively over the entire first year of a new hire's tenure. The childcare provider Bright Horizons re-welcomes employees for months after they join the company. As one employee was quoted as saying, "I never went to a meeting where I was not introduced and made to feel welcome."[7] Likewise, the Office of the Comptroller of the Currency (OCC), a division of the United States Treasury Department, brings in new hires as a group and establishes a cohort identity for them, even though these new hires are scattered in offices across the country. The organization brings back these new hires at multiple times during the first two years, fostering the relationships built at the beginning and allowing new hires to share experiences they encountered in their regions. The extended time frame coupled with the small group approach helps with new hires' cultural acclimation, as these employees have a chance to compare and contrast their cultural knowledge and experiences. Since the organization brings in more tenured individuals to offer advice to cohort groups, the onboarding process also contributes early career support, which we will dig into more in Chapter 5.

Best Principle #6: Think small.
Working new hires into small groups during the onboarding process is a great way of fostering more and deeper connections. Enmeshed in a small group during the first few days or week, new hires experience the firm in a personalized way and are more inclined to engage with the onboarding process overall. Assigning new hires into small groups or cohorts leaves them with a "go-to" peer resource group that can handle their questions or concerns, leaving new hires more comfortable and better able to engage in team-building. Working with small groups requires that firms devote more time and resources to onboarding, as it's more efficient to onboard employees *en masse* rather than in multiple small groups. Small groups might also require additional planning around the composition of the groups. Still, small groups provide the benefit of simulating small work groups—the context in which most new hires eventually spend most of their work time, regardless of overall organization size. Small groups also force new hires to build relationships with individuals with whom they may not have a natural affinity. Relationship building is a necessary skill and one that the onboarding designer should stimulate right out of the gate. Even if you choose not to organize your entire onboarding program into small cohorts, you can take advantage of the learning and interaction that comes from small groups by breaking up your larger new hire class

into small cohorts for different onboarding activities. The technology and strategy consulting firm Booz Allen Hamilton divides its new hire start groups into teams of five or six for several group exercises and simulations. As one new hire noted, "I really liked the interactivity of the table teams and the collaborative work effort. I walked out of orientation knowing four new colleagues much better." Not a bad first-day win.

Similar to the program cited earlier at the OCC, Best Buy has seen clear improvements in the assimilation of its employees through its use of small groups. The firm breaks its five-day initial orientation program into fixed groups of 15 to 20 people and then uses these groups as the central structure of the entire onboarding program. Group members naturally continue to support one another week in and week out. Groups come back together at the 6-month mark for a "celebration" event that provides recognition for early achievements and offers a forum for feedback on how well new hires have been positioned to succeed in their jobs. As the firm has found, individuals are more likely to ask clarifying questions and voice concerns in small groups, and they are more likely to create linkages across functional and geographic divides.

Even if you do not implement small groups, you can still incorporate something of the small group feel by taking steps to personalize the onboarding experience. Google gives its new hires a fun, collective identity by calling them "Nooglers" and lavishing them with special treatment the first week, including a campus tour, numerous lectures from special speakers, welcome balloons and bags of chocolate, "Google Buddies" who answer their technical questions, and special events at which their names are flashed on a television screen.

Although we caution you against going too far and offering new hires a premium experience that is at odds with real-life company (i.e., too much small group attention), taking some steps to recognize new hires and make them feel special can go far in offering the sense of intimacy that comes with being part of a small group.[8]

Best Principle #7: Leverage technologies.
As with cultural orientation, social orientation benefits from the incorporation of new technologies. At management and IT consulting firm Clarkston Consulting, the onboarding team deploys an online site to stay in touch with new associates during the months between acceptance of

job offers and the first day of employee boot camp. New hires can find information about the company, training, and company culture as well as participate in a discussion blog.[9]

Social networking sites can also provide an informal and easy way for new hires to connect with one another. As of this writing, more than 15,000 firms are maintaining Facebook networks, and many best-in-class companies are creating internal networking sites with a familiar look for incoming new hires. Among these companies is Starbucks, whose cutting-edge networking site provides social and career development as well as productivity resources. Modeled after sites like LinkedIn or Facebook, Starbucks' site includes employee profiles, blogs, and messaging capabilities, allowing new hires to interact with other employees and learn information about various teams and programs at the company.

Another, related technology that can potentially help new hires to establish social relationships is the virtual reality experience of the video game Second Life. IBM has begun making use of Second Life as a means of holding virtual corporate meetings. In the words of one reporter, "This isn't the work of teenage gamers interning at IBM. Researchers are looking at the potential business impact of virtual worlds and massively multiplayer online games."[10] Incorporated into a best-in-class onboarding program, Second Life technology can allow new hires to interact with each other in real time before even showing up for the first day. The technology could also allow busy executives to mingle across geographies without spending the time or incurring the expenses required for an in-person social experience.

The good news on the social networking front is that a tremendous number of such tools are available off the shelf, many at no cost. Even if your enterprise neglects to use these tools, a very good chance exists that your employees are building these electronic networks on their own. Harnessing those already in place doesn't only enhance the onboarding experience, it also supports the better building of networks for existing employees. To some extent, you can rely on these electronic networks to naturally form where there is the greatest need and value. But the enterprise can also garner attention around key needs by submitting content contributions that relate to those needs and having leaders participate strategically in online discussions.

Best Principle #8: Involve senior leadership.
In the book so far, we have been making the case for involving stakeholders across the enterprise, up to and including senior leadership. In helping new hires nurture relationships and build networks, senior leadership has a special role to play. Research has shown that new hires yearn to be inspired by the organization and its vision, and nobody is better placed to speak for the organization than senior executives. For many new hires, it is the charismatic and accomplished leader of a firm—a Bill Gates, a Sir Richard Branson, a Steve Winn, a Jeff Immelt, a Meg Whitman, or a Steve Jobs—who makes you want to join the firm in the first place. Senior leaders represent the opportunity that lies ahead for new hires; they ignite new hires' imaginations by talking about their own journey to success within the organization and the challenges and opportunities encountered along the way. New hires benefit from potentially forging personal contacts with people at the top, and the firm benefits if leaders can focus their conversation explicitly on what they want out of new hires. It is not necessarily the senior-most leader (e.g., the CEO) who has the most impact. For many new hires, occupying second- and third-tier leadership positions seems a more realistic goal than becoming CEO, because so few people can achieve that honor. Many new hires are thus more inclined to feel inspired by the stories of lower-level leaders who have beat the odds and achieved satisfying successes.

Although their time is scarce, every leader must make some effort to engage with new hires, even if it is limited to, say, a monthly breakfast with a few specially selected new hires or a regularly organized "surprise" visit to an office with the names and backgrounds of the new hires in hand. At the non-profit IT consulting firm Mitre, new hires receive short personal notes from senior vice presidents.[11] Many professional services firms have successfully involved senior leaders in onboarding and are seeing great results; in this industry, leadership involvement has become the gold standard. Even if leaders only attend events for a short while, they can still have an impact. The onboarding program designer can handle the challenges of scheduling busy leaders by developing a pool of willing senior leaders well in advance of each event, by scheduling events several months in advance, by providing the executives with a one-page cheat sheet with guidance on the importance of and the best methods for engaging new hires, and by formally scheduling and tracking reminders with executive assistants to allow time to find replacements, if necessary.

The senior leadership's participation has an added benefit: It conveys to the rest of the organization that the onboarding program has senior leadership's backing and approval. Firms can give onboarding its stamp of approval in many ways. Yet having a chance to interact with senior leadership conveys the firm's commitment to onboarding and the success of new hires like nothing else can. Hiring managers, mentors, IT personnel, etc. will all get the hint that onboarding matters and it represents a superbly important investment in the company's future on the part of senior leaders. As many new hires as possible should have the experience of getting to know the people who steer the organization and who themselves model the successful maintenance of social networks.

Summing Up

A strong, nurturing social life is both a basic human need and essential for career success. Yet most companies do not help nurture relationship building among new hires as fully as they might, and the organization pays a price. As we have discussed in this chapter, firms need to take a more strategic approach to building relationships. Specifically, they need to include programs that help new hires nourish personal and professional networks both inside and outside the workplace. Such measures cannot guarantee that every employee will be perfectly happy and well adjusted. But a strong social component can increase the chances that more and better relationships will form, leading to higher productivity and lower attrition.

Over the long term, perhaps one of the most valuable functions a strong network can serve for new hires is providing a means of professional development. The relationships that new hires form—particularly within an organization—are available for leveraging throughout an individual's career. This leads us to another pillar of state of the art onboarding: early career support (Table 4.1). As will be seen in the next chapter, providing new hires with the support they need to build successful, satisfying careers is another important way we can redefine the employment compact to benefit new hires while also carving out new value for organizations.

Table 4.1 Interpersonal Network Elements—Sample Tactics

Onboarding Phase	Element	Sample Tactics	Application Advice
Prepare	• Pre-Day one Networking Activities	• In person office tour and cocktail hour • Pre-start company outing (e.g., ball game) • Cohort/small group dinner • Company "Second Life" virtual world simulation • Prestart online social networking (either company developed or utilizing existing tools; e.g., LinkedIn or Facebook) • Provide a list of industry group (e.g., trade associations) and relevant functional (e.g., professional association) events	• Optimal delivery option will depend on support personnel availability and geographic dispersion of new hires • In-person activities with current employee involvement are suggested, as they allow new hires to form personal connections • Online/virtual networking are the most feasible alternative for firms with geographically dispersed new hires • Hiring manager can encourage participation by extending personal invitations for new hire in pre-start phase to join in an upcoming community event
	• Guidance on moving to new city	• Section on new hire portal with Week One tip sheet and check list for key activities • Tips saved on welcome gift company flash drive • Hard copy checklist sent to new hire via mail/email • Wiki for employees or new hires to share feedback and input on the city • Incorporate local events in the company newsletter • Recruiting manager can collect questions from new hires (pre-start) and solicit recommendations from individuals within the firm who might have particularly informed point of view and advice.	• Having a personal resource to answer questions and provide insider advice is optimal, but it requires a high level of resources and is not feasible for all organizations • Web-based guidance or mailing handbook is suitable complement/alternative • Make sure to inform the new hire as to the source of the recommendation. It will be a superbly personal and positive experience to learn that an answer came from an existing employee within the firm
Orient	• Designed networking activities	• "Speed networking" activity with other new hires • Lunch with experienced employees • Post Day-One happy hour/celebrations with current employees, including senior level employees • Affinity group–based networking • Have new hires work in teams during orientation activities	• Ample networking time should be allotted in the Orientation period • These activities should be structured to promote comfort and purpose in interactions and so that new hires have forums to build relationships with both new hires and current employees • Plan networking activities at corporate and the local or team level • Each meeting should have an agenda—to cover an educational aspect—about the company's culture, current position, or strategy

Table 4.1 Interpersonal Network Elements—Sample Tactics (*Continued*)

Onboarding Phase	Element	Sample Tactics	Application Advice
	• Active introduction by mentors and managers	• Prepare the stakeholder maps and use them as a tool to make introductions between the new hires and the existing staff • Mentor or peer sponsor serving actively as a connector within their teams or local assignments • Provide introductions of new hires at team meetings	• Helps navigate the bureaucracy, know who is who, and who one should go to with questions • This is an "active" responsibility for mentors—not just pointing new hire in the right direction, but talking to the person to be introduced so he or she is ready for the new hire's call • Can begin at Orient, then carry through for integrate and excel
	• Distinguish new hires as a distinct group	• Give the new hires a name and establish cohorts	• Naming the cohort helps create an identity for them
Integrate	• Ongoing networking opportunities	• Consortium networking with local new hires from other orgs • Online networking tool on new hire portal (created during orientation, but really used further into tenure) • New hire affinity group events "Lunch and learns" with experienced employees	• Building an internal network should be one of the key new hire goals during the first 90 days, both with other new hires as well as experienced employees and leadership • Programs should provide mechanisms and activities for new hires to identify other employees with like professional and personal interests and build relationships with them
Excel	• Ongoing networking opportunities	• Consortium networking with local new hires from other orgs • Networking tool on new hire portal • New hire affinity events "Lunch and learns" with experienced employees • Personal invite from company leader for coffee, lunch, or dinner • End of year summit—those who have had key successes should be presenting them	• In addition to continuing company based networking opportunities from the earlier stages, orgs may want to provide chances to grow networks within the local community • Joint networking events with new hires at other local orgs are an effective means for new hires to build extra-work relationships and attachments to the local community • Also good for early career support so people can be proud of their accomplishments and show they've made progress

5

PERSONAL PROGRESS
AND PROSPECT: EARLY
CAREER SUPPORT

An investment in education always pays the highest returns.

— Ben Franklin

Cynthia Mills is a role model for other hiring managers. A floor sales manager for an upscale jewelry retailer in New York City, she has done the unthinkable, transforming the high-stress and rapid-turnover sales assistant position into one that retains more than 90% of new hires for two or more years. Several of Cynthia's sales assistants have even gone on to corporate-level management positions. What is her secret? Although it is not a part of a formalized HR process, Cynthia has developed a well-refined early career support program for her new sales assistants.

According to her employees, the early career support provided by Cynthia is unheard of for hourly wage retail sales roles. "On my first day," one recently hired sales assistant told us, "she sat me down and asked me loads of questions: What attracted me to the job? What do I hope to learn? What are my biggest goals? What kind of support do I need? What are my greatest strengths? It was almost like she was re-interviewing me, but unlike any interview I ever had for a retail position, and this was after I got the job. I've worked retail for 14 years and have never encountered such interest in my career development."

After conducting this initial session, Cynthia works with each new hire to create a personal development plan and match them with a more experienced mentor. Over the next 90 days, the new hire and mentor meet weekly to discuss progress, expectations, and goals. Once new hires have demonstrated proficiency in the core sales assistant competencies, Cynthia and their mentors identify "stretch goals" for the remainder of the year that align with the new hire's personal interests and objectives.

What drives Cynthia to devote such time and effort to developing her new employees is her keen awareness of the employer-employee compact. "A manager has an obligation to the new employee," she explains. "You're making an implicit promise to give employees the opportunity to be successful. It's a win-win for everyone. The more successful and happy employees are in their careers, the happier I am in mine. Beyond that, satisfied employees sell more and bring in more revenue for the company—and I do well when that happens. They also more easily and wholeheartedly embrace new initiatives and are more cued into our strategy, the good ones really want to prove themselves, and its best to get them turned on early."

Unfortunately, many hiring managers do not think in terms of a compact between employers and employees. We often hear hiring managers remark that it is a waste to invest in career support and planning before new hires have demonstrated their worth as employees. But this is inverted logic. The truth is that investing early helps distinguish great employees and increases the chances that they will want to stay with the company. Effective early career support programs also yield a higher number of great employees who reach full productivity faster.

Larger and more progressive companies have long invested in high potential personnel, whether it's funding MBAs or providing leadership development coursework. They have embraced the idea that helping employees develop their careers is worthwhile, and indeed, vital from a competitive performance standpoint. This chapter contends that firms should take three steps for Early Career Support in the context of an onboarding program:

1. *Personal Progress.* Engineer a support system that stimulates real and perceived progress throughout the employees' entire first year.
2. *Personal Prospect.* Apply the development and career-planning concept earlier in the employee life cycle; i.e., in the first year.
3. *Access.* Extend the model to all new hires (not just the lucky few).

New hires today seek more than just well-paying jobs; they want meaningful, fulfilling careers. Providing true early career support stands today as the single most important thing firms can do to energize new hires and gain their long-term loyalty and enthusiasm, which is why we label it one of the two power levers. Companies cannot afford to enroll everybody in an MBA program, but they can and need to incorporate a vision of the future into the present. They should provide some measure of assistance—including mentoring, coaching, and counseling—to help establish goals and measure progress against them. They should also provide help assessing career paths and creating a personal plan to *all* new employees throughout the first year. Every month, your new employees should believe that you really care about their success and want nothing more than for them to reach new heights. By acknowledging and supporting new hires in their career aspirations, and by helping them gain a vision of their personal career prospects, companies can redefine the employer-employee compact in a new, healthier way. This is not a commitment for lifetime employment; rather, it is a commitment to personal development with the expectation of greater yield in return. It is a win-win; when new employees make progress, the company benefits in the form of reduced attrition, and higher productivity levels and business performance. Once companies create content and weave it into the fabric of the current business and personnel processes, the incremental cost of widening the net to additional employees is low.

Early Career Support—Where We Stand Today

Initiatives in career development date to the turn of the 20th century, when many companies began to establish in-house training programs for salesmen, engineers, and certain skilled workers. These programs served as a natural extension of orientation into the firm, and they also served a career-planning function, since recruits could expect that completion of training and their standout performance could lead to promotion to the management track and a chance to climb the corporate ladder. These early programs were quite limited in scope, focusing primarily on technical rather than firm-specific information.

During the 1920s, many large companies instituted formal management training programs that were pretty much restricted to college graduates.

These programs typically gave each recruit a series of temporary assignments across the company. Graduates were exposed to the full scope and policies of the company, coming away with the broad, cooperative point of view a manager was supposed to have. Each manager also developed something of an instant network as well as an immediate sense of leadership. Although not called orientation, and certainly not onboarding, these training programs arguably served as an early best-in-class example of many of the Onboarding Margin principles.

Training programs came into their own during the 1970s, when some well-publicized strikes encouraged what came to be known as "job enrichment." Personnel managers and trainers became increasingly professional in their outlook. Ideas about organizational development made their way from universities into personnel departments, encouraging managers to think broadly about how new employees fit into the company.

Despite these efforts, the overall picture was mixed. Many employees received little in the way of job training throughout the 1980s and 1990s, and virtually no attention was paid to their broader career trajectories beyond the deep entrenchment of defined promotion paths. A large majority of managers were falling through the cracks from a development perspective. Clearly the model of survival of the fittest was in play and considered by many as not only fair, but efficient. While big companies still often had special programs for high-potential employees, most of these had shrunk to only a few days, with little individual attention. A Center for Creative Leadership's survey in found that only a third of newly hired managers received development in their new position, and even fewer got special attention from their bosses.

In recent years, companies have offered skills training to employees, hoping to get them productive in their positions more quickly and efficiently. This development was largely stimulated by a perceived shortage of skilled workers and an attempt by companies to distinguish their employer brands amidst the growing demand for knowledge workers. By 2001, some 2,000 firms were sponsoring corporate universities to disseminate cultural information, job skills, and workplace skills like leadership and creative thinking. And this number was projected to grow to almost 4,000 by 2010, exceeding the number of private US universities.[2] According to the American Society for Training and Development, US-based organizations were spending over $100 billion during the mid-2000s on learning and development, with expenditures and hours of training per employee on the rise.[3] A 2008 survey of more than 200 US employers found that almost half "provide training to improve new entrants' workforce readiness."[4] Yet these firms primarily offered job-specific and readiness training, spending less than 20% of training budgets on career development. Among those firms that didn't offer workforce training, spending on career development ran a bit higher—about a third of the learning budget.

To the extent companies across industries have invested in career development, they have introduced a number of useful tools and techniques, including formal and informal mentoring, career paths, career development planning, goal setting, performance feedback, and formal sponsorship within an organization. *Yet these tools remain greatly underutilized for new hires.* Companies offer them only sporadically and do not integrate them within formal onboarding programs. As a result, new hires still struggle to understand what they should do to build their careers, whether inside or outside the firm. Companies, meanwhile, fail to claim the full value that early career support could provide.

Some Common Career Development Tools

- Formal and informal mentoring
- Performance feedback
- Personal development plans
- Goal setting
- Company developed/led training
- Financed secondary degrees and certifications
- Networking support
- Performance feedback and direction
- Functional and industry conferences
- Leveraging diversity and affinity groups
- Career path support
- Formal and informal sponsorship within an organization
- Career fairs
- Coaching
- Introspective skill and personality assessments
- Identification and support of high potential employees
- Career pathing

A few progressive firms have ventured beyond traditional skills training, offering more intense initial training experiences relevant to a new hire's career. The home products retailer The Container Store puts all new hires through a five-day "Foundation Week" that teaches them about products, values, and processes. New hires go on to apprentice with top employees in the firm, and also continue training in "different functions and units" to "gain a broader perspective and to learn about the company's strategic challenges." The firm provides a minimum of 241 hours of training during the first year—far more than the seven hours accorded on average to new hires in the retail industry.[5] Yet as extensive as such training is, even this program fails to offer employees exposure to a broad range of career development resources that a state-of-the-art onboarding program would include so as to achieve the maximum impact.

A 1994 article in the *Harvard Business Review* called for business to move toward a "career-resilient workforce." Observing that the "longtime covenant between employee and employer," under which big firms like IBM offered lifetime employment in exchange for loyalty and decent job performance was a thing of the past, the article exhorted companies to enter into a new covenant "under which the employer and employee share responsibility for maintaining—even enhancing—the individual's employability inside *and outside* the company." In practice, this would mean providing employees with tools, opportunities, and an environment conducive to develop their skills and career potential, as well as managers who "show that they care about their employees whether or not they stay with the company."[6] It is quite clear that companies have not embraced this covenant as far as new hires are concerned.

The case for early career support

Today the need for a new covenant or compact is even more pressing than it was almost a generation ago. If the old covenant was on the way out in the early 1990s, to workers today it is on par with long-playing records or the Big Band sound—a relic of the past. New hires no longer think much about their long-term tenure with a company when they shop for jobs. Instead, they try to get the best salary as well as a job that sets them up for a better job with any employer down the line. In recessions, they take any job they can get or try to keep the ones they have, but when good times return they head to the door.[7] Employee loyalty, in other words, has been utterly smashed. As employees, new hires are loyal to themselves—happy to give value to the enterprise, but only commensurate to what the organization returns back. The absence of organizational loyalty is reflected in a recent survey of 1,400 CIOs (the leadership group that oversees the greatest concentration of knowledge workers in our economy); 43% put retaining existing workers as their top priority in 2010. A great number of professional workers today are not even employees anymore, but part of the large and growing body of independent contractors and freelancers who sell themselves to the highest bidder for discrete projects.

Other numbers relating to loyalty are well known but worth repeating. As of 2005, Americans were projected to change jobs an average of 10 times between the ages of 18 and 37. More recent surveys taken during the global recession that began at the end of 2007 indicate widespread discontent with employers and specific jobs. One 2009 survey of 900 workers found that 60% intended to leave their present jobs and pursue new opportunities as the economy pulled out of recession.[8] Almost 60% of workers in another recent survey reported that "work pressures were undermining their health," whereas almost 80% of high-level employees reported "high levels of stress, more than twice as high as one year earlier." A full 40% felt that relations with spouses and partners were suffering as a result of their jobs.[9] One partner at a New York law firm summarized the situation: "The loyalty of the institution to its people, and vice versa, isn't really there anymore—it's a different animal from what a lot of us were used to."[10]

If the employer-employee compact stands in disarray, starting a conversation and providing support beginning at the point of entry into the enterprise serves as a promising way to reset and redefine it. Disloyal workers did not become that way because of their preference for independence; rather, they were forced to take matters in their own hands as the idea of the corporation as a benevolent caretaker proved weak and unreliable. Pursuing long-term career progress has become a key priority for workers of all ages. According to one recent study, Gen Y and Boomers were looking beyond a paycheck and aiming at personal and career growth. The study found that members of the two generations placed other benefits—including "challenging assignments," "a range of new experiences," and "explicit performance evaluations and recognition"—higher than money.

Slightly less than half (45%) of Gen Y workers reported expecting to spend their entire careers with their current employer, but a majority said they "also want work to bring a range of new experiences and challenges," leading the authors of the study to conclude that these respondents "may be more susceptible to wanderlust than they realize."[11] A 2009 survey by Deloitte Consulting found that 40% of Gen X workers gave "lack of career progress" as a reason for their unhappiness on the job, ahead of job security and inadequate pay.[12]

All of this data, along with anecdotal evidence compiled through our work, suggests that companies would do well to stimulate early career planning and development during the first year—making it available to all new hires, helping new hires to identify better their prospects, and affording new hires opportunities to make gradual, visible career progress. The potentially pivotal role of career development initiatives like mentoring; coaching; career exploration; progress pathing and modeling using career development plans; and skills assessments becomes intuitively clear when we consider the kinds of questions and concerns new hires typically have when they join a new company or step into a new role within an existing employer. New hires wonder about the opportunities that really exist, beyond the entry position, for them at their new employer. They are not just thinking about the standard straight line of progress—staff position, supervisor, manager, and executive. Many new hires join a firm hoping to gain experience and move into a different function. Rather than feeling pigeon-holed in a job that does not reflect their long-term ambitions, they want a clear sense of how they can move from a position that their current resume qualifies them for into one that they dream about. If they enter a firm in finance, can they talk about a marketing role? If they are back office employees, is there any chance they can eventually get out into the field (or vice versa)?

New hires *at all levels* also expect that certain behaviors, actions, and proving competencies will lead to future career progress. But what are the specific requirements? Is it working longer hours? In other words, how does advancement happen? What are the criteria? Questions about career advancement merge with those about the culture, and specifically, the performance values that an organization prioritizes. Often it is the most ambitious, high-potential employees who concern themselves most intensely with performance values. For this group and for all new hires, being proactive and addressing career advancement can temper anxieties and focus the new hire.

Younger new hires harbor many questions about careers and work norms that older new hires might take for granted. Young people with technical backgrounds often feel overwhelmed by the "real world" just after graduation and do not understand how they can ever be effective in their careers. Younger new hires wonder what skills they need to get where they know they want to go. Is it a certification, or international experience, or specific work assignments? What specific elements of a new hire's performance require development for him or her to progress? Younger new hires who happen to know how to build a career within an enterprise start to worry about how to go about obtaining career sponsors. All new hires worry about how to deal with difficult bosses and how to contend with perceived failures on the job. "If I do something wrong, how do I recover, and how seriously does the failure impact my future career prospects with the firm?" Finally, employees at all stages of their careers wonder about how to handle disappointment on the job. If they are uninspired by their current work, will it turn around? Is it worth it to them to stick it out a year or two if they are bored? What do they do to change their experience for the better?

Offering the kinds of career support tools listed in the preceding table addresses these concerns on a number of levels. Organizations help new hires discover the full breadth of the career options available both inside and outside the firm while providing the support required to explore and test those options. With resources such as mentoring and career pathing at their disposal, new hires can develop clarity early on about career path options, and they can begin to plan what they need to do to achieve their personal visions of success. Most importantly, perhaps, early career support helps new hires feel better about their work life, imparting the belief that their career journey will be rich, either within or outside the organization. Any mediocre company can become great, as can any employee, assuming they are on the right path. Offered enthusiastic career support early on, new hires are thrilled to discover their new employer is an organization that will support them on their personal road to success.

Early career support, as we conceptualize it, can be provided by the smallest of organizations. Centralized resources are powerful for larger enterprises, but in a small outfit of 10 employees, all you need is a manager or mentor to take a new hire under his or her wing, provide direction and guidance during Week One, and then keep the conversation going.

Early career support initiatives benefit the enterprise by serving as a catalyst for greater engagement and motivation. Just as companies reinforce consumers about their selection after they make an initial purchase of a given brand, so must companies reinforce a new hire's decision to come onboard. Offering early career support helps new hires see the value proposition of their job from the outset. By demonstrating right away that the organization cares about what new hires themselves deeply care about—their success—firms can more quickly activate new hires to perform enthusiastically and at their best.

In the *Harvard Business Review*'s January 2010 issue, Harvard professor Teresa Amabile presented a study concluding that the number one driver of employee motivation is an employee's experience of progress. As Amabile explains, "making headway in their jobs, or when they receive support that helps them overcome obstacles, their emotions are most positive and their drive to succeed is at its peak."[13] Significantly, the feeling of progress ranked higher than four other attributes that have long been considered top factors—recognition, incentives, interpersonal support, and clear goals.

Given our earlier position regarding the new hires' view of Maslow's hierarchy of needs, we find it unsurprising that progress matters. Progress will lead to job security, the feeling of belonging and being appreciated, esteem, and ultimately self-actualization. When architected to align with the hiring manager's needs, progress will result in recognition, appreciation, and energy for further investment in the new hire. From the enterprise's perspective, progress means that the company mission is being realized—the very reason companies invest in new hires to begin with.

Early career support—understanding personal progress and prospect— can increase new hires' productivity. New hires are motivated to perform better and reach peak productivity quicker, but they also receive help they need to raise productivity levels. Many new hires remain unaware of incorrect behaviors that limit their current progress and long-term potential. Early career support allows individuals to improve their reputations or personal brands within an organization. In many cases, a positive dynamic of productivity is created: The more effectively individuals perform, the more they develop reputations as stars, which leads in turn to still better performance. For younger and more experienced hires alike, greater self-awareness about minor behavioral tendencies that are having a negative impact, such as doing work out of order from a well-established and proven process, or a tendency to use certain language repetitively and to excess, could prove pivotal. Younger hires often do not know the finer points about how best to act, while older hires might retain ingrained habits or skills that do not work in their new organization's culture. Organizations can get employees working most productively by offering early career support that identifies both progress and career-limiting behaviors, intervenes when these behaviors come up, supports employee efforts to transform their behavior, and recognizes positive change when it occurs. Most importantly, firms can help hires work productively by crafting how work is initially "set up" for them—the assignments, the support structures, and the guidance.

Early career support affects attrition by creating an opportunity to turn around new hires who might otherwise have left out of frustration with their current job situation, and also by helping identify lower performers sooner so that they can establish remediation paths. By learning about how they can best develop in the future, new hires can gain a sense of purpose and become excited again about the company. Our own firm hired a high-performing young consultant who had previously worked for another boutique consulting firm. This person performed exceptionally well soon after arrival, so as part of the routine mentoring discussions that occurred, we began having serious conversations with him about his future at the firm. We outlined the timing of different promotions, the compensation rewards he could expect to achieve over time, and the possibility that our firm would pay for his enrollment in an MBA program. Because of his exceptional performance, this employee became a manager in only 6 months. Around the one-year mark, he was so driven that he was already thinking about getting an MBA and was willing to leave the organization to do it. Through our ongoing mentoring process and other early career support initiatives, we were able to reassure this new hire that we would likely sponsor his MBA sooner rather than later. The result: Our go-getter remained happy in his job and has stayed with us. While this is just one person, the example illustrates how informing new hires around career development resources that are available to all can help motivate and engage them about their futures.

Initiating career development early for a broad spectrum of employees can offer firms considerable benefits by aligning strategy and initiatives with employee skills and interests; in effect, creating an internal employment market. Suppose your firm (a large company with a long-established channel) wants to adopt a strategy to develop new channels. You might already have new entrants with career interests in channel development. If you can figure out who those people are and match them to needed skills, you will save money on the external recruiting you would normally do to support this strategic initiative. The existence of an internal employment market unlocks new value for the firm because of the enthusiasm and energy created by making the match.

To see how this might work, consider the professional services firm Booz Allen Hamilton (Booz Allen). In recent years, the company has pursued a strategy of creating and growing a new cyber security business to meet growing market demands. Given the labor shortage that exists for what is essentially an emerging discipline, Booz Allen has had to work incredibly hard to find qualified external recruits. One option the firm has explored: training existing employees in the new skill set. Here the firm's onboarding program has come in handy. As vice presidents participate in Week One onboarding and speak to new hires about their respective businesses, the leader of the company's cyber security initiative can talk about the opportunities that are present for those who pursue additional career development to gain the necessary skills to play in this specific market. In this case, not only are employees gaining exposure to the strategy, with all the benefits to that in which we'll discuss in the next chapter, but new hires learn that cyber security could comprise a promising career opportunity for them if they can get the special interests and requisite skills. Booz Allen is enabling the new hire to self-select and take actions, thanks not only to the information it is providing about the new strategy, but also to the complementary guidance they provide regarding performance values and culture.

Beyond support for a company's strategy, early career support can work wonders for the firm's employment brand, its competitive position, and employees' long-term loyalty. Because career development is so important to new hires, and so few firms currently make the most of it as a part of onboarding, doing so can provide you with a point of distinction in the recruiting community. Firms should be aggressive and entrepreneurial about making career development part of their brands.

We recommend going so far as to put resources available on the intranet titled "If You're Thinking of Leaving" and also to support a frank conversation of relevant issues. Senior leadership could help by taking an interest in new hire career development and talking about career opportunities in a welcome video. Senior executives should offer discussion of their careers, the key milestones, and secrets of their success. Firms might consider offering access to a specialist within the organization who can help new hires transition between roles and organizations. Finally, companies can distinguish their employment brands simply by offering far more extensive access to executive coaching than is currently the norm.

As for loyalty, one 2002 study published in the *Harvard Business Review* found that job security did not contribute most directly to employee commitment to the firm. Rather, "the executives who intended to stay with their companies the longest, and who voiced the greatest commitment, were those whose companies offered them ample opportunities to enhance their employability and to advance their careers." The authors put the basic principle succinctly: "Groom your executives to leave, and they'll stay." They caution that firms cannot just talk about employability—they have to deliver, or else loyalty will quickly evaporate.[14] These findings bring us right back to 1994, and the argument that was made then to create a "career resilient workforce" benefiting both organizations and employees. If offering career development could foster loyalty, it seems obvious that beginning the process early—within the first year of employment—would only help to achieve superior results.

Structural Requirements to Stimulate Progress and Achieve One's Prospect

When a new hire joins an enterprise, *how they are placed* in the organization matters. We identified four structural requirements that affect individuals' experience around progress and affect their ability to reach their

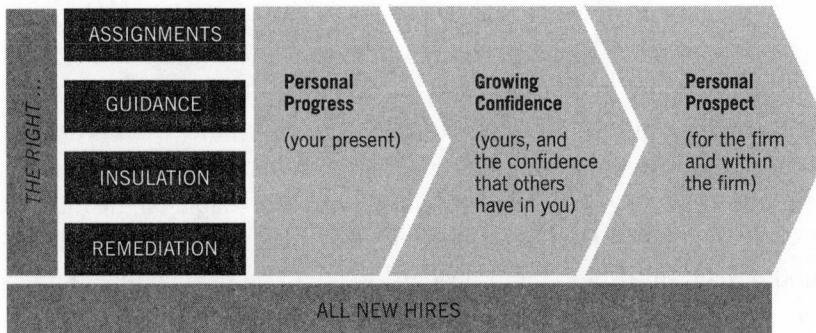

Figure 5.1 Structural Requirements to Stimulate Progress and Achieve One's Prospect

potential, as noted in Figure 5.1; these are Assignments, Guidance, Insulation, and Remediation.

Assignments

Assignments relates to the character, order, and pace by which tasks (defined broadly) are taken on by the hire, whether the most junior employee or the senior-most executive. The onboarding system should require that each hiring manager think through the character, order, and pace of these assignments with the general idea of progress in mind. Set up the new hire to win at every step of the game—in their eyes and in the eyes of peers and superiors. With a real sense of achievement, they will emerge energized, confident, and proud of what they are accomplishing for themselves and the company. Senior hires often enter with an ambitious agenda that they create for themselves or that is dictated by the enterprise. It is critical to counsel these executive or managerial hires to pace themselves. If they are going to succeed, they can't flame out soon after entry. For any level of hire, first assignments should be carefully selected so that they are both valuable and relatively modest.

Guidance

Guidance entails the degree to which the system (and specifically, the individuals who surround the new hire) recognize that the new hire will do better with instruction and advice *as necessary*. A new hire at junior or mid-tier levels may need task instruction, but all new hires benefit more from the managers', peers' and mentors' perspective on the organization culture, performance values, strategy, etc. Taking a "sink or swim" approach and leaving the new hire on his or her own is not such a great tactic. The only thing a hiring manager will likely prove by that exercise is something that requires no proof: that an outsider is far less likely to "get it" than an insider would. Instead, system participants should remain active observers of the things that the new hire is "getting" and the things that the new hire is missing. System participants should be more cautious when the new hire is performing a task or an experience (e.g., presenting in front of one's peers for the first time) that carries risk of judgment by others, and they should provide an additional layer of counsel. Senior leadership should tell system participants that they bear responsibility for helping this new entrant to succeed (and again, everyone's annual assessment forms should reflect this responsibility).

Insulation

New hires—at all levels deserve "insulation"—a layer of organizational protection to help avoid getting in too much trouble too early. Ideally, a new hire reports into someone who has time to take proper care to help the new hire succeed. Given organizational design constraints, a modest leader to direct reports ratio often does not exist. The onboarding design team should examine the enterprise's overall organization and determine which new hire positions remain subject to limited oversight. In these cases, mentors should be made aware of the circumstance, and the system should ensure that the new hire is provided with alternative and sufficient resources and support. At the very least, both the new hire and the hiring manager should understand that the critical "firsts" associated with a given role (introduced in Chapter 2 and discussed further in Chapter 8) require more managerial attention so new hires can experience critical wins.

Remediation

The last piece of structural support is a mechanism for remediation. Too many good people fail because companies do not have the equivalent of an emergency room. Everyone is subject to making mistakes, and anyone may find themselves in either a difficult position or a position for which they were not prepared (sometimes because of weak recruiting and placement). When new hires are not getting the support they deserve, usually the local resource is simply too busy, has conflicting incentives, does not, him- or herself, have the right skills to assist, or is otherwise unavailable. In these cases, the new hire should have somewhere to go to get support. Mentor programs largely exist for this purpose, but in all too many cases, the mentor himself may prove to be disinterested or unskilled. The new hire should not pay the price. Onboarding designers need to provide for a centralized resource to seek assistance. It is simply unacceptable to spend the money that companies do on recruiting and placement and then allow failure because of organizational design flaws. The price is too great.

Effective Delivery of Early Career Support

Now that we've established the critical role of early career support as part of a strategic onboarding program and laid out the structural elements required, let's consider the question of how to do it effectively. Our own experience working with and investigating effective programs across industries has led us to some additional best principles that can help you when introducing early career support as part of onboarding.

Best Principle #1: Take steps to centralize and systematize normally informal career conversations.
Centralizing and systematizing delivery of career information allows for some governance while simultaneously making it easier for new recruits in large companies to locate the information they need. Centralization also helps provide managers with guidance into the needs of new hires as well as into the most helpful ways to offer feedback. Firms like Caterpillar and Lockheed Martin offer centralized materials to provide "go-to" career support and a source of expertise for managers who are planning new programs. IBM and Booz Allen offer corporate learning sites and self-education curricula that provide learning tailored to new hires, making the information more engaging and timely.

An HR manager at the holding company of Sears reported on the benefits of systematizing its previously informal buddy program. In the old days, "no one was assigned as the official buddy [of someone else]—there was no process or list of responsibilities. Because of this, everyone involved thought someone else was taking care of a Buddy's responsibilities, and the new hires suffered." The firm's new buddy system, by contrast, provides standards as well as training (called the "Buddy School") for program participants. "This ensures a more consistent onboarding experienced for all new hires, leading to an accelerated timeframe in which they will be fully engaged, productive members of the organization."

Another prime opportunity for systematization of early career support involves the mentoring programs that many firms currently maintain. Our own research affirms how helpful formal mentoring programs are in integrating new employees by teaching them how to succeed in the current position and how to assess and determine an exciting career forward.

You should remember that a lot of early career support simply involves managers taking the time to speak one-on-one with new hires and offer helpful advice. Just having regular conversation might be a step forward in many firms, and it can be a hugely effective tool for engaging a new hire. The opportunity cost of having conversations is small, as opposed to the large investment that some firms make in delivering formal performance review programs. Conveying one or two helpful hints—a suggestion to take a class, or cuing a new hire into a potentially damaging behavior quirk—can go a long way. If a firm can find a way to activate all managers to observe new hires, think about them, and intervene to help them, both the firm and the new hires will benefit.

A leader in our firm recently participated in a "pulse check" review with a subordinate who joined the company at a mid-management level nine months earlier. As a formal part of the process, the leader had occasion to offer a piece of advice. "You're doing great in many areas," he said, "and you have my support. Yet your career here might be limited, since other senior people in the firm don't see you, and you haven't yet demonstrated contributions to the firm more broadly." This leader advised the new hire to find and take ownership of a project or initiative that, once completed, would give him visibility with senior management across practice areas. Informing the new hire that Kaiser Associates expects employees to make "firm contributions" outside of their client work was a key performance value for us. This new hire thought about it and came back a week later with the idea of co-leading a semi-monthly growth planning meeting. The leader gave him the opportunity, and as a result his profile improved and his career at Kaiser was in far better shape than it otherwise might have been. The initiative that this individual helped spearhead now has new energy and is experiencing progress where it had stalled before. We are realizing the Onboarding Margin in this one instance alone.

This story is a great example of an inexpensive investment making a real difference. All that the onboarding change agent really needs to do here is:

1. Talk to hiring managers about the opportunity and their responsibility to play a special role for new hires; and
2. Modify their company's assessment process to take special consideration and provide special direction for new employees (as compared with tenured employees).

Best Principle #2: Systematizing is no substitute for authenticity.
Even as you take steps to systematize program elements that might already exist informally, make sure not to efface the authentic feel of these elements. Mentorship, for instance, should not be routinized to the extent that mentees lose a sense of their mentors' genuine engagement. It is far better to have a genuine experience than a centralized one that is rote and uninspired. We want all managers to know what to do and when, but if it becomes a perfunctory exercise, all a firm is doing is adding expense without realizing a significant benefit. And given that you are working on a system here for the entire company's benefit, you cannot rely on the goodwill of mentors to take their jobs seriously. For onboarding to be systemic, mentors should have their responsibilities written into their job descriptions, and their performance as mentors should factor into their broader annual assessments. If mentors are held accountable for their performance, they will care about doing a great job.

To understand the tangible difference authenticity makes, consider the case of Robert, a recently hired junior sales associate at a pharmaceutical company. Robert participates in a monthly meeting with his firm-selected mentor to discuss his career development. But because the mentor program is so rigidly specified, the meetings are meaningless. The mentor goes through a five-bullet checklist, and when the meeting is over he goes to his own development plan and checks off that he has conducted the meeting so that he meets his own performance objectives. Since the mentor is supposed to be in contact with the new hire's manager, Robert's mentor sends an email to the manager, yet when he does not receive a response, he fails to follow up.

Unfortunately, that's not all Robert's mentor fails to do. Even though he overheard Robert complaining in the firm's cafeteria about something unreasonable Robert perceived his boss doing, Robert's mentor neglects to talk about it in the mentor meeting because he's relying exclusively on what the five bullets tell him. The mentor is totally unengaged, and so too is Robert. He does not get any real support and ends up with a very negative performance evaluation from his manager four months later. In addition, he feels turned off and isolated in his huge company. If his mentoring interaction had been more authentic, his mentor would have tried to reach his manager until he succeeded. He would have talked with Robert about the negative feedback he'd received from his manager, reviewed the deliverable that had received the criticism, explained the feedback to him, and reached out to the manager to let him know that Robert was working to improve.

So how do you begin to make systemic mentoring authentic? For starters, photocopy this story and share it with your mentors. Put them on notice of what poor mentoring looks like. Establish a standard of quality that you would expect from your company's manufacturing line. Great companies produce great product because they genuinely care. The same needs to be done for mentoring and all other service elements of onboarding.

Best Principle #3: "Amp up" the performance review process during the first year.
While increasing the frequency and breadth of new hire evaluations requires the expenditure of additional resources, it can serve as a strong career support mechanism. Early evaluations can offer new hires an initial sense of accomplishment, something that is particularly important to younger employees. One approach is to offer reviews at the 30-day, 100-day, six-month, and one-year points. But note that the title of this chapter and the label for this pillar is Early Career *Support*, not Early Career *Judgment*.

In amping up the review process, your sole purpose should be to render the new hire more successful and more excited. Increasing the breadth of feedback to include peers, the mentor, and other relevant employees provides a wider scope of information, leaving the new hire with greater guidance.

At the household construction products company Marvin Windows and Doors, new hires receive a "progress report" within the first 90 days. The report distills new hire performance into such categories as work quality, dependability, and judgment.[15]

At Starwood, new hires receive feedback from a circle of about 10 reviewers, not just a manager. Many of the additional reviewers are selected by employees themselves and include internal and external customers and peers. An online tool is used to make the submission of feedback and the aggregation of results easier and more accessible to managers at different levels. This "360-degree" system benefits all stakeholders by providing feedback that captures a variety of perspectives. Starwood can more easily identify individuals for progression planning using the online tool. New hires can better identify which internal career paths are attainable and which skill areas they need to improve so as to get where they want to go. They also gain access to a personal network of resources to help facilitate career support and social and cultural integration into the firm. Finally, multiple channels provide "second opinions" and mitigate the possibility of poor mentoring.

At Bank of America Corporation, executives receive a great amount of performance feedback during their first year on the job as a part of onboarding. During the first week on the job, new hires identify important successes to aim for during the first 90 days. Within three to four months, new hires participate in a "Key Stakeholder Check In," receiving "written and verbal feedback from a select list of their key stakeholders." At the one-year mark, after new executives have already made improvements based on stakeholder feedback, they receive 360-day feedback that helps them understand if their efforts have borne fruit. This feedback "is used along with other data and feedback mechanisms as input in the individual's performance ratings and reviews."[16]

Best Principle #4: Encourage new hires to take ultimate responsibility for their own careers.
Just because a firm accepts some of the responsibility for new hires' career development as part of a redefined employer-employee compact does not

mean new hires do not bear ultimate responsibility. They do, and state-of-the-art onboarding reinforces this message. At our own firm, we tell new hires that they drive their own development. We give them tools, but we do not hold their hands, and we stress that new hires need to be proactive, that they should actively use the tools available to them, and we expect them to help frame the agenda.

At the technology firm Teradata, development resources for new hires are available for self-service on a portal. The firm has managers use this portal to obtain assessment tools, a personal development plan, welcome packets, buddy checklists, etc. Although such a delivery system may not offer the governance of a state-of-the-art strategic program, it at least offers the content and the structure—an enormous gain over most of its peers.

Another company whose program offers new hires tools to manage their own development is Verizon Wireless. The company's intranet provides new hires with individualized career support resources. The site's "About You" section offers specific eLearning modules as well as mentoring information, "go to" resources, announcements of social/team-building events, and a "development manager" that helps new hires chart their career progress, plot career path next steps, and select and register for recommended classes relevant to the job function. This section allows the new hire to personalize and visualize the complete set of onboarding resources.

Starwood's StarwoodONE intranet likewise serves as a central hub for new hires' career development. Employees can reference their development goals in the "About Me" tab. Managers and employees jointly develop five professional goals (e.g., "secure 10 new customers") and three personal goals (e.g., "Enjoy a better work-life balance"). They also access Starwood's corporate training materials and sign up for classroom-like sessions. Learning needs are identified through review feedback, while the system also interfaces with Starwood's software for career planning applications.

Best Principle #5: Encourage new hires to create career development plans.

While creating career development plans are certainly not a new means of supporting employee's careers, not many companies regularly create such plans as part of the first-year onboarding program. We see this as a lost opportunity to take a proven tool and use it to help new hires identify personal prospects and ways they can measure their progress against career development goals.

At Wells Fargo, new bank tellers fill out career development plans at a point between 90 and 180 days, setting expectations and mapping out their future careers with the company. As one report has documented, "initial reactions have been very positive ... and turnover is expected to decrease substantially."[17] This is one of the few examples we've uncovered of a company that has wheeled out career development plans in an attempt to retain lower-level, high-turnover retail employees.

At General Mills, development plans are written out by new hires in their first month in consultation with managers to define the skills that new hires need to develop so as to reach their goals. The manager's input serves as a valuable support mechanism and also a means of helping General Mills meet its own corporate goals. As one 2006 new hire remarked, "It's really important that you write out your development plan because that's what guides you in your growth as an employee." New hires in general come away with a sense of owning their careers even as they benefit from managers' guidance.

Best Principle #6: Make early career support collaborative.
In striking a balance between individual and firm responsibility, onboarding should strive to initiate dialogues and joint planning efforts involving new hires, their managers, and their mentors. Firms like Ernst & Young, General Motors, and Baird have all improved early career support by making it more collaborative. At Ernst & Young, the creation of collaborative career paths has resulted in higher satisfaction ratings for career resources among new hires. At General Motors, coaches work collaboratively with individuals to plan career paths, teach new skills, and improve competencies. The "coaching cadre" is comprised of a clearly identified group of executives, certified during an intensive four-day summit. This has enhanced executive development in career path planning while also helping provide personalized planning to suit the individual's desires and needs.

Chapter 3 illustrated how the new onboarding program at Baird has been used to effectively instill a new strategic and cultural change for the financial services firm. At its core, a key element of this program is the collaborative nature of the onboarding experience. The joining of the new hire into a new team involves not only the team lead, but also the branch manager, the corporate HR "coach," and other senior leaders at corporate involved in the business plan review. Involvement from such a diverse set of stakeholders ensures new hires are well prepared for their new financial advisory careers.

Best Principle #7: Offer a flexible system with multiple safeguards. Experiences within organizations are often uneven when it comes to career development. Some managers might be open to working with new hires on a career development track even if it takes them outside their current career, whereas others are not. To account for variations across the organization, your onboarding system should offer different paths and put the focus on exploration. Firms should offer supplementary resources, potentially even independent career counselors like at a high school or university career center. Should the firm choose an internal resource to serve as a supplemental resource, this individual should be outside the new hire's chain of command and operational role—someone in the talent management, learning development, or HR functions. That way, new hires with poor mentors and managers still gain the benefit of a third option. In many of the companies we have mentioned so far, centralized online resources can serve this function to some extent, as can content such as inspirational case studies for how successful career paths at the organization can unfold. Offering multiple safeguards supports both the guidance and remediation structural elements of early career support.

Summing Up

Remember Charles, the employee we met in the Introduction whose boss quit before he arrived? If his company had offered early career support, Charles would have met with his new manager during the first couple of weeks of employment. He would have articulated where he wanted to go, admitted that he had arrived with higher visions of leading the intended initiative, and informed his manager that he now he felt like a rug had been pulled out from underneath him.

In the wake of such a conversation and the creation of a personal development plan for Charles, his manager might have thought about some new ways to help him achieve his goal—perhaps helping Charles to network with people deploying the initiative, or alternatively, developing some different career paths that would have excited him. Charles might not have left the firm, since his concern about being promoted in 6 months might have been addressed, and he would have known exactly what he would have needed to do to make his promotion happen.

Early career support holds great potential for firms as a part of onboarding, offering not merely a chance to improve retention, but also to heighten new hires' overall enthusiasm and productivity. Most firms today make only limited and late use of career development, seeing it as a reward for employee loyalty rather than what it could be—a powerful means of nurturing it. Even more than social networking, extensive use of early career support could enable firms to gain a competitive edge by redefining the employer-employee compact in a way meaningful to 21st century workers. Combine this with educating new hires on strategy, and providing associated direction (against that strategy), the subject of the next chapter, and new hires are poised to increase the value they can contribute to your company at an early stage in their careers.

Table 5.1 Early Career Support Elements — Sample Tactics

Onboarding Phase	Element	Sample Tactics	Application Advice
Prepare	• Introduce the concept of ECS as part of the employer-employee compact	• Include information in pre-start mailing • Include content in new hire portal and discuss in wikis visited by new hires	• Don't just engineer it in; in addition make a very clear expression of what you are doing; i.e., tell the new hire that you are rewriting the compact; tell him what you are going to give and what you expect in return • Make information equally accessible for new hires regardless of their work location or where they are relocating from • Reinforce the benefit to the new hire of the decision to join the organization
	• Pre-start networking opportunities	• Welcome "call" from hiring manager and/or peer mentor • For college recruits, host networking events (happy hour, dinner) with current employees and new hires where there are several hires joining from the same location	• Allows new hires to form networks before they start, jump starting awareness on ECS • Make sure that representatives from different levels and different functions attend; make sure to instruct the veteran employees that their role is to not just pick up the tab, but to discuss the career objectives and career paths
Orient	• Share unwritten rules and explain how they relate to career progress	• Panel discussion of recent hires to share their experiences: "What I wish I knew when I started" • Designed networking opportunities with more experienced employees • Welcome discussion with peer advisor and/or mentor	• Emphasis is on the "secrets to success" of succeeding in the organization
	• Introduce the concept of a development plan	• Include content in the orientation program • Provide talking points for hiring managers and mentors to discuss the role of the development plan in the new hire's career progression; share personal experiences	• Use of personal experiences to illustrate the benefit of the development plan in others' career development • Make sure that you address the issue of flexibility; some new hires are not ready to set in stone

(Continued)

Table 5.1 Early Career Support Elements – Sample Tactics (*Continued*)

Onboarding Phase	Element	Sample Tactics	Application Advice
	• Provide a career development self-service portal	• Make career development information available to all new hires via a self-service portal	• Providing career support information online will allow all new hires the ability to access information early on, to support their ideas around their prospects for the future • But also recognize that if all that you do is put materials online, but fail to bring it to life (e.g., to make it systemic in enterprise's business processes) you will not fully realize the benefit possible
Integrate	• Develop and utilize the development plan	• Mentors and Buddies provide guidance in writing the new hire's development plan • Review progress at the mentor meeting touch points	• Provide perspective on goal setting and how to take actions against the plan • Incorporate onboarding activities into the plan (such as future networking events)
	• Training — Virtual and classroom instruction	• Customize job skills training based on new hire level and/or function	• Provide new hires with the skills and tools to perform their jobs and make connections with others in their line of work • Provide training through a variety of modes to make it accessible to all new hires regardless of work location and constraints
	• Mentoring (continued through Excel)	• Ongoing monthly career support check-ins with the mentor or peer buddy • Diversity mentoring — allows new hires to receive career support from others with similar diverse experiences and backgrounds • Mentoring Circles — enables new hires to see the future of the organization and what their careers can look like in the future	• Incorporating a variety of tenured staff to share from their own experiences enables new hires to see the "potential" is realistically attainable • Mentors should be looking for early identification of those new hires who may be at risk for departure • Mentors need to be provided with an education and guideline materials to learn what to look for — and how to respond

Excel

• Training – Virtual and classroom instruction	• Provide internal classes and access to external training—even if external training isn't funded by the company, making new hires aware of options will support their overall development • Certification support (could be the actual support of the certification or the introduction of availability when it is necessary in one's career progression) • Quarterly e-learning events to provide all staff including virtual workers, with events customized to their needs and schedules • Recommend functional or industry conferences to attend	• Increasing the use of virtual instruction is essential with a distributed workforce • Incorporating collaboration tools into the learning environment serves the dual purpose of providing individual learning and enhancing connectedness across teams, geographies, etc.
• Performance Management	• Quarterly or semi-annual performance reviews with mentor and manager • Discussion with mentor and manager about the road ahead at the 12-month mark — pre-empt at-risks, provide perspective keys to success at year two	• Emphasize the performance values and compare the new hire's experience with expectations and engage new hires in thoughtful discussion that supports their career progression • Mentor attendance provides new hires with opportunity to ask candid questions and receive advice in a "safe place" following review discussion
• Networking	• An invitation to a personal event with a leader at the six-month mark (lunch, coffee) • One-year learning and networking event • A check-in call with HR (or onboarding team) at the six-month mark	• New hires are encouraged to make connections with others within their business and outside who may be supportive in their future career progression • Reinforces new hires feelings of being valued, supported, and connected

6

"LIMITED UPSIDE IN FLYING BLIND": DRIVING STRATEGIC INSIGHT AND IMPACT

During college, one of the authors of this book, Mark Stein, was fortunate enough to land a summer internship in the corporate headquarters of premium ice cream company, Häagen-Dazs. At the time, with an accounting degree in hand, Mark was planning on a career in finance, and this internship working with numbers seemed like a great opportunity—not least because every day four tubs of ice cream were delivered fresh from the factory line to the corporate headquarters' office kitchen. Water cooler breaks are far more satisfying with ice cream! Most certainly, it was not a bad gig for a college kid in the summer.

After a few weeks on the job, though, Mark's enthusiasm waned. His main assignment was to measure and build by 2 PM each day a 28-page report on the corporation's fulfillment of customer orders. This report conveyed the daily performance and weekly, monthly, and annual trends around product count shortages, flavor shortages, and damaged product count. It contained graphs showing the highest and lowest performing days broken down by distribution center, customer, ice cream flavor, and SKU. The strange thing was that the daily range of performance—for all of these factors—never dipped below 98.20 or rose above 99.40.

Given the narrow deviation, Mark did not understand the point of this exercise. It seemed like he was just spinning his wheels, and as a result, he felt bored and unhappy (except for the incoming fresh ice cream). He grew terribly disillusioned with the prospect of graduation and work at big companies. He even found himself rethinking his career choice altogether.

Everything changed one afternoon when Mark was delivering the report to an executive who stopped and asked how the internship was going. With little to lose, Mark expressed gratitude for the job but frustration with the focus of his work and the report he was preparing. The executive, Steve, quickly got the point and invited Mark to sit down for a talk. As Steve explained, the Häagen-Dazs brand was defined by quality in every regard and at levels unheard of in ice cream category. This quality focus enabled the company to charge a premium price to its customers (largely grocery chains) and get the shelf space it needed to drive growth. To execute on its strategy, the company needed to ensure a top-quality product and top-quality experience—for both the customers (e.g., the grocery store retailing companies) and the consumers who ultimately enjoyed the product. In addition to the best flavors and highest quality ingredients and recipe, Häagen-Dazs had to ensure that every part of the supply chain cooperated in delivering excellence. The company had to deliver the right flavors, in the right quantities, to the right markets, and at the right times. It was unacceptable to send product that had been damaged or that had dropped even a few degrees and refroze in transit from factory to distribution center and distribution center to grocer's freezer.

That was not all. As Steve related, the company had to convince retailers to support its premium brand positioning in its merchandising, care of the product, and final provision of the product (adding a freezer bag to every consumer's shopping bag). In addition, the company preferred its stores to avoid discounting the product's selling price so as to help maintain its premium brand. The brand, in essence, comprised a core operating requirement and central tenant for the company's strategy to grow market share, maximize profit margin, and provide investors with a high return on investment. Steve went on to relate actions he had taken in the course of the summer when noticing tiny inflection points in Mark's reports, and he also reported how people had lost their jobs over the years for neglecting seemingly minor production imperatives. The bottom line: Operational excellence mattered. Analysis of the numbers Mark provided helped managers take steps to maintain high quality and grow shareholder value.

With this understanding in place, Mark's job took on a whole new meaning. When he saw patterns in the numbers, he got excited because he could connect them with something fundamental. Within a few days, Mark became part of the conversation on improving performance. Going back to perform an analysis that nobody else had considered doing, he noticed that one particular retailer had received more bad product than others over the course of the past 6 months. Now things were getting exciting. Mark brought this to the attention of the account manager and the operations lead. Together the managers determined an action plan to ensure that this customer, who didn't deserve sub-par treatment, would not be subject to it any longer. What had started as a disappointing experience eventually led to Mark developing a special interest in his managerial accounting classes the following fall (classes that focused not on financial accounting and more on using accounting to identify improvement opportunities). As he had learned, accounting was not just about adding up numbers; it had a real impact on business decisions, management, and company performance. A single conversation about strategy, done right, transformed his internship and helped determine his ultimate career path. Even without consideration of the free ice cream, Häagen-Dazs had offered the perfect internship experience.

Companies today spend a lot of time and money making sure they get their strategies right. Yet they usually fall short in communicating that strategy to new hires and existing employees alike. According to the tests we've conducted, if you ask five of your peers to articulate what your company's, business unit, or functional strategy is, you are likely to get five answers that barely resemble one another. People are fuzzy not only about what the firm's future direction is, but the reasons behind what the current operations are designed to accomplish. What are we really doing right now? What exactly is our business model? How do we think differently than our competitors, and why? What are we doing to win in the marketplace? Why will it work and what will it do for us? And what impact should these answers have on how I perform in my specific role?

Most firms today do not integrate strategy education into orientation for any rank of employee, lower level or executives. New hires usually get, at most, a cursory presentation of the company's "mission and vision." The presentation tends to contain short statements that amount to watered down "good citizenship" statements—proclamations of how committed the company is to providing opportunity to employees, caring for the environment, delivering profit for shareholders, and "being the best we can be." If a company does provide some level of indoctrination into strategy, it is usually delivered informally and through one-on-one conversations with peers, and mostly this is reserved for executives.

As we argue in this chapter, all new hires should get at least some *substantive education* about strategy as applied to the company, business unit, function, and role, with links forged between these piece parts. Like executive hires, new front-line employees can perform at much higher levels when they understand how their day-to-day work contributes to the firm's overall success, and when they are bought into the actual "action plan." By immersing all new hires into organizational strategies, you can motivate and inspire your evolving workforce, in the process driving key operating metrics such as engagement, job satisfaction, loyalty, productivity, growth, and profit. You can also go further and drive organizational transformation in support of key strategic initiatives.

This last point is an important one. Managers seeking to drive enterprise transformation should help workers understand how their specific actions connect to the strategy. Our greatest aspiration is that this discussion will serve as something of a wake-up call: Driving change is not just about attention-getting measures, like a big investment in new technology or merging with another company. It can and should be about mobilizing the workforce to approach their daily work differently, with new goals in mind. By taking relatively simple steps to communicate strategy better to a key audience—new hires—you can enroll these agents of change and put your firm on the path to real, profound transformation.

Defining Strategy

Although many employees do not understand a firm's strategy, the words "strategy" and "strategic" do get thrown around a lot, to the point where their meaning becomes unclear. What is strategy exactly? What specific topics should companies strive to communicate to new hires when talking about strategy? We like the definition of strategy offered by Gerry Johnson,

Kevan Scholes, and Richard Whittington in their textbook *Exploring Corporate Strategy*: "Strategy is the *direction* and *scope* of an organization over the *long term*, which achieves *advantage* in a changing *environment* through its configuration of *resources and competencies* with the aim of fulfilling *stakeholder* expectations."[1] Working with this definition a bit, we believe that firms should communicate two basic points about their strategy to new hires as part of onboarding: The firm's "win plan" for succeeding in its markets, and the "operating conditions." This win plan should include information about the intended direction and scope of the organization as well as the advantages these yield relative to stakeholder expectations. The "operating conditions" that feed into the strategy refers specifically to information about the firm's markets and competitors (the environment) and its suppliers (resources and competencies). For each of these two broad areas ("win plan" and "operating conditions"), the point is to convey necessary information rather than engage new hires in an extended process of analyzing, critiquing, or forming the firm's strategy. This information needs to be conveyed as it applies at the corporate, business unit, functional and task levels (a configuration mirroring Mark's daily Häagen-Dazs delivery report).

Talking about the "win plan" means alerting new hires to the organization's targets or desired outcomes—goals such as increasing market share, profit margin, and the like. It also means talking about how the organization hopes to achieve these goals. A medical device company might discuss as its win plan getting more customer share by increasing the size of the sales force so that the firm can spend twice as much time with doctors as the leading competitor. An alternate win plan might involve spending twice as much as the leading competitor on R&D to develop a technically advanced product. Another win plan might focus on outspending the competition on clinical trials to create superior proof points on product performance. Still another win plan might involve outspending in a direct-to-consumer marketing campaign designed to create end-patient demand for the product segment and product brand. These are four different strategies for increasing revenue and ultimately share. If you came onboard as a new hire who followed the first strategy, and your old firm had been following the second, then you'd probably find the tactics of your new employer confusing and even misguided unless someone at your new employer explained the tactics and underlying strategy to you. And if you were a young hire without industry experience, you would not understand what you were doing at all (like Mark initially at Häagen-Dazs).

Organizations need to give new hires sufficient context for understanding the win plan by offering insight into the operating conditions that inform this strategy and its execution. Sharing information about competitors, company resources, and decisions associated with allocating those resources is especially important. Many new hires who have not worked in an industry before do not know much about the other players serving a market, including the extent of the competition, how individual competitors behave, and the strengths and weaknesses of each.

One useful approach might be for an onboarding program to break the competition down according to a widely used and fundamental framework in the strategy world—management consultant Michael Porter's Five Forces framework for industry analysis. New hires could learn about the threat of substitute offerings competing with the firm's own; the threat of new players entering the firm's market; how intense the rivalry among competitors is in the industry; information about customer buying power; and information about the bargaining power of suppliers. Since all of these affect the formulation and success of an organization's win plan, communicating them to new hires goes a long way toward rendering the firm's win plan comprehensible in their eyes. Front-line employees especially need this orientation, as they are typically operating along a single thread of the overall strategy and have very little opportunity to otherwise gain a greater perspective.

Let's consider an example of how a company might communicate competitive information. For years, Home Depot had enjoyed a largely uncompetitive landscape, exploiting its scale advantages over smaller local retailers and providing its customers with discount prices and a broad selection of common products. Front-line employees were well conditioned to Home Depot's retail platform and long-term strategy (whether or not if it was ever explicitly taught to them).

Home Depot added a new element to its strategy about 5 years ago when, in response to competition from Lowe's, it decided to differentiate itself by offering customers unique products they could not find anywhere else. Home Depot created an in-house product development function and an entirely new sourcing strategy, investing in company brands and technologies. To execute this strategy, Home Depot needed to bring its sourcing and marketing organizations on board. Yet it also would be well served if all front-line retail new hires in Home Depot's stores understood the new strategy and its significance. Without such perspective, front-line retail hires would never understand the importance, for example, of highlighting the tools and other products that are only available at Home Depot—and specifically what about them makes them special. New hires might have performed such tasks if management specifically directed them to do so, but they would not have done it with anywhere the same zeal unless managers had explained Home Depot's new strategy to improve margins and maintain share against a growing formidable competitor.

Companies should also take care to provide new hires with sufficient information about suppliers. Questions you might answer include:

- Are suppliers exclusive to us, or do they serve all industry players with the same products? Regardless of this answer, employees should understand the implications of the current supply structure.
- What are we asking of our key suppliers? Is it innovation? Low cost? Flexibility?
- Where have we chosen to vertically integrate? Have competitors decided similarly? What are the implications?
- How healthy are our relationships with key suppliers? What are the points of tension?

If an organization could articulate that its win plan relies heavily on having differentiated, innovative products, and that the strategic sourcing (supply) organization should therefore negotiate exclusive deals with suppliers who can provide unique goods with proper incentives, then the firm could execute well against its strategy of being an industry innovator. Behavior on the ground in the sourcing department would change; new hires might try to nurture long-term relationships with suppliers rather than aim at lowest cost no matter what. Customers comprise another especially important component of the strategic landscape. There are many questions to answer here, as part of onboarding. What customer segments exist and which has the firm chosen to target? What does the differentiated strategy look like by segment? What is our relative competitive position within each segment and why? What other choices do customers have when making a purchasing decision? What prospect is there for an industry-transformative substitute emerging for the products our organization sells?

As part of a customer analysis, firms should also clue new hires into key demand drivers. If you operate in an environment with a channel, you will need to explain this at multiple levels; what a new hire may think of as a customer may actually be a channel. What drives behavior at the channel level and with whom is the firm competing? New hires should also understand the organization's brands—what do the brands represent? More fundamentally, what value proposition does the brand communicate in customers' minds, and how does it compare with competitors' brands? How should the new hire's role reflect this brand definition?

Another topic area new hires should know about involves the resources at the firm's disposal to meet its objectives. What are the key resources? What choices have we made to allocate our resources? Is our infrastructure stable or does it require constant innovation and investment? Do we own our supply chain or outsource it? Why? What technical competencies (trademarks, knowledge) can we bring to bear? Without this information, new hires will prove less equipped to think through issues and come up with appropriate approaches. More concerning, they will likely distrust the firm's actions, when in reality these new hires simply do not have sufficient perspective to pass judgment. If your goal is to energize and excite new hires to support company strategy, the last thing you want is a hire unnecessarily skeptical from the get-go.

As you can see, a full and useful strategic discussion (and this is hardly an exhaustive list) is potentially quite extensive—a good reason why strategic education should occur progressively throughout the first year rather than all at once during Week One orientation. In addition to the breadth of the topics, we have plenty of evidence, as earlier discussed, that new hires do not have sufficient context to absorb everything in the first week. You can present strategy during that week, preferably in the form of a two-way dialogue, but at the very least you need to repeat and extend the education throughout the first year as new hires develop the proper experiential context to absorb it. By continuing the discussion throughout the first year and involving company leadership, you get the double impact of not only teaching but also reiterating the company's commitment to the strategy. This can have an enormous effect, raising new hires' confidence and exciting their work ethics, given that they obviously have come to work for a competent and directed team. Given how poorly most companies engage employees around their strategic win plans, you have a very good chance of standing out in stark and welcome contrast to your new hires' last employer.

With understanding and development of a *common view* as the ultimate goals, strategic education needs to focus not only on short-term strategies, but also the longer-term vision. Companies should take care to reveal in depth what the organization aspires to in the broadest sense and how the company's business plan will help them get there. The onboarding system needs to make clear to new hires what the firm is doing right now to pursue the strategy, including where the firm is making investments; where the weak points are; what the firm is doing to address them; and what kind of pressures the firm is under, both short and long term, to realize its strategies. With this perspective in hand, your new hires will be more inspired, have a greater understanding of your company's actions and inactions, and become more confident in their choice of employer and more excited about their future. Most importantly for your stakeholders, the new hires will become *far more effective in helping the enterprise deliver against its intended strategy.*

Aha Moments and Motivation

It is difficult to present hard data about strategy education's impact on the organization's goals, since too few firms have invested materially in orienting employees (much less new hires) to the strategy in any substantive or formal way beyond the senior ranks. However, we know from our experience working with winning and struggling companies alike on business improvement initiatives that strategy conversations radically improve the chance that the group will have an *"Aha moment"* and either form the critical operational insight or come to support an insight that a group member has already advanced. Both outcomes offer huge advantages.

Strategy implies action to achieve the objective set forth by the plan. To the extent an organization requires its workforce to think and act on behalf of the enterprise, understanding the strategy and the underlying strategic landscape will make all of the difference between achieving random and intended outcomes. Empowering the organization to understand the strategy creates leverage for the organization and radically reduces wasted energy that is applied in conflict with the plan. Moreover, the very process of socializing the organization's understanding of its strategic landscape and its associated strategy with new hires helps fine-tune the strategy as opinions and insights come to the table in the course of discussion.

As Figure 6.1 conveys, strategic orientation and immersion helps yield the Onboarding Margin by carving out value in three distinct ways.

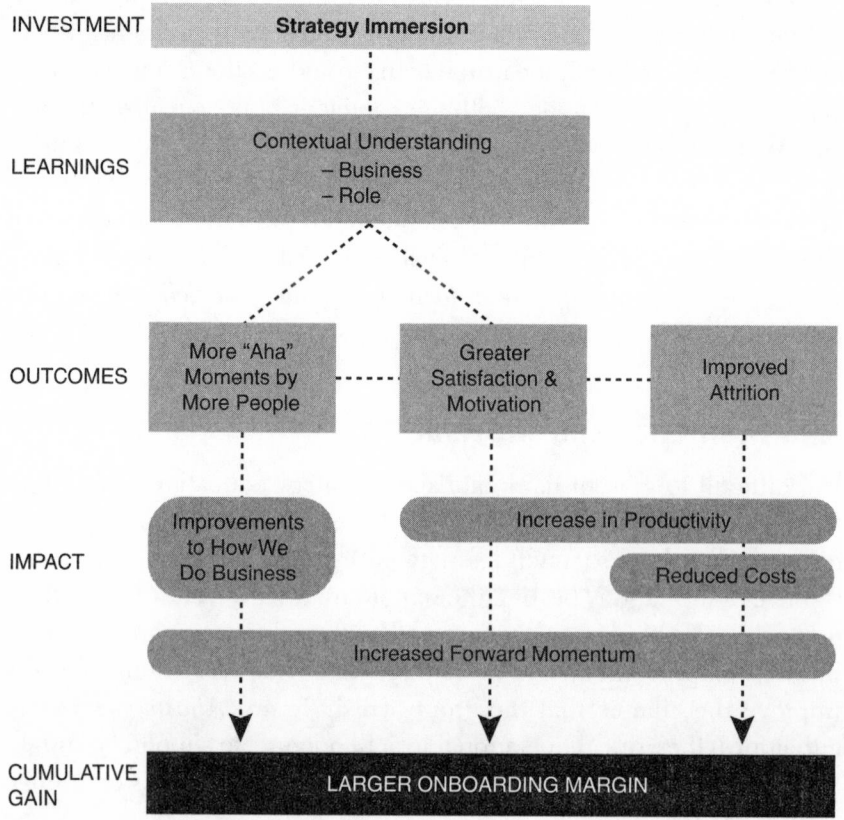

Figure 6.1 From Immersion to Impact

The more versed employees become in the strategy, the more they begin to regard their everyday work through that lens. They begin to notice elements of their jobs they didn't before and tie these elements to the strategy. They also start to ponder their experiences and observations on the job, leading to "Aha!" moments when they realize parts of the business process that are inconsistent with strategy and discover improvements that can push the strategy forward. These eureka moments in turn have the derivative effect of improving how the organization does business—whether by serving customers better, meeting additional customer needs, or developing more efficient work processes.

A great deal of data exists to support the idea that any employee can potentially help improve an enterprise. Toyota has a system in place that queries front-line employees for ideas on how to execute the company's strategy. The result: More than a million ideas a year[2]—and despite recent product safety issues, a company renowned for continuously improving and innovating its product design, features, and operational effectiveness. Google News originated from a little tool that one of the company's developers devised in the wake of 9/11 to help himself find news about the event.[3] Now while this single employee at Google may have had a personal need for his news service, it ultimately required an understanding of Google's strategy for this personal project to become a major competitive force, one that many argue is largely responsible for challenging and reshaping the news and periodical publication industries.

Google's leadership simplified its strategy and widely communicated it with a single sentence that it refers to as its mission: "to organize the world's information and make it universally accessible and useful." We cannot tell you if Google News' originating employee in question understood this strategy, but it was put out there loud and clear. If Google's strategy hadn't been circulating in some form, the chances that this innovation would have made it to the marketplace and in such a strategically consistent form would have plummeted. It would have required dumb luck—not something leaders can afford to rely on.

Beyond leading to "aha moments," we've seen strong anecdotal evidence suggesting that the sharing of strategic information has increased motivation and led to positive results. During the economic downturn of 2008, when many firms were laying off employees and many companies saw employee engagement at an all-time low, one new mid-level employee at a mid-sized company we know of remained engaged and happy with his job (and of course there were likely others). This individual had been given information about the strategic context by his mentor, so he understood why he had been spared from layoffs and what the company was doing to weather the storm. Further, he understood how his daily work helped the company execute its recession-era strategy. Because this employee was committed enough to the firm and really wanted to help it succeed, he took it upon himself to share this strategy with his peers and more junior employees, helping get them engaged around the long-term opportunities at the company despite the current disruptions. From our work with this company, we learned that his behind the scenes conversations helped sway a number of unhappy employees to stay, helping this company continue to deliver on promises during this stressful period and remain healthier than the competition.

Conversely, we have also seen situations in which firms have discouraged the sharing of strategic information and seen the morale of individual new hires suffer as a result. One new hire, an experienced executive assistant, had become adept at serving as the "gatekeeper" for the busy executives whom she served in her past employment, largely because of her knowledge of company strategy collected in the course of her 15 years at the company. Understanding the roles individual executives served relative to the company's goals, she understood who needed to be seen right away, who or what issues could wait, and how to support prioritization for the executives' agendas. At her new company, her "onboarding" consisted of showing her where the kitchen was, how the executives liked their coffee, how to answer the phones, and when to feed the fish.

Eager to succeed, this employee introduced herself to others in the office and made a point of learning about strategy on her own. At one point, she emailed the management team and asked to speak with them for 10 minutes to get a better understanding of their individual roles and how they all fit into the big picture. Upon receiving this email invitation, her hiring manager called her to tell her this was not a good use of her time. She reminded her that she supported the CEO and CFO, not the other functional leaders, and that she should not stray beyond her standard job duties. Not surprisingly, this superb executive assistant chose to leave her new job within one month. Her hiring manager had not only failed to deliver an onboarding experience worthy of their needs; this manager's lack of appreciation of strategic education caused her to actually resist when an entrepreneurial new hire brought the need for it to her attention.

Some of our clients have found strategic orientation a valuable means to prevent anticipated declines in motivation. One of our clients, a technology company, traditionally gave most employees an assigned workspace in the corporate office. Over the last several years, as their business model changed, they found that more of their staff were spending a greater majority of their time working on-site at customer locations and other transient locations outside the office. This transition, coupled with growth demands, was putting pressure on the company's real estate needs. There was no more space to grow at their current location, yet the average staff member only used their offices one-third of the time.

Our client decided to merge a business strategy—providing better service to its customers by working more closely with them at their locations—with an operational strategy of transitioning the headquarters workspaces into "hotel-ing" sites. Employees wouldn't occupy permanent workstations; rather they'd have a "locker" of sorts for storage when in the office as well as a workstation reserved for the duration of their stay. As you can imagine, this change might have aroused dissatisfaction among employees, who generally enjoyed being able to come back home to personalized workspaces. However, with careful articulation of the strategy, the company was able to win over employees and prevent major disillusionment around this strategic move. Employees saw that the move made sense, for it would enable the company to serve its clients better and grow without much additional capital investment.

New Blood

Another important way strategic orientation benefits a company is by operating as a driving force in support of either a newly determined "business transformation" (initiatives in which entirely new business strategies and/or outcomes are pursued) or "organizational transformation" (initiatives to change how a company thinks or behaves). Farmers Insurance, for instance, wanted to focus the attention of field employees on customers. To affect that strategic change, the company revised its training program to include not just experience with live customer interactions, but also immersion in the kind of industry knowledge vital to understanding and executing a company's strategy.[4]

Oddly, when seeking to realize a transformation, most managers have severely underutilized their employee base to drive change. Companies generally seek to avoid tackling organizational transformation; when they do attempt it, they take a top-down, command and control approach with limited results. A common approach is to acquire another company or change leaders—options that deliver very moderate results. Given our earlier reference to the Attrition Law of Thirds (because of attrition, you will turn over a full third of your work force every three years), we hope you can see how onboarding represents an amazing opportunity to enlist new hires into a transformative strategy.

If your company is anything like most, this line of thinking probably diverges starkly from how you generally view new hires. Often hiring managers responsible for a strategic shift view new entrants as something of a necessary evil. They only accept the idea of relying on new hires once they discover that veteran employees are too busy with existing assignments and the requirements of running the current business to participate in change-related activities.

Let's make this notion of onboarding as a pathway to change more concrete. Consider a US-based cable television company. Thirty years ago, players in this market operated as legal and licensed local monopolies; the cost of digging up streets and laying cable was so great that no company would do it without an exclusive contract with the local municipality. Once a cable company obtained this contract, no great impetus existed for it to provide superior customer service or innovate the product. As local cable operators started to merge with one another and achieve greater scale, they gained negotiating leverage over suppliers (content providers) and spread the other operating costs across more households.

By the 1990s, new forms of competition—satellite television, DVDs, the Internet, gaming consoles, fiberoptic competition from Verizon and AT&T, direct to consumer distribution models such as Apple's iTunes, among many others—slowly but surely chipped away at the exclusive domain that cable companies enjoyed for so long. This new reality has forced cable operators to become much more concerned with customer service. But how do you improve customer service dramatically?

How do you transform an organization that had provided very low levels of satisfying customer care into one that takes as its daily mission providing superior service to customers? This is where onboarding can play a huge role.

Companies that have been doing business a certain way for a long time tend to have employees conditioned to do things the old way. By contrast, organizations interested in change can hire new employees primed and ready to behave in a new way. What this "new blood" requires is information about the transformation and how their role fits in. They also need the strong support of leadership that sees this incoming class for what they are: Brand-new and expensive capital investments with great potential. New hires need to understand that they are change agents; otherwise, they will not know how to relate to veteran workers they'll encounter on the job. If you can provide these things, you'll find that new hires can push transformation farther on account of their open-mindedness and willingness to listen, their motivation to perform and prove themselves (they just got the job after all), and the knowledge about best practices, trends, and technology they bring from prior experiences.

Strategic knowledge empowers new hires to make proactive choices in support of the new strategy. It is easy to see the importance of indoctrinating a newly hired executive into the strategy of a transforming company—typically, strategy becomes central to the discussion and evaluation during the recruiting process. What is less obvious to management is the benefit that comes from indoctrinating an average new hire. Strategy orientation allows the typical employee to be more connected to the strategy and therefore further it through his or her everyday activities. No longer is the job transactional; with understanding of the strategy under his or her belt, a new hire is on a mission.

If your company's strategy is to be your industry's lowest cost provider, then it might make great sense to reduce working capital needs, minimize interest expense from all bank lines of credit, eliminate any cost that is not necessary and minimize all others, and go to market with the lowest possible price. If your organization can explain this strategy and the importance of a given tactic—e.g., lowering interest expense by reducing your line of credit to your new employees in the collections department—then new hires might help push the strategy forward by leaning on customers to pay their bills quickly.

Alternatively, if your company is pursuing a strategy of premium service and premium pricing, then you can imagine how important it might be to communicate that strategy to your collections department. Although collections remain critically important, greater customer accommodation on payment terms is likely far more appropriate than it would have been in the first scenario. Not providing this context will very likely impede the company's chance to deliver on its strategic plan — and this is true even when new hires perform functions that at first glance do not seem most relevant to the strategy.

In speaking of strategy immersion's impact on change, or indeed, in speaking to any of the benefits that such initiation might bring a company, it's important to acknowledge that some new hires might not care about strategy at first. Perhaps they don't feel incentivized enough to care, or perhaps nobody has gotten them to care about strategy in the past. It is the job of onboarding (the collective whole of the onboarding stakeholders) to give them the motivation and incentive they need to care. If you talk about strategy with the employees, some will get it and will be moved by it. Guess what? You just activated drive and ambition. You have also just given new hires — even those with low-level, hourly wage jobs — reason to believe that their employer is a company at which they can build a career (or if nothing else, keep their job, as this employer may actually have a business plan that will result in job growth). If only a small number of new hires — say, 5% — get the strategy and run with it, you will see a big payoff in terms of "aha" moments, higher productivity, and an organization more aligned with its strategy of transformation. You will realize a bump in your Onboarding Margin, and you should be proud of its impact.

Making New Hires Strategic

Now that we've established how powerful strategy immersion can be, let's consider how a company should incorporate this orientation as part of a state-of-the-art, strategic onboarding program. In other chapters, we've provided "best principles" drawn from our experiences working with and researching best-in-class onboarding companies. In this case, since few if any companies have incorporated it as part of onboarding (one more reason why it constitutes a golden opportunity for a firm interested in gaining competitive advantage), what we offer here are our "best principles" for establishing strategy orientation based on our general organizational development and performance improvement experience.

Best Principle #1: Don't be afraid of sharing the strategy.
It's important that we address the perceived risks associated with teaching business strategy to your employees. You might think that the more of your strategy you put out in the open, the greater the chances your competition will learn of it. We believe that the benefits far outweigh the risks. You already have employees, contractors, suppliers, and customers who talk to your competition, not to mention ex-employees. Your company already likely posts company performance against key performance indicators (KPIs). Also, analysts may already cover your company. And, we can assure you that if you have a distinct strategy your competition has already figured it out from the actions that your company has taken. Knowing your strategy is quite different than being able to execute it or being able to guard against it. And you likely have legal protection on your side in the form of non-disclosure agreements with your new employees. The bottom line is that the risks associated with letting new hires into the tent are far smaller than the risks of keeping them away from it. You can always limit how much depth you share, and you can also parse information on a need-to-know basis (albeit with a potentially limiting impact on the Onboarding Margin). Overall, we encourage you to share and realize the benefits that come when your new workforce contributes as much as possible to realizing your strategy.

Best Principle #2: Provide rich examples of how other employees have delivered on your strategy.
Providing illustrative examples is one of the best ways to teach concepts to new hires, and this is certainly the case with strategy. We advise showing new hires the impact that individuals have had in furthering the strategy through their own work. Ideally you should show two kinds of examples: (1) the standard fare that shows how work activities are aligned against the strategy; and (2) examples of employees making independent decisions in the course of their work because of, and in concert with, the strategy. Examples can come from any area of the business, and the more you gather, the better. Ideally, you can select and craft these stories so that every new hire has a chance to see themselves in the stories. At a minimum, take care to provide stories that cover the largest groups of employees:

Front-line, customer-facing employees; back office/administrative; pro-duction; management, etc. With the second type of examples, you should demonstrate how the individual worker's actions went beyond their ordi-nary roles and responsibilities, how this worker included others in their ini-tiative (including gaining buy-in), and how this worker's actions made a real difference for the company and its strategy. Stories about "aha" moments might prove most interesting and make the biggest impression, yet examples depicting everyday activities will pay off, too.

Here is an example of the kind of story you might share: At a mid-sized company, the leadership team regularly engaged employees in strategy discussion regarding the key areas of focus for the firm. At one of these meetings in early 2008, the president shared key strategies the company would pursue for revenue growth as well as some of the activities that were being taken to reduce costs in non-strategic spend categories (i.e., the com-pany was happy to cut costs in areas that were not going to drive revenue growth). Not long after this meeting, one new employee had an idea to help with the cost-cutting strategy. His roommate was a computer pro-grammer and worked for a firm that provided outsourced IT support. In swapping stories about their respective days at work, the employee real-ized that outsourcing IT might well work for his own company, lowering costs and providing better service. The firm had grown so large that its IT staff could not serve everyone's needs; when something went wrong, it always took too long to fix. The new hire recommended his idea to the leadership. After some additional investigation, the company determined that it should indeed outsource IT, resulting in material cost savings as well as service improvements. To make your stories successful, all you need to include is the strategy set-up, idea, actions, and outcome.

Learning about stories like this, individual employees will imagine them-selves in the position of the entry-level employee. They will understand in concrete terms how they can make a difference. They will be more moti-vated to share creative thinking so as to help push the strategy further.

Best Principle #3: Incorporate periodic formal strategic insight interviews.
Your system should implement a formal process to capture your new hires' insights around strategy. This process might begin during Week One with an initial welcome interview similar to one we advocate around culture.

Formal follow up discussions should be scheduled and can take place at the 6-, 9-, and 12-month points. At all of these meetings, the conversation should run in both directions, with the new hire's manager or mentor first gauging the employee's understanding of the strategy and then asking the new hire to share his or her ideas. These ideas should include suggestions to inform any revisions to the strategy, but with greater focus on business unit, function, and role-specific related issues, and they should also include ideas for how to better execute the current strategy.

By engaging new hires in this way, the conversation reinforces a key principle of the new employer-employee compact: That the company truly cares about the new hire's opinions and ideas and is willing to invest in the time to hear them. Reinforcing that the company cares is important not merely because it helps the new hire to feel good. "Truly cares" means that your company is going through this exercise because it expects a contribution of significance from the new hire community on this front. The "expects" part is important; there is no need to put undue pressure on your new hire class, but you should set an expectation early (ideally in the recruiting stage) that the company believes all employees can potentially to contribute to its plans. You should communicate this upon the new hire's arrival, throughout the various orientation communications, as part of the broader onboarding conversation, and most certainly in the core periodic check points. Employees will come away more motivated than ever to do their best because they feel that they are being listened to and that the potential exists for them to make a real difference.

Solicitation of strategic insights can also take place in the form of an open-ended survey as opposed to an actual interview. For larger enterprises, insight collection/synthesis is obviously easier with electronic collection, and as long as you have a very strong analyst reviewing the submissions, it can be an efficient and effective exercise. We strongly suggest that you collect strategic insights live in the form of discussion with a mentor or managers; that way, you can in the same forum provide feedback and together make plans with the new hire to socialize or take action on the ideas. Here are some questions we recommend covering:

1. Do you believe you have a good understanding of our company strategy? Business Unit (BU)? Functional? How would you explain it?

2. From your perspective, how are we (the organization) succeeding at executing against these strategies?
3. Do you have any ideas that may help us in executing the strategy?
4. Have you encountered any challenges or hurdles in trying to perform your role in the organization?
5. Have you had any exceptional "successes"—when everything came together and you could see our strategy in action in the work you and/or your colleagues were performing?

After the conversation, the manager or mentor should determine with the new hire what appropriate actions the company could take as a result of the new hire's ideas. The hiring manager or mentor should also take notes during the conversation so that during a subsequent pulse check or formal interview, the discussion can resume and the manager/mentor can learn if the new hire's experiences or perceptions have changed.

Ideally you will initiate these exchanges as a distinct discussion, separate from other activities. If this topic becomes a single line item as part of a periodic performance review, than the scope of the strategic discussion will likely be minimized, since other topics at the meeting will likely receive greater airtime.

Best Principle #4: Make use of stakeholder maps.
In our chapter on social networking, we advised that managers help develop stakeholder maps for new hires, identifying specific individuals whom the new hire should approach for specific needs or with specific ideas. Another way to talk about strategy to the new hire is to pull out a stakeholder map and explain how each of these stakeholders will work in concert with the new hire to achieve strategic goals. Using the stakeholder map, and an accompanying organizational chart, helps make the different layers of strategy (corporate, business unit, etc.) visual for new hires; you can literally connect the dots for the new hires as to who is doing what in the organization and why. At the same time, you will also be supporting another part of onboarding, the forging of social connections.

Best Principle #5: Unveil the strategy in layers.
Since strategy is highly detailed, organizations will do best to unveil it progressively and in layers. That way, new hires will not feel overwhelmed with

information, and they will have proper context—as noted in Figure 2.7 and accompanying discussion—to make sense of it.

We advise beginning the strategy immersion portion of onboarding with a discussion of the broad, high-level strategy. In the weeks and months ahead, the conversation can then proceed to cover in more detail the new hire's role and how it supports the overall strategy. It can also explore how the new hire's function/organization fits in to executing the strategy. When working with the stakeholder map, we advise beginning with organizations that most closely relate to the one to which the new hire belongs and then spiral out from there. Later on in the onboarding year, managers should customize conversations, organizing them in a way that makes sense to the individual new hire's role and position in the company.

Best Principle #6: Be honest and realistic when talking about strategy.

Do not go overboard trying to inspire your new hires. Do not turn strategy conversations into mere sales pitches. Authenticity inspires, not smoke and mirrors. Think of *The Wizard of Oz*: In the end, there was no fancy wizard orchestrating events, and the real actions of individuals became inspirational. The CEO and other senior leaders are key here: Honest, heartfelt messages from the firm's leadership are more than enough to inspire individuals; you simply do not need the hype. If leadership can acknowledge that they have made some trade-offs and tough choices, for better or for worse, new hires will have more confidence in both leadership and the underlying strategy. They will feel motivated to help out because of the collective sacrifices that have already been made. They also will not wind up disillusioned down the road when false expectations raised by the CEO have failed to come to fruition. If leadership prepares new hires for challenges and the road ahead, new hires will feel more inclined to rally. They will be more patient when the company encounters bumps in the road. And they will be more willing to forgive leaders for any mistakes or poor judgments they make.

Best Principle #7: Frame strategic thinking as a skill that employees can develop and that will benefit them in a knowledge economy.

There is a reason strategic thinking stands today as one of the most widely discussed skills and concepts in business literature: Companies rarely succeed if they don't have a good strategy, and a good strategy will not emerge if companies don't have employees adept at plotting strategy.

In a knowledge economy, workers' intellectual skills become more prized assets than the durable goods companies produce. As Peter Drucker noted in his book *The Effective Executive,* knowledge workers produce with their heads, not their hands, creating ideas, knowledge, and information.[5] Organizations are already investing in their human capital by offering more robust training and development programs. Teaching your new hires strategy and strategic thinking as a skill that will enable employees to produce ideas is another way a company can support the new hire's development.

It is a clear win-win: The organization is preparing its people (or assets) to "produce" more of what is needed by the company to succeed in the future, and the individual gains a valuable skill that makes him or her more marketable when changing companies or simply more successful within the same company. Yet companies need to articulate this to new hires. That way, new hires will possess a stronger sense of participating in and benefiting from a new employer-employee compact.

Best Principle #8: Clue new hires into your strategic priorities.
Not all parts of the strategy are as fixed as others, and not all are prioritized as highly. Part of our firm's strategy is to have a congenial workplace where young people can learn a lot and work hard. We decided to locate our office in the heart of downtown because we thought new hires would find this neighborhood more attractive. If our lease comes up for renewal and our rent doubles, we might be willing move our offices to an alternative location, even though being downtown is part of our people strategy. We might compromise because a greater strategic priority might be to improve our profits. To understand our company, new hires need to understand how our firm thinks through these issues and how we make decisions that befit our strategy. This nuanced discussion empowers new hires to begin to become a more effective steward and activist of the company's strategy, as they are equipped to think and act in harmony with the enterprise's intended path.

Companies need to articulate what their strategic priorities are. That way, they can organize their own efforts to support the firm's more important strategies when these come into conflict with less important ones. The more new hires understand the priorities, the less they will need to run to superiors to ask for clarification or guidance. And more importantly, the less frustrated they will become, as they will be able to avoid misinterpretation of company actions and intentions. When the strategy is well communicated, organizational efficiency improves, whereas new hires feel more empowered and gain more confidence in their own decision-making abilities.

Summing Up

Even more than other onboarding components, strategy immersion for rank-and-file employees remains uncharted territory for most firms. Yet the opportunities are huge. Similar to high-potential executive hires, low- and mid-level employees feel empowered and motivated when they are able to connect what they do every day with the organization's higher purpose. Engagement increases, and with it productivity and the Onboarding Margin. As an extension of early career support, strategy orientation stands as an important way of redefining the employer-employee compact in a way beneficial for both the company and the new hire. Organizations can realize benefits from strategic onboarding without strategy orientation, yet alerting new hires to the bigger picture remains necessary if companies are to squeeze the most value possible from their onboarding programs. In ways we have suggested, strategy immersion (Table 6.1). works together with social networking, cultural mastery, and early career support; it is the organic meshing of all four that allows for the greatest impact.

So far we have covered the four key topic areas that a strategic onboarding program should include so as to unlock vast new value for organizations. Yet all the thoughtful program content in the world will not do much good if the company fails at execution. Onboarding must be systemic and of extended duration if it is to achieve optimal results, and this means having adequate processes, technologies, and resources in place to coordinate the different players so that the program appears seamless and of superior quality. An onboarding program also needs a system in place for measuring stakeholder performance and holding players accountable for fulfilling their onboarding functions. Like the system of blood vessels assuring that muscles in the human body have the oxygen, nutrients, and other elements they need to perform, administration and governance serve as the life support system for a state-of-the-art onboarding program. They allow enlightened organizations to integrate new hires and prepare them for success, so it is imperative that as a program designer you get them right.

There is a more fundamental point here. The new hire compact that we discuss in this book implies that the entire enterprise cares about the new hire's future, not just his or her boss. To enact this compact, we have to build into an enterprise's system a model that ensures that the entire enterprise will attend to the new hire's success. Organizations have to commit themselves at the deepest levels to retaining the people they bring onboard. They have to put the onus on themselves to identify at-risk people and take steps to remediate problems and turn them around, so as to retain new hires as strong, productive employees.

In the end, the goal becomes to reduce recruiting activities—not because of company stagnation, but because we are more successful with the ones we already brought in. This means putting senior leaders in charge of overseeing the program's success. It also means that companies should make sure they've devoted sufficient administrative and governance resources to onboarding—not just dollars and people, but tools and technology. What those resources are and how a progressive enterprise might deploy them to greatest effect is the subject of the next chapter.

Table 6.1 Interpersonal Network Elements—Sample Tactics

Onboarding Phase	Element	Sample Tactics	Application Advice
Prepare	• Pre-Day One self-education on company, culture, values, and strategy	• Include the annual report in the new hire package—a version with call outs for what is most relevant to the new hire and his or her role	• Personalizing the information by use of notes/call outs makes information more relevant and reinforces "valued connectedness"
Orient	• Introduction to company strategy by leaders	• When firm leaders get up and introduce themselves, in the leadership message, they need to share more information about the strategy—real time, and updates on what doing to execute against it	• Leaders should go into the strategic mandate and how the various components of the organization work together to achieve it—going beyond mission and vision
	• Break down the strategy by organizational element and functional area	• Hiring managers conduct conversations with new hires explaining how their organization supports the broader strategy and the individual's role • Use the stakeholder map to illustrate the key players in the strategy • Compare and contrast company strategy to that of the new hire's former employer, if appropriate	• Incorporate content around how employees had an effect on strategy • Use illustrative examples from various parts of the business so that each new hire can find an element that relates to his or her role
Integrate	• Continue to incorporate strategy content into discussions with new hires	• Conversations with mentor at three-month touch-point • Brown bag discussions with experienced employees from a variety of businesses and functional areas • Managers and/or mentors conduct debriefs following any company-wide strategy related announcements	• Strategy is unveiled in layers, as new hires gain more context • Relate strategy to the new hire's role • Cover all the key content areas: competition, customers, supply chain, brand, etc.
Excel	• Capture the new hire's perspective on strategy	• Conduct periodic strategic insight interviews with the new hires • Incorporate as a discussion topic into the regular new hire summits	• Soliciting new hire's perspective supports both teaching the strategy and reinforcing feelings of "valuedness"
	• Continue to incorporate strategy content into discussions with new hires	• Continue discussions with mentor at regularly scheduled intervals • Brown bag discussions with experienced employees from a variety of businesses and functional areas • Managers and/or mentors conduct debriefs following any company-wide strategy related announcements	• Strategy is unveiled in layers, as new hires gain more context • Relate strategy to new hire's role • Cover all the key content areas: competition, customers, supply chain, brand, etc.

7

THE ONBOARDING MARGIN LIFE SUPPORT SYSTEM: ADMINISTRATION AND GOVERNANCE

You are not alone if your company's onboarding process is administratively disjointed. On the surface, processing new hire paperwork; outfitting recruits with the necessary supplies, access, tools, and development resources; assigning new hires to a team, a mentor, and a first assignment; among many other requirements, seems basic. It should be easy to manage, right? Unfortunately, it's not.

At most companies, this process requires tight coordination between stakeholders in almost every function—people who typically lack a formal reporting structure for this activity or accountability to each other. At a minimum, Recruiting, Security, IT, Facilities, Payroll, Legal, Benefits, and the new hire's manager must play a role in welcoming the new hire. The remainder of the year, a systemic program provides administrative coordination (and direction) for the new hire, hiring manager and system-wide participants, assuring that they can complete training, acclimation, acculturation, skill progression and recognition, progress in role, career development, and performance review activities. To pull it off, you need not only the right technology, people, and resources in place, but a system of governance to measure performance, ensure that all system participants play their role properly, and assess consequences if they fall short.

It is true that flawless onboarding program administration will not by itself materially affect the Onboarding Margin (i.e., productivity or retention). If all that you invest in is cleaning up onboarding administration, you will not likely realize any material return on investment. Even if the administrative process is broken, and no real governance exists, new hires will eventually receive their equipment and gain access to required systems and tools, albeit while experiencing frustrations, annoyances, or unnecessary cost. Further, program administration can be a thankless task; it will only garner attention insomuch as things go wrong. So why bother?

Seamless program administration plays a critical role in ensuring that higher-impact early career progress and support, networking, and development are properly executed. If system participants do not inform and guide new hires toward the key resources available to them and do not play their part more broadly, new hires are far more likely to miss out on learning or developmental opportunities critical to their success at the company. And although program administration alone may not make or break a new hire's experience, flaws in execution represent one of the most common "gripes" that you hear from new hires. "They weren't prepared for me," new hires say. "I didn't even have a place to sit." "I had no idea where to go or what was expected from me." "My manager wasn't even in the office the whole first week to meet me." We have all witnessed these initial impressions tarnish a company's reputation as an employer of choice.

The motive we most commonly hear about for improving program administration is wringing cost and wasted energy out of the process. Automation and centralized oversight can simplify and standardize the onboarding experience and reap significant cost savings for the organization. As senior management realizes the cost benefits, many of our onboarding clients find that improved program administration builds momentum, generating the capital and organizational energy to attack higher-impact program upgrades. Governance, meanwhile, is essentially a higher-level form of administration. It ensures that the firm is doing what the program design says it should do; i.e., address the most critical issues uncovered in the diagnostic. It also involves evaluating on a regular basis (we recommend annually or upon conclusion of a business cycle, whichever is shorter) whether the program design remains the right answer and assessing consequences to participants for failing to perform according to required standards. It is simple: You can have sufficient administrative resources in place, and all the right content, but if you do not have governance, your program will fall short of delivering the value the enterprise deserves with this human capital investment.

This chapter provides general guidelines for governing and administering a strategic onboarding program. It also relates practices we have seen applied to great effect at our clients' companies and at other leading-edge onboarding organizations. Putting state of the art administration processes behind the programs you choose and executing these programs with excellence clearly means accruing some cost. By now, though, we hope you will consider these costs in their proper perspective, seeing administration and governance as enablers of the great opportunity that onboarding represents. Program administration and its continuous improvement are the foundation for implementing a new employee compact, and as such, a worthy and important investment in your company's long-term future.

Onboarding's Administrative Needs

Here is some great news: Your enterprise already possesses the skill set it requires to administer onboarding properly. One thing many successful companies excel at is operational excellence—repetitively doing the same thing over and over again with efficiency and reliability. Large companies are especially adept at simplifying and making routine processes for scale and scope advantage, which is precisely why they often cannot undertake dramatic change all that well (often the skill set of smaller firms). Yet the majority of big companies have not applied this skill to the particular function of bringing onboard its new hires. They've refined and systematized processes that relate to production or serving customers, but where onboarding is concerned, the slate remains largely blank.

For processes to become routine and effective, in the sense of delivering consistently great outcomes, you need to:

1. Determine the process objectives.
2. Document the necessary steps for the process.
3. Simplify and optimize the process for cost, service level, and time objectives.

4. Administer the process.

5. Embed a continuous improvement system for the process.

Within the human capital world, we have developed strong administrative processes for things like recruiting, performance assessments, promotions, compensation, benefits administration, labor utilization, and succession planning, among many others. So what does proper administration of onboarding look like?

Let's start with Week One and the preparation leading up to Week One. Administration means organizing and overseeing the numerous preparation and orientation processes—getting everyone's security, legal, confidentiality, and compliance forms taken care of efficiently and completely and delivering information to new hires (company policies, benefits, etc.). It also means giving new hires tools they need to do their jobs, including business cards, computers, mobile phones, telephone extensions and voicemail, email addresses, email system distribution groups, security access, and much more. It includes preparing the new hire's manager about the new hire start date and prepping the department on the new hire's background, strengths, weaknesses, and objectives. It includes determining the new hire's first assignments and providing the necessary orientation.

At the childcare provider company Bright Horizons, everything is ready upon the new employee's arrival, including nameplate, security access, phone system, email, desktop, and paperwork.[1] Unfortunately, most companies do a far less comprehensive job prepping for and delivering Week One, and people do talk about it. Many HR task leaders presented with the task of addressing onboarding are told to focus on this world—in our view, a short sighted approach to onboarding. Managers in charge of onboarding notice the griping (from both the new hires and the hiring managers), and they in turn talk about the organization's failures. This is a good thing; managers *should* clean up those processes to take wasted cost out and improve the experience for the new hire and the hiring manager. Still, we have not seen many companies truly do the basics well, and as a result some low hanging fruit is sitting there for the taking. But we want to repeat again, don't fool yourself or your team. Improving Week One administration won't materially impact retention and productivity. If new hires are aligned on objectives, love their jobs, find the work fulfilling, enjoy their manager, are inspired by career opportunities, and understand the culture, they will without any question forgive the company for not performing optimally on Week One administration.

As we have stressed throughout this book, proper onboarding administration goes way beyond the largely one-time only, transactional activities of Week One. If you have a mentoring component of your onboarding program, you'll need to administer this component on an ongoing basis (assignments, content, direction, oversight, timing, etc.). Every time a new hire gets a mentor, the mentor requires notification and information about the mentee's background and the desired mentoring focus. Recruiting managers always know things about the new hire's point of view coming into the organization, but in most companies today nobody captures this information and effectively (and routinely) provides it to the mentor or, worse, the hiring manager.

In a well-administered mentoring program, a process will exist to collect information from the recruiter and hiring manager, store it in a centralized place (perhaps by leveraging existing software systems), offer it to the mentor alongside guidelines for how to run mentoring meetings, automatically schedule mentoring meetings on an ongoing basis, and dispense reminder notices as appropriate. This process would also organize more formal meetings at the key check points (e.g., 90-day, six-month, nine-month, and annual reviews), instructing mentors to discuss the culture and discuss development opportunities for the new hire, both in areas where the new hire needs to improve and in areas of special interest to the new hire. Without this process, the program will underperform (and from our experience, it will materially underperform). On the other hand, a well-administered mentoring process can provide a great experience from the outset, getting new hires off to a positive start at the company. As mentoring goes, leading corporations are increasingly doing a number of things to systematize effective mentoring, including:

- Putting formal programs in place to identify at risk (those that risk failing but should not) and high performing individuals (those with great prospects, so long as the organization does not fail them);
- Mandating frequent mentor meetings during onboarding to handle new hire concerns and monitor progress;

- Creating "mentoring circles" that provide multidirectional flows and feedback loops, thus expanding the perspectives available to a new hire; creating vertical, multi-generational "mentoring families" to mitigate the possibility of poor mentoring;
- Using goal and strengths input to align mentors with mentees, thus improving engagement of both by creating a sense of unique "fit" from the first day; and
- Providing guidance to mentors on the issues that they need to be discussing, the timing of the discussions, and the actions that they should take.

Mentoring is just the beginning. Almost everything we've covered in the last four chapters requires ongoing and *thoughtful* administration—performance management, task assignment, team assignment, pulse checks, buddy programs, affinity groups, networking events, and content updating on the web site and other media. In addition, program administration supports the systemic nature of onboarding over an extended period. Mentoring and buddy programs, for instance, need to unfold seamlessly in conjunction with the new hire networking program. Content across the organization needs to be updated and disseminated periodically and appropriately so that it is up-to-date. One of the senior leaders in an organization we once worked with opened a presentation to new hires with, "Well, I've never done this before, and they didn't give me any materials, so I'll just wing it." In a world-class onboarding program, just like a world-class assembly plant or retail center, "winging it" doesn't cut it; firms need infrastructure in place to ensure that people and processes across the organization are coordinated and have the fresh, high-quality material they need, when they need it.

Companies need to coordinate mentoring with ongoing learning and development events. They need a system that determines new hires' learning needs and matches them to the resources, and the mentor needs to be part of this process. Such a system will assure on an ongoing basis that the firm possesses the right resources to meet new hire needs. Timelines and centralized checklists for development opportunities will be sent out to new hires, and completed courses will be automatically entered into the new hire's profile for later reference. Reminders will be sent out to new hires and their hiring managers. All of this is plenty of work, yet if the proper resources are not there, the firm's investment in mentoring and learning and development programs does not provide nearly as great a return as it might otherwise.

To give you a sense of the myriad administrative tasks required to execute a state-of-the-art onboarding program, imagine you are sitting down with a new hire and explaining to him or her all the elements of the redefined employee compact that you are promising to provide. As an important aside, we strongly suggest that you take this step; i.e., have actual conversations about this with new hires so that they fully understand and appreciate the commitment the firm is making on their behalf, as well as the responsibilities that they, the new hires, accept when entering the compact. Even a partial list of the firm's promises as part of the employer-employee compact suggests the breadth of the administrative burden that accrues during onboarding:

The Firm's Initial Promise to the New Hire

- We will provide you with the tools you need to get the job done: A computer, a work space, a phone/phone number, email, supplies, tools, equipment, safety equipment (personal protection equipment), etc.
- We will ensure that (if offered) benefits are handled smoothly.
- We will ensure that your new manager (and team) are ready for your arrival.
- We will assure you that a manager who oversees the onboarding program is available to answer questions that may arise.
- We will provide you with an onboarding buddy—someone who is at your level or is not long from having been a new hire themselves to help shepherd you through the process and serve as a resource for questions.
- We will provide you with knowledge about company learning and development resources at your disposal for establishing your career and setting out your career development.
- We will help you make connections with others in the company so that you can hear from others their "secrets of success," make connections that may help you with your job performance, help you understand the strategies of the company and how the various units support each other in execution of those strategies, and make friends with similar professional and extracurricular interests.

- We will help you get settled in this new city—where to live, where to "play," and how to meet others outside of our company who are in your industry.

- We will tell you how your role fits into the big picture: What the company strategy is and how you support it, who the various role players within the company are and how they support successful execution of the strategy, how and why our strategy differs from that of the competition, and what this means for you.

- We will provide you with progressive work assignments, so that you can achieve gradual success and make steps to achieve your personal prospect.

- We will provide you with regular "pulse checks" throughout your first year to find out how you are doing—how you are acclimating, how you experience your role and your network, how your understanding of your role and the strategy is progressing, and how we are doing in delivering on the promises we made to you during recruiting and Week One.

- We will provide you with many opportunities to learn company culture and strategy and to interact with other professionals. These opportunities will range from formal "traditional classroom" type training to "on demand" training you can access via Inter/Intranet, to mentoring, small group discussions and networking, net forums and blogs, and one-on-one conversations.

Now, these are pretty significant promises! Few if any firms possess an onboarding department, but looking at the preceding list, you quickly realize why such a department might be desirable. Of course, if your firm lacks resources for an entire department, you can always limit the workload by prioritizing which onboarding elements your firm offers and assigning responsibility to an existing entity within your organization. But the key is that it does become an expressed responsibility for that organization and/or individuals. All program elements require at least some level of administration, so the administrative resources (and supplemental external resources) you have available will help determine your firm's priorities and the depth and breadth of your program. More on this in the next chapter on diagnostics.

Managing Administration Properly

To manage administration properly, we recommend that you implement a Provisioning and Administrative Support process that runs from the hour of offer acceptance all the way through the greater of the new hire's entire first year or complete business cycle. This process needs to include all the materials and support necessary for a new hire to work well in his or her position. Certain materials, such as laptops and badges, should be ready by Day One, whereas others such as site-specific supplies and support will be provided later. Still other materials, such as reminders and organization for the performance review process, mentor meetings, learning and development activities, the remediation of at-risk employees, benefit support, and other program elements should run continuously.

Firms should take care to account for all of the "behind the scenes" activities that need to take place so as to support program execution throughout Year One. They should develop process flows and checklists to provide process owners with the necessary tools, guidance, and support to execute new hire activities during each program phase. To ensure that administrative processes do not get lost in the course of rolling out various phases of an onboarding program, these processes should be laid out explicitly as part of the formal program blueprint described in the next chapter, and they should run concurrently with all phases of the onboarding program. Writing administration into the blueprint formally recognizes logistical support needs and provides insight into possible provisioning gaps in the various phases. It also enables seamless process hand-offs across the four phases, all the way from Prepare to Excel, thus ensuring consistent support for new hires throughout the first year.

State of the art administration does not just involve planning and allocating for logistics and coordination; it also means deploying technology. To handle some administrative tasks, many firms have turned to off-the-shelf—and to some extent customizable—onboarding software. Software is great at helping firms arrive at a standardized approach for common tasks. Software packages vary, with many of them also serving as platforms for distributing learning materials to new hires, hiring managers, and other stakeholders. Some packages automate only certain relatively simple processes, such as providing benefits information or allowing new hires to fill out and submit forms for procedures such as obtaining a security badge. More sophisticated software might handle onboarding activities throughout an entire year, managing workflow and keeping managers and new hires on schedule with key onboarding activities such as mentoring meetings.

Evidence suggests that integrated talent management software suites can offer large gains when applied to onboarding, streamlining processes and seamlessly transitioning new hires to the rest of the talent management software. A 2007 Towers Perrin presentation cited that one major US telecommunications company used technology to onboard 12,000 new employees in just four weeks. The onboarding process began far in advance of the new employees' first days of work thanks to online tools that automated traditional paperwork, saving the company time and money. In addition, new employees were able to begin acclimating themselves to their new work environment, developing a sense of excitement and engagement. As the 12,000 employees began work, the software they had begun using before their first day became their portal for all training, performance management, and promotion planning. The integrated software suite quickly assimilated new employees and took some of the burden off the company's onboarding team.

Onboarding leaders such as Starwood, Starbucks, and Booz Allen use software to manage onboarding processes. Starbucks' deployed system includes automation of administrative processes; training and orientation roadmaps; web-based portals for new hires, HR/administrative staff, and managers; and reporting of key analytics. The career planning tool offers individual new hire career profiles detailing goals and experience, integrated with destination planning roadmaps, manager inputs into employee profiles for additional talent assessment and management, and site-building tools to promote and match internal career opportunities to employees. The software allows for many advantages, including improved time-to-productivity, forms efficiency, better ability to track metrics, and scalability without the need for significant additional resources. It has been reported that Starbucks saw a 1 to 2 percent improvement in retention following implementation of the software and the associated support practices.

Other software platforms feature onboarding and career planning modules that integrate with other human capital life cycle modules; e.g., automated recruiting processes. The software includes analytics and measurement of new hire orientation activities, process map development tools for activities automation, and implementation best practices. Client constructed as well as commercial software include features that provide design and implementation tools for identifying and developing top performers, workforce management tools to redeploy internal talent, career path planning tools, and a "talent record" database that details development and performance information for each new hire. This database allows HR managers to search for internal candidate matches when positions open up, and it also includes tracking and reporting tools. Overall, the software allows for much greater efficiency in the performance of administrative tasks, especially as relates to the transition from recruiting, new hire documentation, and internal candidate searches. The software is fairly easy to implement and is compatible with many current systems. Since commercial packages have already been created, HR staff can focus on other, higher value tasks with a more strategic focus rather than designing a new program from scratch. Various packages offer different levels of customization and flexibility. Of course, many clients elect to develop platforms internally, providing for even greater degrees of customization.

Our own clients have had great success in automating parts of their onboarding programs, particularly by front-loading many normal Day One or Week One administrative activities before Day One—what we often call "pre-start" or "pre-boarding" in the Prepare phase. Time to productivity increases because the firm can start working on other key onboarding components, such as strategic education or networking, on Day One rather than spending time on benefits or other "basic" elements that have been pushed forward to a pre-start time frame. There is greater compliance and a more complete "paper trail" with these online delivered processes. Also, having new hires engage with the firm (and accomplish both pre-start work and learning) can further excite the new hire about the new job in the days and weeks before starting and allow you to more effectively "prime the pump" and hit the ground running. Software can also engage new hires by helping them to plan for and even establish cohort and other relationships of interest before Day One via social networking.

The key element of onboarding automation, especially as relates to pre-boarding, is the new hire portal. Access to an online portal can facilitate logistics, educate the new hire about the firm, make a new hire feel welcome and connected, and outline what to expect on Day One and beyond. Companies should conceive of the new hire portal as a core tool used throughout the first year and transitioning into other development tools as Year Two approaches. Although all portals will have a back-end interface for system administrators, the most effective portals will have interfaces (e.g., emails, alerts, planning and background tools, guides, etc.) for all core participants of the onboarding program (e.g., hiring manager, facilities, security, IT, mentors, etc.).

Upon offer acceptance, the portal needs to excite new hires by articulating what is in store for them at the company. The portal should expose new hires to all the development tools the company will provide. It should also provide guidance as to how to hit the ground running and how to increase chances for success. Positive *as well as negative* case study profiles really work well here. Cultural acclimation, perhaps in the form of blogs or video addresses from the CEO, should appear, as well as social networking features, initial training modules, and forms management. Companies can also post helpful items such as schedules, important phone numbers, and go-to resources.

Throughout Year One, intranet portals should provide links to all resources for addressing new hire needs, including instruction on how to resolve common problems and challenges encountered early in one's career, guidance on development planning and training curricula, and reminders for key milestones and events. In other content areas, the portal should conform closely to new hires' interests. The portal should cover professional and personal interests associated with joining the firm, such as information about where to live, school systems, how to find resources of interest, etc. Finally, the portal should express the brand of the onboarding program, maintain an authentic voice, and instruct the new hire on his or her responsibility for helping to assure the program's positive outcome.

In addition to content, firms should consider the messaging, rich media elements, and functionality of portal sites for new hires. If the site is not dynamic and if there is not value and a sense of activity and community, it will likely not receive much traffic or attention beyond that which is necessary to complete required paperwork and tasks.

Governance Structures

If companies require proper administrative resources to reap onboarding's full value, they also require governance and accountability mechanisms to ensure that the program works as intended. Without administrative resources in place, you're leaving money on the table. If you have administrative resources without a governing and accountability mechanism, then everything you've tried to build is at risk. You may have the ability to execute processes, but you'll be doing the same thing again and again without reviewing it to know if it's working (i.e., meeting the original objectives, let alone the most current objectives). We have seen firms waste large dollars by failing to build a governance component into their onboarding program. More often than not, companies do not hold anybody accountable for onboarding, in large part because no single department oversees the whole program. These companies pull together cross-functional teams, which is great on the front end from a diagnostic and design perspective but ultimately insufficient from an oversight and management perspective. Exceptions do exist; we've seen companies that maintain piece part accountability; e.g., holding IT accountable for delivering computers or phones on time. Yet limited accountability comprises a mere shadow of what companies should implement so as to reap the full Onboarding Margin described in Chapter One.

Proper governance requires that as a first step you designate individuals with clear governing authority. We recommend a governance model with clear roles and accountabilities. A steering committee might provide strategic oversight, while below it an onboarding Center of Excellence might oversee programs and keep on eye on how well participants are performing and the return stakeholders are receiving. The Center of Excellence should also monitor content and delivery, including the ongoing development and updating of program curriculum and portal content. Companies should designate an "Authenticity or Integrity Czar"—a person who understands and encourages frank and genuine communication (e.g., calling the aspirational just that instead of portraying the aspirational as the "here and now").

Below both of these groups, local onboarding coordinators should take charge of coordinating orientation for local offices and teams, ensuring that the new hire's team and broader community is prepared to support key activities. Local onboarding coordinators also are tasked with reminding support personnel and ensuring compliance with key activities, such as networking and mentoring. A second group reporting into the Center of Excellence, regional onboarding coordinators, oversees firmwide orientation activities; schedules learning and development facilitators, senior leaders, and panelists; and coordinates any community events (e.g., "New Hire Summits" or networking events within the industry). A third group, Provisioning, provides access to the new hire portal and prepares equipment, other tools of the trade, and access to resources (including security access to the building) for Day One and beyond. A fourth group attends to the unique design elements that exist for new hire segmentation (e.g., by level and experience, but business unit, by geography, etc.).

Learning centers of governance structures

Some firms make use of corporate universities and learning centers as a means of centralizing the training portions of onboarding under a single authority. At these firms, corporate universities become the hub for resources and training relevant to new hires, providing early opportunities for employees interested in learning and development. New hires gain access to coursework supporting their career development through leadership courses taught by senior management and other "guidance-counselor" based models. This approach demonstrates commitment to new hire development, and the centralized governance structure allows for more resource delivery than programs fragmented across departments or business units. Interaction between new hires and senior leadership instructors provide networking and stronger relationships across levels. New hires are also able to network with seasoned employees in shared courses.

Setting up a structure like this does require a significant investment in additional learning resources as well as reorganization of career support functions into a central organization. We recommend that you make employee participation in coursework mandatory, and that feedback loops exist between university and senior leadership (to align with business goals) and between the university and new hire managers (to capture learning needs). Mandatory participation puts more pressure on designers to create coursework that is relevant, effective, and valued by new hires, hiring managers, and peers. Without proper resources and attention to relevance, you run a great risk of wasting valuable company resources.

Real-life examples of governance structures

At equipment manufacturer Caterpillar, the corporate university is tasked with identifying and meeting new hire learning needs. Departmental learning managers develop learning plans and maintain dual reporting relationships with the departmental HR officer and Caterpillar University, while the University offers mentor and career coach training. Clearly defined training centers help engage new hires in career development and offer them the possibility of continued advancement, learning, and career progression. The firm's Leadership Quest onboarding program, available to selected management recruits, is predominantly taught by senior executives and tasked with the mission of helping young leaders understand Caterpillar's global market and its challenges early in their careers. Pilot implementation of Caterpillar University's "Making Great Leaders" program was so successful that it was rolled out among all 7,000 of the company's leaders.

At Lockheed Martin, the corporate university—called the Center for Leadership Excellence—serves as the central training facility for new hires. Six levels of curriculum address all employees' needs, from new hires up to senior leadership. Participant evaluations measure quality and ensure high standards (presenters scoring less than 4.5 out of 5 are not invited back). Learning is tied to mandatory training for specific programs, and an employee's review processes evaluate training progress and program eligibility.

Another governance structure modification made by some leading edge onboarding programs involves designation of a team within the governance structure to handle issues associated with the employer brand. Starbucks ensures a maximum return on process improvements through its Employer Branding team. With expertise in branding, HR, and onboarding, the team develops a branded strategy to provide a unique onboarding experience and ensures that the "Starbucks Experience" is a strong brand externally as well as internally. Employer Branding representatives attend staffing and development planning meetings to ensure maximum ROI for new program rollouts. The group monitors the employer brand and considers branding ramifications of all process improvements, with an eye toward not merely preventing damage to the brand, but finding new ways to maximize benefits.

Starbuck's Employer Branding team reflects the firm's recognition of the significant retention value of appearing as a "best-in-class" employer. Employer branding establishes a sense of prestige that motivates individuals not merely to work at the company, but to stay there. As you think about governance of your employer brand, consider the segmented audiences that exist. You will need to maintain an overall umbrella employer brand and also have the opportunity to engineer unique brands for important new hire segments (e.g., front line hires, campus hires, manager hires, executive hires, etc.).

Measuring Onboarding Success

Beyond implementing a proper structure of oversight and accountability, governing an onboarding program entails mobilizing measurement tools and processes to determine if program elements are performing as desired (effective against the objectives and at the expected pace). If your firm judges it critical to have a certain program element, and if all new hires participate in this part of the program, then you need to measure the program's performance by department, geography, and level. Otherwise, you have no way of knowing what needs improvement, nor can you determine the shortfall's underlying cause. Even if your company is realizing desired results, you need to confirm that the program element has produced the benefit as opposed to some other factor. It is a completely inappropriate use of resources to continue investing in something if it isn't creating the desired outcome.

In designing measurement systems, we advise measuring performance levels in ways that reflect the new hire's perspective and that of the hiring manager (and for senior managers and executives, that of their peers). Again, companies only hire people to help managers get a job done. If hiring managers do not see greater new hire effectiveness, then onboarding is not working. We might be offering new hires a more attractive employer-employee compact, but fundamentally, we're not doing onboarding to make people happy—we are doing it to improve enterprise performance. If we do not see improved enterprise performance, then there's no improvement and no reason to do onboarding.

Impressions matter. Individuals other than the new hire community will interpret your onboarding brand. If hiring managers don't believe onboarding delivers serious outcomes, they will see this as just another administrative task, and they will not participate or encourage new hires to participate. Onboarding program designers need hiring managers' buy-in, so they should create a metric system around their needs. Also, firms should continually improve and update the onboarding programs; that way, hiring managers will continue to see the program as productive and remain excited about participating and supporting it.

As management guru Peter Drucker promoted, "What gets measured, gets managed." As onboarding continues to grow as an HR management discipline, expectations to measure performance are increasing. Specific metrics tracked by onboarding leaders across organizations can and should vary depending on companies' unique onboarding program objectives. Many companies are relying on both qualitative (surveys, focus groups, etc.) measures and quantitative (cost-savings) measures and blends of the two (perceived time to productivity) to assess the value created through onboarding.

In addition to enterprise-level metrics, more advanced onboarding programs apply metrics to employees responsible for delivering program components. Programs committed to measuring success and ensuring accountability are also developing metrics for each group of onboarding team members. These data prove invaluable for identifying areas of strength and opportunities for improvement.

As stated earlier, one of the onboarding Program Manager's chief responsibilities is to monitor program performance and ensure that the enhanced program is meeting intended objectives across the organization. Often the program will require tweaking in a few areas post-implementation, and it will most certainly require periodic updates to meet changing organizational priorities. By the pilot stage, the organization should already have new hire and new hire manager surveys in place as well as initial baseline measures to monitor program effectiveness and satisfaction. Although these will prove important inputs, leading programs typically track a number of additional metrics and indicators—data that surveys cannot necessarily glean.

The metrics tracked by your organization will depend on your program's organizational objectives. If your program seeks to increase your ability to recruit top talent from undergraduate programs, one metric you may want to track is intern conversion yield; i.e., the percentage of interns who receive and accept an employment offer. If your initial diagnostic revealed that new hires maintain a low level of connectedness with other employees in the organization, you may want to track how designed networking activities in the enhanced program impact new hires' feeling of connectedness at several key points throughout the year.

Before implementation, you should consider the full range of data needed to measure program performance, and you should ensure that you possess the proper mechanisms to gather this information on an iterative basis. Although this list does not necessarily contain all of the metrics your organization should track, onboarding metrics tend to fall into the following key categories noted in Table 7.1, and each can be segmented by new hire business unit (BU), function, and level.

Numerous methods exist to view metrics so as to examine performance comparatively across the organization. Taking new hire Onboarding Satisfaction as an example, managers often find it most meaningful and actionable to focus on groups. These inter-organizational comparisons allow the Program Manager(s) to identify particular types of new hires who may be having a below average experience, as depicted in Figure 7.1.

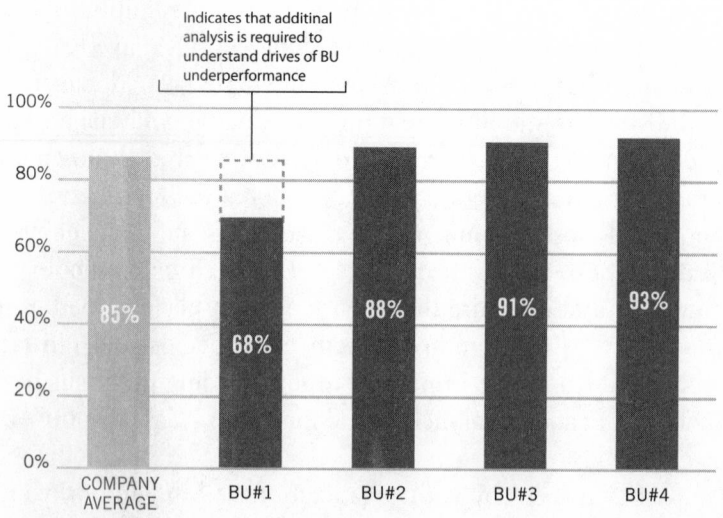

Figure 7.1 New Hire Satisfaction by Business Unit

Table 7.1 Sample Metrics Dashboard Approach

Metric	Data Source	Analytical Value	Application
1) New Hire Job Readiness	• New hire manager survey questions on new hire "job-readiness" following the initial training period	• Gauges the extent to which new hire orientation and training activities are effectively providing Managers with "job ready" new hires	• When coupled with qualitative manager feedback, enables onboarding program leadership to identify specific business units/functions in whch program element and training components can be improved to increase job readiness
2) New Hire Portal Utilization	• IT data on the number and frequency of new hires who are accessing the portal	• Measures the usefulness and value of the portal from the new hires' perspective	• Enables onboarding program leadership to consider further enhancements/features for high-traffic areas of the portal • Enables onboarding program leadership to identify low-traffic areas of the portal, where new hires may be neglecting to self-educate on key information
3) New Hire Satisfaction by Survey Period	• New hire survey data	• Provides visibility into specific periods of higher and lower new hire satisfaction throughout year one	• When coupled with qualitative new hire feedback, allows onboarding program leadership to consider potential phase-specific enhancements to increase new hire satisfaction
4) New Hire Satisfaction by Onboarding Region, Business Unit and Function	• New hire survey data	• Provides visibility into comparative new hire satisfaction across onboarding regions, business units, and functions	• Allows onboarding program leadership to identify and address drivers of lower performance in specific onboarding regions, business units, and functions
5) New Hire Satisfaction by Level	• New hire survey data	• Provides visibility into comparative new hire satisfaction across new hire levels	• Allows onboarding program leadership to determine whether additional new hire activity customization is needed to address the unique needs of distinct new hire audiences

(Continued)

Table 7.1 Sample Metrics Dashboard Approach *(Continued)*

Metric	Data Source	Analytical Value	Application
6) Overall New Hire Satisfaction	• New hire survey data	• Measures the extent to which new hires are satisfied with their year one onboarding experience	• Provides onboarding program leadership with overall gauge of program performance that can be benchmarked against the legacy onboarding program
7) Improvement in Intern Conversion Rate	• Data on percent of interns who accepted offers extended	• Measures the impact of the onboarding program on intern conversion yields	• Enables onboarding program leadership to determine whether the program is having a meaningful impact on intern conversion • When coupled with qualitative intern feedback, enables onboarding program leadership to consider intern-specific program enhancements
8) Overall New Hire Connectedness to the Organization	• New hire survey questions related to feeling connected, supported, and having a network within the organization	• Measures the extent to which new hires feel connected and supported	• When coupled with qualitative new hire feedback, enables onboarding program leadership to identify needed enhancements that will drive greater new hire support and networking opportunities
9) Improvement in New Hire Retention	• Annual new hire retention data	• Measures program effectiveness in improving new hire retention relative to the prior year	• Enables onboarding program leadership to evaluate retention program impact on new hire retention levels
10) Program Return on Investment (ROI)	• Annual new hire retention data and recruitment cost per hire data • Annual program delivery cost data	• Provide gauge of recruitment cost savings due to improved new hire retention	• Enables onboarding program leadership to evaluate retention and delivery cost savings of the new onboarding program relative to the legacy program
11) New Hire Time-to-Productivity	• New hire manager survey data	• Provides insight into the average number of days it takes new hires to reach the minimum expected output for their new job	• Allows the onboarding program leadership to assess the effectiveness of the program at providing new hires with the minimum skills needed to perform their new jobs

Before Implementation, the program manager should have a clear plan in place for gathering data on a quarterly or semi-annual basis, as well as a performance dashboard that rolls up the relevant data cuts for easy comparison and analysis. As an example of a dashboard, CheckFree, a provider of electronic services to the financial industry and today a part of Fiserve, has implemented an "onboarding excellence scorecard" measuring "efficiency, quality and attrition, process completion, and associate satisfaction during all phases of onboarding." The system divides onboarding elements into distinct tracks (e.g., recruitment production, transition and mentoring, retention), and each month process improvements are generated for each track to drive onboarding metrics.[2]

Figure 7.2 provides an example of a metrics dashboard that links and forms the relevant data cuts for the Program Manager.

In developing metrics and a performance dashboard, onboarding designers should assign responsibility to individual participants for each metric, thus tying key onboarding players, including managers, mentors, and trainers, to the broader onboarding program's success. New hire tasks and objectives should also be clearly defined and tracked as a metric. Onboarding objectives and timelines should be codified for all new hires, while managers should collaborate with each new hire on an individual basis to define specific onboarding objectives and chart the new hire's career development progress. Ownership and responsibilities should be clearly defined, and a new hire's performance against his or her onboarding objectives should help comprise a basis for early career performance evaluation. As we noted when discussing early career support, it is important for the new hire to demonstrate progress over the course of his or her first year as a key element of the new hire's development.

Companies should also hold hiring managers, human resources, and other key players accountable for the completion of objectives. Objective completion and execution rates should be treated as a metric for assessing the success of the entire onboarding program, as this ties program success to the individual onboarding objectives of each new hire, providing for personalization of experience and allowing new hires to attain desired onboarding goals in a proactive way. Onboarding responsibilities should be written into the job descriptions of the role participants and should comprise part of each participant's general formal performance assessments.

Program Management Metrics Dashboard

New Hire Satisfaction

New Hire Satisfaction by Survey Period

	Past 6-Months	Current 6-Months
Day 2	95%	97%
Day 30	92%	94%
Day 90	89%	91%
Day 365	86%	88%
AVERAGE	91%	93%

New Hire Satisfaction by Region

	Past 6-Months	Current 6-Months
Northeast	88%	86%
Great Lakes	90%	98%
Midwest	91%	95%
Mountain	93%	94%
Western	95%	93%
AVERAGE	91%	93%

New Hire Satisfaction by Function

	Past 6-Months	Current 6-Months
Sales & Mktg	89%	91%
HR	85%	87%
F&A	96%	98%
Corporate	88%	90%
Services	95%	97%
AVERAGE	91%	93%

New Hire Satisfaction by Level

	Past 6-Months	Current 6-Months
Intern	89%	97%
Campus	91%	90%
Experienced	93%	92%
Executive	90%	92%
AVERAGE	91%	93%

New Hire Connectedness

New Hire Connectedness by Survey Period

	Past 6-Months	Current 6-Months
Day 2	93%	95%
Day 30	90%	92%
Day 90	87%	89%
Day 365	84%	86%
AVERAGE	89%	91%

New Hire Connectedness by Region

	Past 6-Months	Current 6-Months
Northeast	86%	84%
Great Lakes	88%	96%
Midwest	89%	93%
Mountain	91%	92%
Western	93%	91%
AVERAGE	90%	93%

New Hire Connectedness by Function

	Past 6-Months	Current 6-Months
Mktg.	87%	89%
HR	83%	85%
F&A	94%	96%
Corporate	86%	88%
Services	93%	95%
AVERAGE	89%	91%

New Hire Connectedness by Level

	Past 6-Months	Current 6-Months
Intern	87%	95%
Campus	89%	88%
Experienced	91%	90%
Executive	88%	90%
AVERAGE	89%	91%

New Hire Job Readiness

New Hire Job Readiness by Function

	Past 6-Months	Current 6-Months
Sales & Mktg	91%	93%
HR	88%	90%
F&A	85%	87%
Corporate	82%	84%
Services	76%	84%
AVERAGE	83%	86%

New Hire Job Readiness by Region

	Past 6-Months	Current 6-Months
Northeast	84%	82%
Great Lakes	86%	94%
Midwest	87%	91%
Mountain	89%	90%
Western	77%	81%
AVERAGE	85%	89%

New Hire Time-to-Productivity

New Hire Time-to-Productivity (Campus)

	Past 6-Months	Current 6-Months
Sales & Mktg	4.2	3.5
HR	3.8	3.7
F&A	4.2	4.1
Corporate	1.9	3.7
Services		1.9
AVERAGE	3.5	3.4

New Hire Time-to-Productivity (Experienced)

	Past 6-Months	Current 6-Months
Sales & Mktg	4.5	3.2
HR	4.1	3.4
F&A	4.5	3.8
Corporate	4.5	3.4
Services	2.2	1.6
AVERAGE	3.8	3.1

New Hire Attrition

New Hire Attrition by Function

	Past 6-Months	Current 6-Months
Sales & Mktg	12%	11%
HR	6%	5%
F&A	5%	4%
Corporate	8%	7%
Services	13%	12%
AVERAGE	7%	7%

New Hire Attrition by Region

	Past 6-Months	Current 6-Months
Northeast	10%	9%
Great Lakes	4%	4%
Midwest	3%	2%
Mountain	6%	5%
Western	11%	10%
AVERAGE	6%	5%

New Hire Attrition by Level

	Past 6-Months	Current 6-Months
Intern	11%	10%
Campus	5%	4%
Experienced	4%	3%
Executive	7%	6%
AVERAGE	7%	6%

Intern Conversion Rate

Intern Conversion by Function

	Past 6-Months	Current 6-Months
Sales & Mktg	85%	88%
HR	63%	66%
F&A	76%	79%
Corporate	95%	98%
Services	76%	79%
AVERAGE	79%	82%

Row labels (left margin groupings):
- New Hire Survey Measures
- Hiring Manager Survey
- HR / Recruiting Data
- Metrics Derived from / Measures

Figure 7.2 Sample Metrics Dashboard Tracking Sheet

In a lesser way, an onboarding element should also be written into the job responsibilities of all senior employees who interface with new hires. To be systemic, onboarding needs to be part of the organization's fiber, and for that to happen, established employees need to bring the "onboarding ethic" and values to life. Unless formal responsibilities clearly address onboarding, this process risks devolving into a rote exercise with little meaning or impact.

Integrated process automation and tracking software can support the efficiency and effectiveness of metric evaluation. HR can input training completion and training rates, while web-based self-assessment tools for new hires help monitor productivity/capability assessments, objective tracking and completion rate, equipment receipt, and satisfaction surveys. Starbucks uses its onboarding software suite to track metrics like Time to Complete Training, Time to Capability, Time to Receiving Equipment and Tools, and Retention. The telecommunications company Sprint Nextel uses automated reporting software to track metrics such as the following:

First-year Retention,
Time to Training Completion,
Time to Productivity, and
Time to Receiving Needed Equipment and Tools.

Senior management monitors these metrics regularly and reviews them annually, setting objectives for the following year. As a result of the implementation and tracking of key performance metrics, Sprint Nextel has seen a stronger onboarding program that has driven quicker productivity and higher retention. Time to productivity has decreased by more than 30%, and retention rates have risen by more than 20%.

Incorporating onboarding into existing feedback mechanisms, such as departmental and annual corporate surveys, can provide important insights from untapped sources. Drawing opinions from a broader pool of participants provides greater perspective on the role of onboarding in the corporation and increases awareness. It also elicits feedback and ideas that may otherwise be overlooked.

HR might insert questions directly pertaining to new hires, such as, "Was your computer delivered before you arrived?" or "If you could change one thing about the onboarding experience during your first year, what would you change?" Tenured employees might be asked, "In your experience, how prepared have new hires been for their jobs?" and "What could be done to better prepare new hires for a job in your department?" To quantify performance, you should structure questions for scoring along a low to high answer set spectrum, you should render sample sizes large enough to cover each employee segment in a statistically significant way, and you should take measures on a regular basis, allowing for comparative results and trend analysis.

Using feedback to measure success

Best-in-class onboarding firms have developed innovative techniques for gaining regular and actionable feedback data. Starbucks promotes open, employee-initiated communication about onboarding; new hires can provide feedback, express concerns, or request new programs through Starbucks' Mission Review System, which guarantees employees a response. Similarly, any new hire can write the CEO and receive a guaranteed response. Starbucks invests in this form of feedback on the belief that employees who feel they can express their beliefs will prove less likely to become frustrated and quit. "We realized that as we grew we increasingly needed to hire different types of employees, mainly corporate employees," one Starbucks program manager told us, "and we found that these communication tools were some of the best ways to ensure that their needs were being met." Use of employee-initiated feedback helps uncover process improvements by tapping the ideas and feedback of all new hires. It also helps boost Starbucks' employer brand higher, since communication serves as the main driver behind such employer brand rankings.

Verizon Wireless measures individual feedback as the chief determinant of onboarding program success. The company queries new hires before onboarding about their expectations and then surveys them during and upon completion of the program. The firm also uses town hall meetings and web seminars to identify process gaps. Unlike most firms, Verizon views onboarding process development as an organic experience that should evolve so as not to remain stagnant. HR monitors feedback on a monthly, quarterly, and yearly basis, using permanent feedback mechanisms to improve onboarding experience continuously. Measurement of individual feedback in this way increases responsiveness, provides the means for change, and also provides a means for testing pilot programs. Of course, for this to work a firm needs permanent feedback mechanisms as well as tools sufficient to collect and interpret feedback.

Finally, General Mills ensures the responsiveness of its onboarding program by fielding frequent and regular surveys as a component of company-wide climate surveys. Corporate-wide results are gathered every two years and used to plan new program rollouts. Progress in addressing concerns raised during the corporate-wide survey are evaluated with more focused status updates in the off-year when a complete survey is not taken. Departmental climate surveys are conducted more often as required by departmental needs to gather more specific insights. Surveys include questions about onboarding effectiveness, career support, planning programs, and training needs. The firm also gauges onboarding through new hire process evaluations at the end of each onboarding phase. All of this yields a responsive and constantly improving program. It allows for new hire input, and it also ensures that the mechanisms for change remain in place, allowing for early adoption of innovative practices. Measuring program performance in this way requires a survey infrastructure, tools to conduct status reports, and tools to track changes in survey results.

Summing Up

Onboarding administration and governance might not be sexy, and by themselves these elements will not provide the big value boost that onboarding as a whole promises. Yet administration and governance underlie the success of any program and comprise a vital part of the new employer-employee compact that firms can and should offer through onboarding. To realize the Onboarding Margin, the onboarding experience and program must be systemic; this means firms must implement the administrative means to coordinate stakeholders and take actions across the firm, and they should also implement the mechanism for assuring compliance and continuous improvement in the program's workings.

As consultants, we have witnessed too many initiatives fly out of the gate only to falter for lack of sufficient administrative resources. Often a project team is assigned to develop a process, and then the team disbands for the next assignment without leaving resources in place to maintain the program with up-to-date information about strategy, organizational structure, resources available, etc. By contrast, best-in-class firms assign people with senior authority, experience, and knowledge to determine if everything is aligned, and they also put mechanisms in place to upgrade the program as necessary. Someone must do these things; otherwise, they do not get done, and programs suffer.

We have examined the four pillars covered by our model for successful onboarding as well as the underlying organizational requirements for bringing them to new hires. Yet deciding which program elements to include, how precisely to execute them, how to link them to one another, when to roll them out, and who to involve is by no means an easy task. Given limited resources, how should a firm weave onboarding elements together in a way best suited to the organization and its own strategic goals? The two chapters that follow outline a process for successfully conceiving, designing, and selling in a strategic onboarding system. We start in the next chapter with what we regard as that ever-important, but frequently neglected, initial phase, diagnostic investigation and analysis.

Part Three

THE ONBOARDING
DESIGN PROCESS

8

GETTING STARTED: CONDUCTING A PROGRAM DIAGNOSTIC

Most organizations have a distinct set of onboarding needs. Some battle high attrition or low time-to-productivity, whereas others need to ensure effective knowledge transfer between legacy and new employees. Still other organizations are spending way too much on onboarding (or more specifically, the front-end administrative piece of onboarding) and need to make processes more efficient to wring cost out of the system (see our Onboarding Objectives table in Chapter 1). Because every organization's circumstances and goals are different, it's important when designing an onboarding program to catalogue what a company currently does to orient employees and assess the best opportunities for improvement. Unfortunately, the vast majority of organizations do not devote enough time to taking stock of problems and opportunities. As a result, they either fix the least important problems, or they come up with improper solutions to the right problems. Their redesigned programs fail to meet expectations, and they wind up with poor returns on investment and decreased organizational commitment to address onboarding as a performance improvement opportunity.

To succeed with onboarding, organizations should begin the design process with a diagnostic assessment that identifies the main problems onboarding can address, the size of the opportunities, the root causes behind the problems, and the most practicable solutions given the organization's unique circumstances, operating conditions, and constraints. Performing this assessment not only helps an organization arrive at the best result; it also helps designers sell the program into key stakeholders in an organization. The exercise also allows you to objectively determine if onboarding renewal merits investment in the first place. (We have found some cases in which performance was strong and the business case for additional investment weak.) After exploring in more detail why the diagnostic phase is so important, this chapter offers a rigorous four-step process for measuring the opportunity, determining a program's highest value improvement areas, understanding the root causes and focus areas, and beginning to galvanize stakeholders behind wide-reaching, systemic change.

Don't Skip the Diagnostic!

When designing an onboarding program, many companies feel an impulse to skip the diagnostic process and put something in place that has worked elsewhere. They want that silver bullet answer—the all-powerful set of "best practices"—and see no need to spend valuable resources on a drawn-out analysis of their needs. Yet rushing to embrace a best practice without taking the time to determine its suitability to your company is a horrible idea. The ancient Greek phrase "Know Thyself" inscribed at the Temple of Apollo at Delphi guides us not merely to success in life, but in onboarding, too.

The rush toward best practices has been fed in recent years by onboarding's emergence as a topic in the human capital community and press. Articles advising HR specialists how to jump on the onboarding bandwagon often appear in online communities and blogs. A few onboarding conferences have emerged over the past few years. At these events, discussion threads and interest areas commonly center on questions such as, "What best practices do you employ?" and "How do you convince management that this is important?" We know from reviewing these articles and speaking with publishers of this material that way too little analysis goes into determining which practices become "best practices." We usually find that most of these supposed "best practices" are tactics that sound attractive but have not been assessed for their efficacy. These might better be considered "progressive practices." One recent *Wall Street Journal* article reduced the process of "acclimating newcomers" to a few easy tips, such as "make space," "find face time," "inform your staff," and "set goals."[1] Taking such an article at face value, it is easy to see how managers new to onboarding might accord the discipline a limited scope and regard starting a program as simply a process of collecting and deploying what others have done.

A best practice only helps if it matches your company's unique circumstances and objectives. Under different conditions, a best practice developed by another company could prove useless, and worse yet, a drain of valuable resources. Many want to copy what Apple does, but that technology firm possesses skills, competencies, culture, and objectives that most other firms do not. We have to obtain their skills and competencies and match their objectives if we hope to adopt a behavior or technique of theirs with any success. As part of a thorough diagnostic process, we need to evaluate whether the variables at play in other, benchmark organizations resemble ours closely enough to appropriate their best practices. If not, then we need to determine whether we can take an existing best practice and modify it to fit our actual culture, operating conditions, and skill sets.

A proper diagnostic analysis helps us to arrive at the right priorities. Most companies have limited budgets for onboarding, and better onboarding could potentially address a wide variety of business issues and objectives. We beg you, as practitioners in the field, to be intensely strategic in devising your program objectives. You can design a program that is well run, appreciated, and recognized but that does not deliver appreciably on any defined onboarding goals. A strong diagnostic phase allows companies to go beyond just offering new hires an "enhanced and cool experience" and devise a combination of program elements that creates maximum value.

Apple does not follow blindly what other firms are doing when it comes to onboarding. As we've seen, the firm has gained notoriety around the Web for greeting new hires with an exciting, high-concept welcome packet. In incorporating this tool into their onboarding, the firm did more than give new hires an amazing experience. It devised this tool to teach new hires about the brand, and specifically, about the kind of experience the firm wanted new hires to provide its customers. Apple's welcome packet supported a key business strategy: the pursuit of customer centricity. Another firm might pursue an entirely different strategic orientation, which would lend itself to different tools and a different message. If General Motors places strategic emphasis on building high-quality, durable products, its onboarding packet might be, say, constructed of a durable material. The company could then go on to express the importance of durability, and even link the ideas of building durable vehicles and durable careers to its objective of regaining industry leadership. Or maybe it wouldn't have even offered a welcome packet and instead chosen to invest its greater onboarding budget in a higher-impact area identified as critical in the diagnostic. In the vast majority of our first meetings with prospective clients, we encounter designers at the earliest stages of a renewal effort who come primed with action items spawned from reading about other companies' tactics.

Taking time to take stock when designing an onboarding program produces better onboarding because it allows firms to consider solutions keyed not merely to the opportunities and problems at hand, but to the *underlying causes of these problems*. As part of a strong diagnostic process, onboarding designers determine the root causes of problems by conducting an analysis that correlates experiences, existing tools, programs, and processes with particular outcomes. The designer might ask: Which experiences and processes of ours have resulted in this level of productivity for a certain category of hire? In another case, a firm might determine that a large majority of new hires possess a very limited network after 6 months of employment. The diagnostic process might reveal that this is because the company quickly deploys new hires on remote tasks and does not provide them with any real means to build relationships within the company. The designers of an onboarding program could then incorporate solutions that address new hires' lack of proper social exposure and relationship-building forums.

In many cases, companies can detect specific underlying causes behind a particular problem rather than the sort of generic causes implied by a knee-jerk focus on "best practices." As we saw in Chapter 4, one large client of ours was puzzled that their young hires were leaving after a year. The root cause was quite specific—many recruits at the company had to relocate to the corporate headquarters, and too many found it hard to fit in culturally and find peers with common interests in the new city. One solution was to coordinate with other big employers in the region to help new hires establish social relations and also to invest in affinity groups that might help new hire segments feel more connected.

Think, too, of the new hire at a tech company we described in Chapter 3, the one who had a really good idea yet committed a faux pas in sharing it publicly. The problem in this instance was clear, but not the underlying cause. The temptation was to pin the blame on this employee for "not getting" the culture, whereas in truth this new hire was a smart person who erred because her prior employer had established a culture of public debate and had not established propriety around ideas. In such a situation, a diagnostic process might uncover three things: first, a frustratingly high failure rate of experienced new hires (an outcome); second, an organizational need to bring in a large number of experienced managers given important growth initiatives (an organizational objective); and third, exit interviews and job performance reviews indicating that, above all else, many failures centered around not learning the culture soon and well enough (a root cause).

This outcome, objective, and root cause analysis would enable program designers to arrive at appropriate solutions. One solution might include a longer cultural orientation (using techniques that fit the business processes and rhythm of the company), a centralized oversight group that actively monitors new hire acclimation at key determined milestones, and quick education and instruction for hiring managers and peers on the problem's impact and nature. With this last piece in place, existing employees might prove less inclined to write off an experienced new hire as "disappointing" or "hopeless," and more energized to help the new hire adapt to the organization's unique mix of performance values. All three pieces of this prescription should be implemented in a gradual, systemic fashion—baked right into the organization's processes. Although we're not discussing yet the process of specifying these design attributes (we are still in the diagnostic phase), it is important to remain aware of them. The diagnostic phase includes assessment of current systems that contribute to current problems and can later be affected to make the program systemic and therefore effective.

Beyond helping organizations craft an onboarding program that applies real solutions to material issues, the diagnostic phase helps change agents sell in the program to diverse stakeholders. Performing an initial analysis of a firm's current challenges and opportunities provides HR specialists with data they need to drive change, including quantification of the size of the challenge and the size of the prize. The process of obtaining information during a diagnostic phase involves consultation with functional and business unit leaders, which in turn enables their enthusiasm down the line.

Performing a diagnostic analysis provides the onboarding change agent with a baseline against which to measure progress—essential for obtaining buy-in for ongoing investment. Development of a complete onboarding solution cannot happen at one pass; typically it requires a staged implementation. To obtain permission (and budget) to progress to the next stages, change agents need to show the great distance the firm has traveled thanks to onboarding relative to an initial position. And if onboarding is not bringing progress, simply knowing as much empowers you to revisit your onboarding design and figure out where it is going wrong. You need to activate a set of metrics during this diagnostic phase and establish a very clear baseline. As discussed in the last chapter, we recommend that these baseline measures capture numerous inputs (satisfaction levels, retention rates, etc.) for the appropriate segments of your new hire population (by level, business unit, race, gender, etc.) and from the perspective of both new hires and hiring managers.

To understand just how helpful information gleaned during the diagnostic can be in assuring both intelligent design and institutional acceptance, consider the following scenario involving a national health care firm with which we've worked. In discussions with the company, we discovered that attrition for the commercial side of their business—the sales and customer service departments—was slightly better than the industry average of 12%. Initial management commentary around discussion of attrition amounted to, "We do well here—just look at the industry average." Digging deeper, we started to discover some very interesting nuances. First, the firm experienced great regional disparity in attrition. Some regions experienced 4% attrition, whereas some were at 22%. That suggested that some regions were doing an exceptional job and some a poor job at onboarding new employees. When we examined the picture closer, we also discovered that the region that had the highest attrition was the same region of the country that was experiencing the *highest* rate of unemployment (at the time, 2008, the national economy was in recession). And here's the real kicker: The highest three attrition regions were also the ones experiencing the greatest customer turnover. Not only was attrition costing the company in labor expense, but it was also costing the company in customers and revenue.

Additional analysis revealed that customers' frustration with service personnel turnover was contributing to account churn. Moreover, effective practices in certain regions had cropped up, and these could be applied to high-attrition regions without much problem or cost (e.g., transferring the tools and techniques and a little education for the challenged managers). All of a sudden, what had started out as a "feel good" HR initiative got the attention of the CFO and the EVP of sales and became a critical mission to improve revenue and control costs during a prolonged recession.

Now imagine if the HR leader had not conducted this deeper analysis but simply brought forward some generic onboarding improvement practices to these same departments after attending an onboarding conference and learning about best practices. If this HR leader approached the head of sales and asked him or her to implement time consuming and possibly expensive new onboarding programs, the head of sales would likely have shown little interest; after all, he or she is way too busy contending with declining sales in a very challenging environment. Selling-in an onboarding program involves answering the question, "What's in it for me (the *"wiff'em"*). By performing a thorough diagnostic up front, onboarding designers can identify areas of great opportunity and develop the hard-edged business case that serious organizations require to drive wide-ranging change. And if you cannot build a real case for onboarding after a diagnostic process, then you should not be doing it.

Conducting a System Diagnostic

In our work with leading companies, we've developed a four-step process for conducting a diagnostic evaluation of a firm's onboarding efforts. The four steps are:

1. Internal discovery
2. External benchmarking
3. Opportunity identification
4. Obtaining organizational validation and buy-in

In running through these steps, you need to take a long-term view, starting at the hour of the candidates' acceptance of your job offer and running through the greater of the new hires' first year employment or a complete business cycle for your business. You also need to assess all four pillars of the onboarding framework, as well as the administrative and governance resources available to support onboarding. You need to evaluate not only the designed and formal program elements of onboarding, but also the entire range of experiences that the new hire and new hire managers have. Finally, we recommend that you benchmark against best-in-class and key competitors (either industry competitors and/or regional employers that compete for your labor talent, regardless of industry), which helps in evaluating your performance relative to critical benchmarks.

We now take a closer look at each of the four steps in turn. Although we'll present the diagnostic phase here as a neat linear process, in practice it can unfold in a far more fluid and uneven fashion. The diagnostic can also be performed in a way that does not result in a bogged down *"analysis—paralysis"* exercise. Internal discovery will sometimes yield intuitive knowledge of the root causes before the formal analysis of the data. More generally, diagnosis has an iterative or circular character, unfolding gradually and on an ongoing basis. What follows is best regarded as a model of a proper diagnostic process rather than as an iron-clad depiction of what the diagnostic phase will look like for your organization.

Internal discovery

As part of internal discovery, members of an onboarding redesign team should do two things: Assess the current state of the program and identify the organization's actual greatest needs so as to prioritize key onboarding opportunities.

Understanding the current system activities, tools, and resources that exist for new hires in their first year helps us diagnose the root causes of program underperformance as well as dissatisfaction among new hires and managers. As the diagnostic process unfolds, it also allows you to compare what you have with best-in-class and competitor programs, and later on, to measure your own progress against the baseline. Some organizations have pre-existing process flows, checklists, and new hire guidebooks that outline the program's current state. Others need to go through the process of mapping out the current state to develop an understanding of all the touch-points and activities that exist as new hires go from offer acceptance to orientation and then into their business unit or function. Put differently, these firms need to understand all the *critical* "firsts" that do so much to shape new hires' impressions of their new employment.

Representative Key "Firsts"

- First administrative problem
- First on-the-job mistake when no one notices
- First on-the-job mistake when peers notice
- First on-the-job mistake when the boss notices
- First personality conflict with a member of the team
- First time having a conflict with a supervisor
- First time the new hire calls in sick
- First time an outsider asks the new hire who he or she works for (Remember how important esteem is according to Maslow?)
- First personal victory
- First team victory
- First time new hire gets recognition or fails to get recognition
- First time the new hire faces a situation where he or she didn't know the answer
- First conflict between the new hire's two separate reporting lines (e.g., functional and business unit)
- First company-sponsored social event
- First time closing on a sale
- First uncomfortable encounter
- First time the new hire is presented with gossip about his supervisor
- First time the new hire commits an ethical violation
- First time the new hire witnesses an ethical lapse
- The first time the new hire presents the company's value proposition to a customer
- The first time the new hire speaks at a meeting
- The first time the new hire *leads* a meeting
- The first stretch assignment for the new hire
- First time witness to a company layoff
- First time doing work unsupervised
- First time having to sell an idea to colleagues
- And so on

Developing a process flow or activity diagram is often the best means of taking stock of the system's current state and the business processes central to a new hire's experience. In the activity diagram, we can outline the key process owners that support new hires at each step. A diagram like this helps the design team define roles, responsibilities, and needed process-level changes once the enhanced program is designed.

As you assess a program's current state, it is helpful to gather information about how much the company currently spends to onboard on an annualized basis. This helps you identify opportunities for cost savings, places where your company is currently under-investing, and the appropriate ways to prioritize so as to achieve an optimum return on investment.

Once you know what your program's current state entails, you need to assess how well your current program activities, tools, and resources meet

---

Common Diagnostic Data Elements

- Census of current employee base
- Census of recent new hire activity (e.g., three-year history)
- Attrition data
- Promotion performance
- Projections of new hire needs (numbers and special skills or other organizational development needs, such as ramp up requirements to support growth areas)
- New hire performance reports
- New hire ands new hire manager satisfaction reports
- Job offer acceptance rates
- Results from any "engagement level" studies that may exist
- Exit interviews
- Results from any recent hire focus groups or surveys
- Other data requirements to be determined at outset of project
- Fresh surveys, focus groups, new hire manager interviews
- Online community chatter (e.g., LinkedIn, Facebook groups, R&D communities)

the needs of new hires, managers, and the organization as a whole. Here the point is not merely to look for program elements that are failing to deliver, but also program elements that are working well. Identifying internal pockets of "best practices" can prove extremely helpful in many situations, since we can often find ways to leverage these best practices for use within the firm as a whole. Just as with external benchmarking, however, you should evaluate each internal best practice to make sure that it fits the needs and circumstances of diverse corners of the business. Here are some common sources of data to consider when performing an internal analysis.

Onboarding designers need to conduct internal interviews with key corporate, business unit, and functional executives. It's important to interview these individuals to understand better the primary strategic initiatives and what they most require out of the new crop of talent. By interviewing these leaders, you will not only learn about key business and human capital priorities that should be a focal point for your design, but you will also have the chance to win over these leaders to support the effort with the resources necessary to build a program that can deliver against these needs.

Of course, you hire new people in the first place because managers need to accomplish certain goals and they believe their current resources are not sufficient. These hiring managers are the most important stakeholders, and you need to determine how they think new hires are falling short. These interviews need to be exploratory. They need to not only cover satisfaction levels and ideas for improving the onboarding system but they should also produce:

- An outline of hiring managers' own business objectives. It's important to understand these not simply as line items; rather you need to know the *nature* of the challenges that hiring managers tackle. You also need to explore how managers believe current entrants are falling short and how they could be better equipped.
- An overview of the administrative and business processes with which the new hires and their managers have contact. This will help you understand the challenges of being successful as a new hire as well as the systemic elements of business operations you need to leverage in the redesign effort.

In addition to conducting interviews, we also recommend conducting surveys with hiring managers and recent new hires so that you can quantify your findings. Later on, you can then use these numbers as a baseline against which to measure the impact of your enhanced onboarding program.

Ultimately, organizational needs tell us what specific goals our enhanced program must support. One company we worked with—an electric utility—was expecting 40% of its current workforce to retire within 10 years. This was a very scary scenario considering how much technical know-how this retiring base represented. The company wanted to ensure that company culture, performance values, know-how, and skills survived the transition from legacy to new employees. To service this need, the enhanced onboarding program incorporated two key components: (1) an increased number of opportunities for new hires to build relationships with experienced employees; and (2) a knowledge transfer program enabling these company veterans to impart their accumulated know-how on a formal basis throughout the entirety of the first year. Another company forecasted a 200% increase in employees over the next five years in a rapidly expanding business unit. Here the program redesign focused on educating the new hires on the underlying strategy associated with the growth, the demands that the growth was putting on the business, and the skills necessary to meet those growth demands. All of this was achieved by segmenting new hires into the key areas of intended functional and business growth.

As far as new-hire needs go, many organizations pursuing major program redesign efforts lack sufficient onboarding surveys in place to help guide the redesign effort. Ideally, you would query new hires and hiring managers at different points in their tenure with the company, most likely the 30-, 60-, 180-, 270-, and 365-day marks. When setting survey points, consider time periods that recognize completed business cycles and natural anniversary milestones. You can also brand surveys to associate them with formal phases designated for your onboarding program. Surveys need to include demographic questions (e.g., queries about gender, race, previous work experience, new hire level, function, business unit, etc.) or they otherwise need to correlate with respondent data from centralized human capital information systems. This information will allow you to segment out responses into distinct groups of new hires, providing necessary instruction on how to customize your solution.

Think carefully about which demographic components to include, as this helps determine the quality of your insight and associated program customization. In general, a sampling approach will suffice to get the job done. However, you should consider the brand value of engaging all new hires in the survey activity. If the surveys are designed to speak from the perspective of the new hire and hiring managers, you get an additional benefit—a chance to convey to new hires that your firm cares about their success and takes seriously its role in assuring it. This is a message every new hire and hiring manager deserves to receive.

In evaluating an existing program's performance, the onboarding design team should also consider how far the program compares with state-of-the-art program characteristics described in Chapter 2. Does the existing program offer tools, experiences, and support in all four pillars over the first year? Are these tools customized to the needs of key new hire groups? Are the key stakeholders in the program participating enthusiastically? On an even greater level of detail, do program elements incorporate the Best Principles described in Chapters 3 through 6?

External benchmarking

Once your organization has assessed its onboarding program's current state, the next step is to catalogue the program elements and techniques deployed by leading onboarding programs and that of your competition. Again, members of your onboarding redesign team should resist the urge to simply expropriate "best practices" without further analysis. When looking at a specific best practice, your team needs to try to understand what is *behind* the practice—the root causes that the company was trying to address as well as how the best practice related to the firm's unique strategic objectives. Finally, your onboarding design team needs to consider best practices and comparative performance metrics through the lens of your own firm to determine if they fit strategic needs and organizational constraints.

Depending upon program objectives, you might also want to evaluate onboarding programs at your chief labor competitors in the recruiting marketplace, typically leading employers in your region(s) or leading employers in your company's key functions (e.g., the leading companies who recruit product marketing talent if you are a consumer product company). Properly executed, onboarding can distinguish a firm in the eyes of new hires and provide competitive advantage in recruiting this top talent. Speaking with transfer employees from other peer organizations is a great place to start. Some companies also choose to conduct highly detailed peer benchmarking analyses to develop a clear differentiation strategy.

Suppose you represent Caterpillar and you are seeking engineering talent that can enable you to design a whole new tractor that is less costly or that uses hybrid technology. In deciding which companies to benchmark against for recruitment purposes, you might consider Toyota or other companies looking to bring hybrid technologies, as well as other leading engineering organizations like Lockheed Martin, GE, Intel, or Google. Similarly, if you're trying to bring in top MBAs, you might want to look at how consulting firms, leading marketing companies, and top investment banks are approaching onboarding, since these are your prime competitors for talent. If you are in an industry in which your corporation hires regional talent, then you need to look at who else is competing for that same talent, including smaller, regional firms that at first glance would seem to be in a different league than your own.

Opportunity identification

With a good sense of best practices and competitor practices in hand, we now need to analyze the data so as to identify the most important opportunities and come up with recommendations. This part of the process has several steps. First, you should conduct a quantitative analysis of the gap, if any, between your current performance and both your desired performance and external benchmarks. Such analysis should be done for specific geographies, business units, and functions; that way, you will understand the diverging needs and performance levels of different parts of the organization. You will also be able to identify areas across the organization that require greater investment and prioritization. You might even wind up deciding to focus on only one part or cross-section of the organization (for instance, one business function) so as to realize the most business impact. Once you have determined where the gaps are and their size, you should determine the root causes behind these gaps. This in turn

Table 8.1 Sample Framework for Identifying Program Objectives

Example Organizational Goals	Example Program Shortcomings	Example Onboarding Redesign Objectives
Strengthen Senior Leadership pipeline	• New management-level hires lack effective career development support or mentoring relationships with company leadership • No formal mechanism exists for identifying and nurturing "top performers" early in their careers • Career path and promotion opportunities are not clearly outlined for new management-level hires	• Develop tools and resources to ensure management-level hires understand their career prospects with the organization and have the necessary Senior Leadership support to achieve their development goals
Transfer knowledge and company culture from retiring "Baby Boomers" to future generation of employees	• Campus hires indicate that they have limited opportunity to form relationships with and learn from with more experienced employees	• Provide forums and structured networking activities that enable new hires to develop relationships with more tenured company employees
Become more competitive in regional recruiting marketplace	• New hires indicate that the organization has only a modest employment brand in the recruitment marketplace • Onboarding program is not a clear differentiator for prospective hires	• Develop a brand for the enhanced Onboarding program that can be promoted as a key employment differentiator in the recruitment marketplace
Increase new hire time-to-productivity	• New hires at all levels believe the organization could do a better job of communicating "unwritten rules" and job expectations	• Provide more robust early career support and job skills training to better prepare all new hires to meet organization expectations

leads us to determine where the opportunities lie for improving the onboarding program. Table 8.1 provides a sample framework for identifying program objectives.

Some of the opportunities you choose to address might have originated from the internal and external best practices uncovered during the prior research phases. Others will have emerged during the course of internal discussions that are not in practice elsewhere. You will need to decide

decide which of these the company might plausibly (and profitably) apply throughout the organization. It is important to determine investment priorities, balancing the potential impact with the cost or degree of difficulty in implementation. You should also consider which opportunities might lend themselves to early wins, since these can help to build or gain momentum and thus make buy-in for later phases more likely.

In evaluating possible opportunities, team members should take care to identify operating and business model constraints that limit an onboarding program's shape or scope. Constraints are helpful since they focus the design process; it is just as important to know what *cannot* be changed in implementing a new program as it is to know what can or should change. A new onboarding program needs to challenge some organizational assumptions, but clearly some things will remain untouchable.

One financial services firm we have worked with realized it had two constraints as it went about re-defining its onboarding program: It knew that company field representatives would remain in the field; and it knew that growth opportunities for employees would remain limited given the fairly flat organization required by the firm's business model. Recognizing that the firm had few sales management positions, and that most new hires therefore faced limited long-term career prospects of upward mobility and increasing responsibility with the firm, this company could focus on offering most new hires career training and networking as a part of onboarding. Meeting other sales personnel in the company who have had long, prosperous careers without moving into "management," and gaining access to the communities they would serve, new hires could understand and feel better about their careers while simultaneously beginning to build relationships that could turn into future sales prospects.

Organizational validation and buy-in

Even as your redesign team tries to diagnose problems and come up with possible onboarding solutions, you should begin the work of selling the rest of the organization on onboarding. The earlier you can get leadership, stakeholders, and broader system participants to buy in, the more support you will obtain for implementing the kind of broad change that a strategic onboarding program requires. We strongly recommend engaging key stakeholders from the start of your process. Enable them to evaluate the current state of onboarding, educate them on the potential and prospect of the Onboarding Margin and the typical objectives of onboarding programs, allow them to participate in hypothesis generation, and encourage them to set forth possible improvement opportunities. That way, they will enjoy more ownership over solutions and be able to articulate in a compelling way the key changes that will emerge from onboarding redesign. Focus especially on convincing stakeholders who feel threatened by an onboarding redesign, since these individuals are those most likely to resist meaningful change.

Taking Shortcuts ... and Starting Off Right

The preceding model represents what we regard as the best way to pursue a rigorous diagnostic process. If you lack the resources to pursue a process as involved as this, we would recommend the following shortcut (although recognize that it is a compromise). Find an appropriate group of representative stakeholders, educate them on onboarding, and instruct them to develop a set of hypotheses about the opportunities, problems, and root causes surrounding onboarding. Validate these hypotheses by testing on a spot basis. Even better, you can supplement these efforts by cherry-picking pieces of the above diagnostic approach that fit your resource levels, time frame, and circumstances.

This is a less rigorous approach, but it can certainly produce an excellent result. In any case, it is far better than skipping the diagnostic. If your initial analysis yields results that inspire a high level of confidence, then you are all set. If you remain unsure as to the proper course, then you should pursue the deeper analysis we have outlined.

We recommend that all firms perform this simpler, initial exercise before proceeding to the main diagnostic process, as it will help target the in-depth analysis. If you are tempted to forego the longer process even though your firm has allocated adequate resources for a diagnostic phase, you should bear in mind that the small group of stakeholders you have initially assembled might well get it wrong. In marketing, companies learn a lot from proper market research, even though they feel from the outset that they possess an intuitive grasp of consumers. Top tier marketing companies know that relying less on intuition and more on customer insights makes all the difference in driving results that lead to industry leadership. The same holds true here. If you can afford the research, you're better off avoiding the risk that you've missed something big or wasted money on the basis of a false assumption.

Summing Up

Before your firm can hope to unveil a state-of-the-art onboarding program, it must take care to gain organizational self-awareness. Do not just grasp at the onboarding "best practices" you read about online or in trade journals. Kick off your onboarding redesign process with a rigorous diagnostic phase that catalogues the onboarding measures currently in place, compares them with those at competitor and best-in-class firms, and identifies realistic opportunities that get at the root causes of problems. Pursued with integrity, the diagnostic phase can help focus a program around a few key objectives among the many that onboarding can viably help you meet. A diagnostic phase can also serve as a fulcrum for beginning to generate buy in and support from stakeholders across the organization.

Once your redesign group has settled on a few key opportunities to pursue with onboarding, you are likely to feel a sense of excitement and momentum around the program you plan to develop. It is tempting to jump right in and start putting programs in place. That would be a mistake. Given how all-encompassing a truly systemic program is, it is vital that you take the time to develop a highly detailed blueprint of what your new onboarding program will look like as it is rolled out over multiple phases. You cannot just put tactics in place haphazardly; you need to create a plan, just like an architect does when constructing a skyscraper. The next and final chapter shows you how to create a compelling onboarding blueprint and then begin the process of transforming your organization.

9

DRIVING
IMPLEMENTATION—FROM
BLUEPRINT TO IMPACT

In 2008, we helped strategy and technology consulting firm Booz Allen Hamilton as it set out to renew its onboarding system. This rapidly growing firm of 22,000 employees works with clients, including government agencies, corporations, institutions, and not-for-profit organizations to "deliver results that endure." Booz Allen considers its employees its most valuable asset; therefore, attracting, developing, and retaining talented people is essential to the firm's mission.

Diagnostic analysis of Booz Allen's redesign showed that though many employees were enjoying their work, they felt less emotional connectedness (what we call "valued connectedness") with the company than management would have preferred. The firm's rapid growth, accompanied by a dispersed workforce, created obstacles and inconsistencies in onboarding processes and programs. Recent and unprecedented growth also challenged the scalability of Booz Allen's existing onboarding processes, technology, and systems. To support the firm's operations while balancing significant growth demands, the onboarding redesign team realized it could cut its recruitment demands (i.e., reduce the number of new hires it would need) and costs if onboarding protocols helped employees more effectively and rapidly understand their roles, become productive, and recognize their value. The team also concluded that the new processes should incorporate a concept for better connecting the aforementioned off-site staff as well as helping develop a bond with Booz Allen itself that would ultimately add value and reduce attrition.

A number of ideas circulated as to how the firm might improve the onboarding experience for new hire intake. Proposals included fostering more consistent experiences among new hires, doing more to help experienced hires understand the culture, and building early wins with structured networking opportunities. Booz Allen dedicated considerable resources to the diagnostic phase of its redesign, working to assemble a representative team that cut across functions, business units, and geographies. This core team focused on formulating hypotheses and gathering internal data that was then analyzed to help prioritize the opportunities. Over time, a collective vision of a new onboarding program that would better serve the firm took shape. Executive Vice President and Chief Personnel Officer at Booz Allen, Horacio Rozanski, spoke of priorities and vision for the new program: "Developing an onboarding program that captured and conveyed the culture of Booz Allen was paramount. It is critical to us that our new hires understand and internalize the firm's core values." The redesign team eventually concluded that cosmetic changes to specific onboarding program elements were unnecessary, and that the more significant opportunity involved enhancement of Booz Allen's basic relationship with new employees.

Booz Allen has long distinguished its employer-employee compact by providing hires an opportunity to work on challenging, high-impact/important projects—a distinction reflected in the firm's strong employment brand. In fact, the company had won numerous awards for its employment value proposition.[1] Still, the team realized that if they could expand this compact and offer hires even greater support, then hires could realize an even greater sense of the opportunities available as part of a career at Booz Allen. Their loyalty to the firm would increase and attrition would decrease. Booz Allen's new onboarding program would be designed to not only show new hires all the resources available to support their long-term development; it would also provide significant value during the first year by offering experiences that engaged them on these issues. Additional value would come via associations and a sense of community that the onboarding program would nurture among the firm's 22,000 highly talented employees, who represent an array of skill sets and expertise. If onboarding could foster meaningful connections between new hires and Booz Allen colleagues, the hope was that new hires would be happier working at the firm, and therefore perform better, provide more value to clients, and ultimately drive business growth.

It's one thing to come up with clear program objectives, but quite another to implement change. The latter requires a solid project management effort that addresses the business case created during the diagnostic phase, translates it into a coherent blueprint, and executes on this blueprint. As we have discussed throughout this book, onboarding can only attain the Onboarding Margin if it's fully systemic rather than a series of standalone tools and programs. The complexity of changing and integrating business processes while still maintaining business operations requires thoughtful blueprinting and an ongoing effort to gain organizational buy-in around the blueprint. Just as an architect tasked with redesigning an entire building drafts formal plans to help organize all the changes that renovation will require—while simultaneously gaining stakeholder and building owners' support for those changes—so too must change agents within an organization execute a formal and detailed plan. This is critical to identifying the key issues and achieving success. This chapter offers some general advice for bringing onboarding redesign efforts to fruition, using Booz Allen and its award-winning onboarding redesign as an illustrative example.

Creating a Blueprint

In Booz Allen's case, development of a blueprint took place after a critical second phase of the diagnostic process: Stakeholder Analysis. Upon gaining consensus around program opportunities and objectives, the team began work documenting the requirements of each stakeholder group mapped as essential for Booz Allen to more successfully onboard new hires. Given the organization's size and complexity—the firm has more than 45 regional offices across the United States that serve three markets and span more than 15 different business areas—the list of requirements reached into the hundreds. It quickly became apparent that most of these line items didn't actually drive new hire excitement or create new strategic value for the business. Rather, many of them were administrative items that merely needed to be addressed—important tasks, but not the essence of what makes onboarding desirable for a business.

Booz Allen's cross-functional working team (with participants from each of the business units and from different levels within the enterprise) was divided into six separate teams, each responsible for drafting its own version of what an improved onboarding experience would look like. As a result of this approach, the organization minimized a rush to "group think" around possible answers, thus expanding the number of fresh ideas and approaches. Each team represented deep company expertise as well as unique experiences relevant for tackling the opportunity. Although the teams performed some external benchmarking, they put far more energy into understanding Booz Allen's operating conditions, culture, resources, and business plan than to mimicking what other firms had done with similar programs.

The teams presented their ideas to each other and created a process for selecting the best ideas and designing a cohesive story line for the new hire. A plan was created—the program blueprint. In general, program blueprints provide the overarching design architecture documentation for an onboarding program, enabling all design and stakeholder participants to coordinate along a single, comprehensive design. Possessing a single design ensures that all elements support the intended objectives. In our experience, the most successful system redesign efforts start with a clear plan and vision of what the future state will look like. They also articulate a timeline and demonstrate how the organization will meet its goals.

The blueprint defined onboarding for the new hire and the hiring manager and determined the timeline for onboarding. It included a detailed outline of all new hire activities, tools, technologies, and resources the firm would offer as part of onboarding. It also explored how onboarding would integrate, in a systemic fashion, with other human capital programs and the firm's overall business processes. An outline of resources required was included, as was a detailed budget and straw man overview of roles and responsibilities. Aimee George-Leary, Director of Learning & Development at Booz Allen, spearheaded the blueprinting activity. "A comprehensive blueprint enabled the team to gain a shared vision of the future state of onboarding while also acting as a tool to allow our stakeholders visibility in the program goals and objectives." The blueprint described the findings from the diagnostic and connected each of the pieces of the new onboarding program to specific objectives and evaluation metrics. This blueprint was then socialized outside of the working team to secure early buy-in and feedback. Team members were enthusiastic about presenting the overall work product, and leadership embraced their approach as an important investment that would benefit the firm, which was now going to address longstanding challenges and create an even more effective engine to drive future growth and attain business objectives.

When designing blueprints, it's critical to approach the exercise as if you were designing a set of architectural drawings for a building renovation. The initial pages paint the picture at a high level, while subsequent pages cover specific areas in greater detail. With these architectural plans in hand, key stakeholders can efficiently review and refine the structure while team members building the program can ensure that the building's integrity is maintained even as reconstruction takes place.

Since redesign efforts often require an iterative process of consensus building, it's important for the blueprint to capture the high-level consensus around objectives that the diagnostic phase produced. As a designer, you can do this by including the matrix described in the last chapter that maps organizational goals against current program shortcomings. You can also create a document that describes the conditions and constraints, the program opportunities, and target outcomes.

Booz Allen used this document to illustrate the core objectives that surfaced during the diagnostic:

- A consistent program experience
- Increased affiliation with Booz Allen
- Increased employee engagement
- Reduced time to productivity
- Reduced attrition

Realizing that new hires were having different onboarding experiences, the redesign team decided that Booz Allen should implement more consistency across onboarding efforts. The team also learned that participation in existing onboarding program elements was lacking in certain areas of the firm, so the onboarding program blueprint needed to address the underlying deficiencies, include measures to help hiring managers recognize the value of onboarding, and outline a plan for producing high-quality content that manifestly added value. Finally, the program needed to improve productivity by giving hiring managers the resources and guidance they needed to have more meaningful conversations with new hires during the first year, covering issues and topics that the diagnostic work revealed as being important.

In addition to objectives, the blueprint should also reflect agreement about the new program's scope. Given the nature and extent of an organization's diagnostic findings and available resources, it may not be possible to tackle a full Year One program redesign for new hires across all areas and levels of the business. Being overly ambitious in a redesign effort can dilute the impact of proposed enhancements or cause them to fail outright in meeting overall program objectives. Companies can also benefit from identifying what they consider the gold standard and make incremental improvements against achieving something similar; both the finished product and interim steps and gains along the way should appear in the blueprint. Numerous ways to segment redesign efforts exist; Booz Allen's work on this front was largely focused on prioritization based on impact as determined by the detailed diagnostic process. Organizations can choose to focus on certain categories of new hires (e.g., campus hires, field employees, corporate, etc.), certain new hire levels or functions, certain business units, certain geographies, or certain phases of the Year One program.

Once teams have a strong understanding of program objectives and scope, they can go on to create the high-level program blueprint. Booz Allen's team started with the four-phase framework outlined in Chapter 2 and defined objectives for each stage, incorporating the principles outlined in Chapters 3 through 6. Booz Allen's high level blueprint (Figure 9.1) broke down early orientation into two phases (firm-wide versus local). Note the clear distinction between the firm's existing program and the new onboarding program.

Program designers should take care to modify and update timing and objectives to fit an organization's core business cycles and other specific operational needs. Next steps can then focus on cataloguing the full range of design options that will meet objectives in each phase. Booz Allen's experience also illustrated the importance of early efforts around fostering creativity and putting forth as many ideas as possible; teams can prioritize and vet later. Inspiration can come from best-in-class and peer company programs, suggestions from recent new hires, pure creativity on the part of design teams, or consultation with outside advisors.

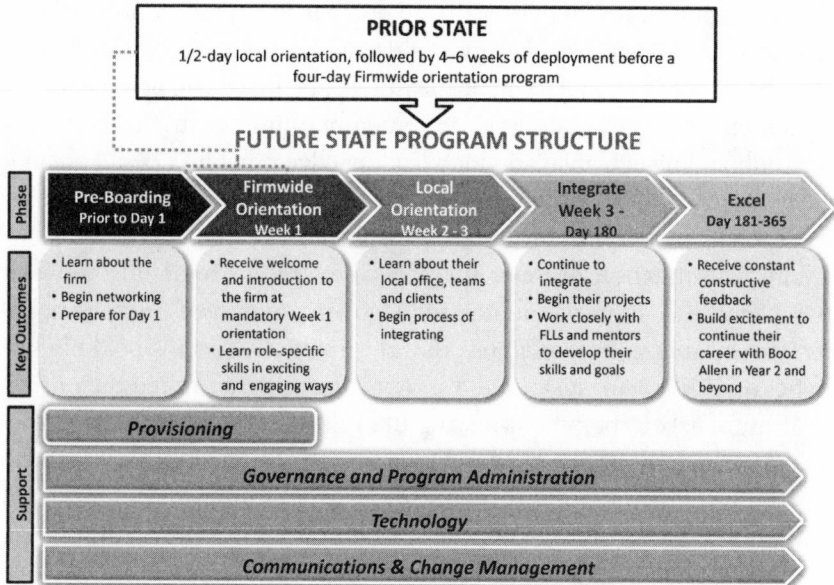

Figure 9.1 Future State Program Structure

Next steps at this point in the process include adopting *design thinking* methodologies (e.g., empathetic design, observational research, etc.). To help with brainstorming or organization, teams can perform a *Retained—Added—Done differently—Eliminated* (RADE) exercise, which includes brainstorming phase-specific program elements that should be *Retained* in existing form from the current program; *Added* to the current program, as an entirely new item; *Done differently* than it's done today, but retained; and *Eliminated* from the existing program. These decisions should of course be made with the framework determined as a result of the diagnostic.

For each program element, teams can also conduct an Impact Exercise that determines each business process that touches it. This can allow you to determine where and how to integrate the program into the fiber of the enterprise's core functions and operations, thus increasing the program's systemic nature. As designers, the ultimate goal here is to create a program that appears distinct from the rest of the firm and its processes *only* when the blueprint or navigational aide is pulled out and it is possible to see how the program fits in with the larger business system.

After creating a working list of design options, teams can prioritize them, making sure that each activity, tool, and resource generated links to a specific phase objective; that it can be measured; and that it can be successfully implemented. It's also important to remember: Just because a "best practice" onboarding activity works for a leading-edge program doesn't mean it will conform well to another company's culture or business system or satisfy *their* specific highest priority onboarding objectives.

The prioritization exercise involves allowing for trade-offs between impact and ease of implementation. Many teams choose program activities, tools, and resources whose initial implementation is possible but that cannot likely be sustained over time. Booz Allen relied on a prioritization matrix to begin comparing the relative feasibility and value of particular design choices. Many program redesigns look to combine "low-hanging fruit" and more ambitious, high-difficulty/high-reward elements. Other efforts focus on designing and implementing quick wins and then move on to the more challenging program elements once they've realized cost savings or gathered more organizational support. Teams can benefit from determining which specific criteria to use as the basis for prioritization. As Vince Gonzalez, Senior Employee Development Manager at Booz Allen, notes, "Organizing our program design elements, and collaborating on determining priority across our variables, allowed us to balance quick wins, ease of implementation, and high impact to create answers we not only felt good about but also intuitively knew would have positive and lasting impact on the process we were trying to improve." Upon conclusion of the exercise, what results is a series of "best bets" using the prioritization matrix, which can then be selected for the program blueprint.

In determining priorities, it's also often helpful to incorporate input from a champion member of the organization's broader leadership. Senior executives have preferences when it comes to onboarding elements, and including them when possible facilitates organizational support for the entire effort. Political considerations aren't the optimal criteria for making prioritization decisions, but in the real world support from a top leader can make the difference between the overall program's success and failure. As a caveat, program designers should ensure that the team doesn't compromise and pivot priorities around an element that the diagnostic shows will have a limited impact. This can mean a team might not achieve the initial results that will allow for implementation of more important and costly program elements over time.

Booz Allen's design team emerged from the prioritization process with a decision to implement the program in four distinct phases, introducing the most critical program elements first and then building on these items in the following three phases. The team divided introduction of the four pillars across the four phases, designating in each phase whether there would be "light," "medium," or "heavy" concentration (from a design and deployment perspective) on that content area in a given phase. Under this model, each deployment would build on the progress of the prior one. Assignment of program elements to an earlier or later phase reflected a number of considerations, including whether the content area was a steering committee mandate, where it resided on the prioritization matrix, and whether other elements not yet considered required introduction of this particular element first. Light elements were easily deployed foundational elements that would meaningfully enhance the current program; medium elements were incremental elements that added functionality to the program; whereas heavy elements were final-phase elements that delivered a gold-standard onboarding experience and offered the promise of delivering the Onboarding Margin.

In creating a blueprint, teams should proceed to outline specific new hire activities, tools, and resources that will support each program phase. As further support for the program design, effective blueprint documents for any organization development system should include:

- New program objectives
- A clear link between the design and current program deficiencies
- Enhanced program phase elements
- Expected outcomes
- An integrated work/build plan (by wave and implementation timeline)
- A governance and operations model (overview and guiding principles)
- Systems and technology requirements

- A change management and communications plan
- A summary of high-impact changes and framework with stakeholder messaging
- A detailed business case for change, including an ROI calculation
- A governance/operations model
- An outline of roles and responsibilities for initial and ongoing initiative personnel
- A program development budget and preliminary ongoing program delivery budget
- Program metrics and associated measures

In Booz Allen's efforts, the main body of the blueprint specified the new program brand (what the program should express and accomplish, not just the logo and tag line), the program phases, the group owners, the high-level metrics for evaluating program success, and the change management strategy. It also included a Timeline Activity Matrix outlining activities organized by our four recommended program areas of Cultural Mastery, Interpersonal Network Development, Strategy Immersion, and Early Career Support.

One final part of blueprints worth highlighting is the detailed governance and operations model. Booz Allen opted for a centralized structure framed around a formal "Center of Excellence." An appointed lead person oversees operations and metrics for the program, assisted by a number of other individuals responsible for pieces of the program. A firm-wide orientation manager designs and oversees the ongoing orientation strategy, oversees coordination of Firmwide Orientation (e.g., panelists/speaker scheduling, etc.), and ensures a smooth transition between firm-wide orientation and local office orientation. A pre-arrival manager designs the ongoing pre-arrival strategy and oversees portal content updates, touch points, and technological notifications and handoffs. A local team orientation manager designs and oversees ongoing local and team orientation strategy, ensuring consistency and facilitating program-related communication between regional managers. Regional strategic HR managers partner with local and team managers to ensure regional and team needs are actively met. They also work with managers in local

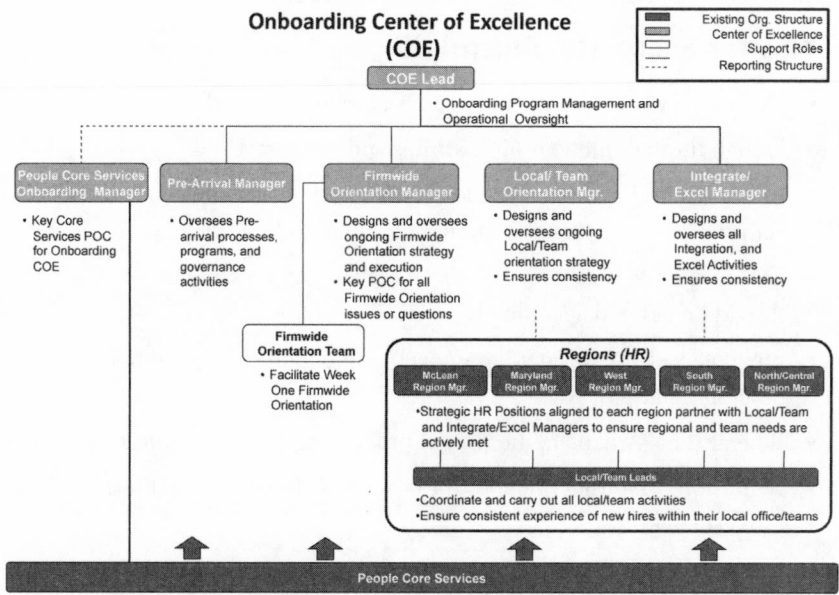

Figure 9.2 Onboarding Center of Excellence

offices and teams to coordinate local events and ensure participation in regional events (Figure 9.2).

Booz Allen's blueprint included provisions to monitor and measure progress on an ongoing basis. The blueprint specified the collection of objective and subjective data from program pilots, the engagement of program participants in conversations to extract critical feedback, and the deployment of surveys that measured stakeholder participation, new hire engagement, job readiness, and productivity. Additionally, a comprehensive metrics dashboard would be monitored on a regular basis to ensure that program performance met the needs of new hires, frontline managers, and the firm. Data sources for the enhanced program metrics dashboard would include participant survey data (new hire surveys, hiring manager surveys), human capital analytics data (new hire attrition and demographics data), new hire portal user data (percent of new hires accessing site, usage trends, etc.) and other data (course enrollment statistics, benchmarking data, etc.).

Tips for Successful Blueprinting

- Determine what matters—Focus on goal setting and performance metrics
- Design through the lens of new hires and managers
- Inform yourself—If you lack design experience, educate yourself and get informed via articles on design concepts and methodology
- Embrace customization—All new hires are not the same, so content should be tailored accordingly
- Integrate well—Consider the impact (and opportunity) on other programs and processes
- Be realistic—Articulate the risks of proceeding under the *status quo*
- Be flexible—Consider options for how much to take on, not just "gold standard"
- Quantify opportunity size in meaningful terms to your stakeholders
- Answer *"What will it take to get the job done?"* and ask for resources
- Answer *"What will it take to sustain?"* and ask for resources
- Design to help the business areas achieve their business objectives
- Ensure that executive champions are onboard before proceeding

Developing Program Content

When attempting to develop content based on your blueprint, consider the full range of tools, technology, resources, and content elements required to deliver the program seamlessly. Assemble a content development team that includes representation from across the organization. Many organizations assemble a less representative team, and this is unlikely to yield the best results. At a minimum, we recommend creating a part-time advisory committee with representatives from each business area or function, instructional designers, the IT department, field members from HR, and a representative from facilities. The business area representative should not only bring to the table the "local" culture of their respective business areas, but also the business goals of those business areas.

To realize the Onboarding Margin, think about how this class of new hires can help the business area achieve its mission, and build around that. We also recommend including in advisory roles: A leader from the company (and business unit) strategy group; the chief talent officer; regional talent delivery leads; recruiting leaders; functional and business unit HR or learning leaders; and an internal communications leader.

With content design underway, designers should take care to leverage existing HR programs to the extent possible. While existing programs will often need enhancement or updating to reflect the guiding principles of the new onboarding initiative, they can serve as an excellent starting point. If you haven't yet done so as part of the diagnostic process, take inventory of all existing HR programs and materials, including training modules, performance review systems, mentoring programs, firm social events, orientation content, and Web content, and think about linkages between these groups and activities. Often, we see pre-existing links between onboarding and learning and development, recruiting, human resources, and training programs. Identify opportunities to include locally owned initiatives within the larger onboarding umbrella.

Having touched on the importance of customizing onboarding to specific new hire segments, at this point in the process it's important to develop a baseline of content that serves as a basis for knowledge and is common across all new hire groups while also identifying content that needs to be tailored to the needs of certain key new hire segments. Organizations should pay special attention to groups of employees it has more difficulty recruiting as well as those who fall into "feeder roles" to senior management positions. Offering program elements to one group of new hires and not another can prove sensitive. Ideally, everyone would receive the full range of premier services, but the reality is that the size of your content development team, your timeframe for producing new content, and the cost of delivery will require prioritizing segments that would most benefit from customized material.

Given the large number of participants who typically assist with content development, it's critical to outline roles and responsibilities for everyone at the outset. With roles and responsibilities clear, the team can begin identifying materials needed for each constituency to deliver against their responsibilities. Mapping delivery roles and responsibilities also addresses frequent pain points, such as key handoffs between onboarding

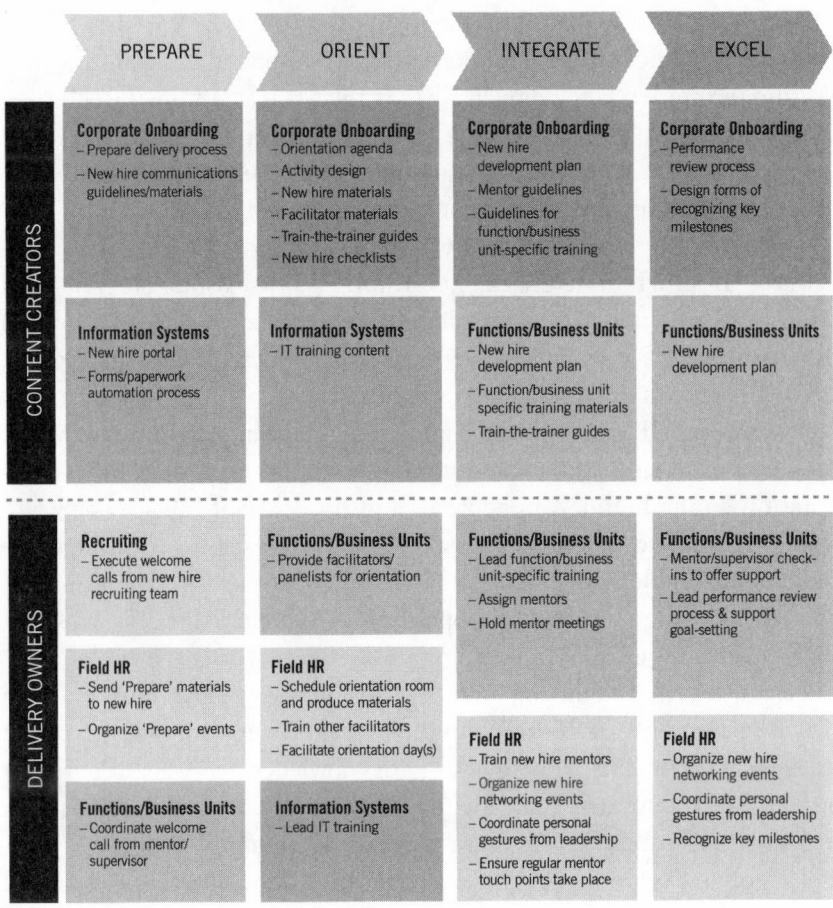

Figure 9.3 Onboarding Delivery Model

constituencies or decisions around centralized vs. business unit/function delivery of content. Figure 9.3 provides a sample of breakdown of roles and responsibilities by phase.

Similar to Booz Allen's, successful onboarding initiatives tend to develop and pilot new content in progressive stages. Staging allows for greater efficiency by encouraging content development to take place for upcoming reviews even as key stakeholders are reviewing previously developed material. Staging also prevents teams from taking on too much at once, allowing for learning opportunities and gaining momentum over time.

Wave I Development Activities

Phase	Category	Wave I Focus	Summary of Sub-element Development Activity
Pre-boarding	New Hire Portal Educational Material	Light	• Upload educational material from Orientation
	New Hire Portal User Experience	Light	• Introduce initial version of on-boarding program identity • Design user interface with static new hire journey map and progress meter
	New Hire Portal Personal Connections	Medium	• Upload preexisting welcome video • Upload preexisting information on networking
	Personalized Welcome	Heavy	• Develop and implement guidelines and approach for welcome phone call from recruiter and manager as a requirement for all new hires
	Enhance Administration and Communications (Provisioning)	Medium	• Create checklist and process for all administrative activities (including materials and equipment for Day 1)
	Account Creation (Provisioning)	Medium	• Develop and implement manual process for account creation and notifications
	Forms Automation (Provisioning)	Medium	• Upload downloadable forms on portal for new hires to print and complete
Firm-wide Orientation	Firmwide Orientation Delivery Model	Heavy	• Design and develop new delivery model for Firm-wide Orientation (e.g., regional vs. centralized) • Make Week 1 participation mandatory for all new hires
	Pre-existing Orientation Content	Medium	• Re-examine pre-existing elements and reconsider any content redundant with portal
	New Orientation Content	Light	• Develop and implement new hire panel • Develop and implement program identity reinforcement content (i.e., introduction to program and how new hires will be supported)
	Engagement Readiness Course Content	Medium	• Re-design engagement readiness course content and approach
	Increased Networking and Connectivity	Medium	• Develop and implement initial guidelines formal networking activities
Integrate & Excel	Upgrade Performance Assessment	Medium	• Develop and implement guidelines and process for 30/60/90 day formal touch points with manager and integrate with annual assessment
	Increased manager Role and Accountability	Medium	• Define and implement guidelines for increased manager role / accountability
GOVERNANCE, CHANGE & ADMINISTRATION: Initiate Change Management; Define end-state governance model			
PROGRAM MEASURES: Develop & Deploy Initial New Hire Survey			

Figure 9.4 First Phase of Four-Stage Program Rollout

Developing content in stages can also make budgeting for and financing a systemic program more feasible. Figure 9.4 shows Booz Allen's activities for the first phase of its four-stage program rollout. Notice how the firm broke down development activities by onboarding phase, focusing on pre-boarding and orientation.

Given its concern with new hire *valued connectedness*, Booz Allen's first stage featured a revamped first-week new hire experience that highlighted the connections among Booz Allen employees. The company determined that the value of connections *within* the firm acts as a proxy for the value of connection *to* the firm. Using interactive and simulation-based learning activities, new hires explore a range of content around the firm's mission, sources of differentiation, core values, and ethics. New hires also learn how the firm is structured and what its mission is in serving clients. New hires collaborate with one another in teams of five or six, navigating the content by engaging in activities, scenarios, and knowledge sharing. These teams work together much as they will in the real workplace—as a diverse group of staff from all levels and areas of expertise. A simulation called "Engage" immerses learners in a realistic consulting engagement preview, teaching them what to expect during a typical client assignment (an important "first"). A workshop called "Your Career, Your Legacy" explores critical factors for a successful 6-month assessment. New hires also build a social impact map to represent their evolving personal network, and they begin creating a personal development and integration plan for their first 6 to 12 months. A new hire portal supports the experience, providing guidance and modular learning activities on key firm-related topics as well as introductory videos from senior leaders.

When developing content, it's important to develop a clear plan and the underlying materials to support change management within the organization. A best-in-class approach to change management and internal communication requires soliciting input from onboarding stakeholders early and often. Input mechanisms such as a cross-functional steering committee can help gather detailed design and program input. Keep in mind that reviewing and incorporating this feedback is likely an iterative process. Nevertheless, collecting regular input throughout the process of executing a blueprint is critical if diverse stakeholders are to buy into a truly systemic program. Consider developing a regular "news cycle" about the onboarding initiative. During the development phase, team members should develop documentation that the team can use during program implementation to inform the broader organization about the initiative's goals and likely impact.

In Booz Allen's case, the enhanced onboarding program was communicated as part of the firm's two-year People Strategy Initiative. "It is critical not to short-change the investment of time and resources an effective communication and change management strategy will require," advises Chris Holmes, Program Manager of Onboarding at Booz Allen. "Be intentional about your communications to stakeholders across your organization: a comprehensive communications plan will begin informing a small but key group of senior stakeholders at the onset and become progressively more broad, complex and detailed as program development progresses." The Booz Allen team leveraged both top-down and bottom-up communication vehicles (memos, meetings, webcasts, firm intranet, etc.) to market and increase awareness of the program. The firm's onboarding program was also communicated throughout the organization via development and release of a video piece. To further the external employment brand, the initiative is being widely marketed through the Booz Allen web site, webinars, conference presentations, and articles in HR and Learning and Development publications.

Piloting and Implementing Your New Program

Like any major program rolled out across a large organization, a strategic onboarding initiative should roll out after the design team has sufficiently piloted the program. These pilots can take place concurrent with ongoing content development to allow ample time to collect feedback and make changes before broad scale implementation. Organizations can choose to pilot in selected regions or business units, by phase or new hire type. During the first stage of its redesigned program roll out, Booz Allen piloted new program elements with three separate groups of about 30 new hires each, each group spaced a month apart. The first group received the firm's new, week-long orientation (including simulation-based learning activities), the second received the new orientation plus a new pre-boarding experience, while the last group received new iterations of both these program elements.

During and after pilots, the design team should gather feedback not only from new hires, but from all relevant stakeholders. The design team, and ideally the stakeholders, should observe and analyze all onboarding activities delivered in the pilot and converse with process owners and new hire support personnel. They should also conduct surveys and focus groups with new hires and new hire managers. By observing the pilots, the design team can determine what works and what doesn't, what delivers the greatest excitement and offers the greatest educational value, and what elements are not being delivered as intended. Design teams can also use the pilots as a chance to provide feedback to and coach individuals responsible for delivering the program. Many of these individuals will continue to play a role in the onboarding process after implementation, so engaging with them now can enable them to develop better delivery expertise.

Piloting in select locations or among specific new hire segments can allow teams to benchmark pilot performance for the enhanced program relative to areas of the organization that still receive the old program.

Consider whether new hire satisfaction is higher or whether specific program elements can be improved to increase new hire satisfaction.

In Booz Allen's case, the piloting phase offered important guidance. Overall survey results surpassed expectations and yielded glowing responses (e.g., "I normally hate this stuff, but I had fun and learned a lot!"). Yet respondents also pointed to elements of the firm's new program that needed improvement, such as information on Booz Allen's functional teams, which was perceived to be too scarce. Program designers also learned that they needed to update their messaging to clarify learning objectives behind program components. Ratings from the second pilot group surpassed those in the first group.

Pilots enable you to test not only content, but also those operational processes that will support the program over the long term. Chris Holmes observed that pilots were critical for successful implementation at Booz Allen: "Once our content reached a certain point of maturity, we were able to increase the aperture of the pilots to include technology and process support. Increasingly more complex pilots broadened the scope of our test-bed to include other functions such as technology, recruiting, and help desk support."

During the pilot stage's second half, design teams should begin preparing to implement the program operationally across the broader organization. Prior to the broader rollout, teams need to create an implementation task force to help coordinate change management and training for process owners (e.g., recruiters, hiring managers, mentors, etc.) and support personnel. The implementation task force should begin pre-implementation activities during the pilot phase to ensure that no momentum is lost between the pilot stage and implementation.

As pilots are concluding and the implementation team is rolling out the program, it's critical to again return to the task of change management. For this purpose, the implementation task force includes a communications leader who can educate the organization about the program. This person should maintain strong connections with senior management, since ensuring the support of organizational leadership is vital to success. Many communications leaders choose to adopt a top-down approach, communicating the onboarding message to senior leaders in business units or functions who then pass on information about onboarding to program managers, role players, and other experienced employees.

At Booz Allen, the implementation team developed a compelling "road show" presentation that brought the message to key local offices once the team had secured buy-in from the organization's key stakeholders. The presentation was given in person at around a dozen offices with large populations of incoming new hires and by webinar at an additional 14 offices. "The road shows provided crucial early buy-in from stakeholders and senior leadership across the business," notes Holmes. "However, and perhaps more importantly, these sessions also served as a means for establishing an essential channel for ongoing communications and feedback with our regional counterparts across the country."

Results

Within a year from the start of the diagnostic phase, Booz Allen's program was off the ground and running. The firm had established a new welcome portal to foster pre-arrival activities, revamped its firmwide orientation, and initiated internal efforts to get diverse stakeholders behind onboarding. With these measures in place, the program had already met several of its goals and business objectives. Results from new hire surveys and interviews indicated that the online portal and the enhanced program curriculum were contributing to increased levels of new hire job readiness and engagement. More than 95% of survey participants acknowledged the program's positive impact on their impression of the company, reinforcing their decision to join Booz Allen. New hires note that they feel "fully prepared to do business with clients and co-workers and fit into the Booz Allen culture after coming through this course." A full 96% of participants rated the enhanced onboarding curriculum, ROI, instructors, and program logistics higher than comparable components of the firm's legacy onboarding program.

The firm also saw productivity gains associated with increased new hire job readiness levels. Doug Carter, Senior Vice President at Booz Allen, remarks that "new hires emerging out of this new onboarding program are some of the most prepared I've seen in years. Their understanding of the complex Booz Allen structure, our service offerings, and our methodologies and approaches ensures that we are able to deploy them swiftly to client engagements with the assurance that they will be able to effectively meet client demands." A four-hour instructor-led orientation class was converted into digital, interactive content available on the portal—eliminating instructor costs, participant travel costs, printing costs, and facilities fees. Other savings yielded from the portal include the elimination of printing and mailing costs associated with the new hire welcome packet, which is now available online for all new hires the day they accept their employment offer. Additionally, the portal's automation of new hire data collection has yielded substantial process and labor cost savings.

Based on early data, Booz Allen expects its program will improve the firm's retention rates. Reduced attrition will likely result from the enhanced onboarding program as early as Year Two, since new hire decisions to stay or leave the firm typically occur at the end of the first year of employment. In 2010, the firm won a Bersin Learning Leaders Award for Excellence and an ASTD Excellence in Practice citation for this onboarding redesign. Without question this effort has made an impact on its employment brand and is paying dividends.

Booz Allen's enhanced onboarding program was successful for a variety of reasons. First, key stakeholder involvement during the design process generated early initiative acceptance and adoption. "Our process of socialization and vetting not only the completed products, but also the work in progress allowed us to incorporate real-time feedback, ensuring our program sponsors' and stakeholders' recommendations and direction was fully integrated. Ultimately this streamlined the design and development process and added significant value to our work," notes Vince Gonzalez. Second, using a waved approach to development, piloting, and implementation permitted the organization to adopt specific gold standard best practices while ensuring ROI gain and continuous organizational momentum and support throughout the process. Third, development of program governance, provisioning, and administration frameworks and support tools contributed to ensuring consistent delivery of a high-quality onboarding experience for new hires.

What sets Booz Allen's onboarding program apart from other similar initiatives is the program's integrated and systemic approach, which leveraged existing integrated technology platforms and performance management systems at the company. By making use of Booz Allen's existing social media tool, the onboarding program encourages new hires to network with their colleagues. Furthermore, deployment of an online new hire portal streamlines program processes and eliminates the need for paper-based welcome kits and automated data collection. Meanwhile, a cohesive identity defined the program, promoting accountability and participation and creating value for the new hires, their managers, and the firm in general. Most importantly, managers are given instructions and tools on how to engage their new hires, drive their progress, and raise their awareness of potential pitfalls. One manager at Booz Allen indicates that the revised onboarding program "takes a more holistic approach to the process. Before, onboarding was narrowly focused on one thing—firmwide orientation—and that was it. We lost sight of the big picture. Now, there is a whole host of tools and activities for new hires and Frontline Leaders that should occur before and after firm-wide orientation throughout that first year."

Summing Up

All of these results were possible because Booz Allen was willing to invest in the right diagnostic. The firm took the time to develop a systemic approach, reflected in a comprehensive blueprint, and it executed methodically around that document. As this chapter has laid out, companies can realize success more readily by organizing onboarding design efforts around a clear plan. Otherwise, organizations may fail to realize the full extent of their Onboarding Margin. Booz Allen devoted substantial resources in terms of time and energy to craft its blueprint, but if your organization lacks these resources, don't panic. We've participated in success stories with some organizations working with fewer resources. The most important thing is a robust diagnostic, a commitment to drive change, a creative vision of what your institution can accomplish via strategic onboarding, and a strong resolution to get the job done.

CONCLUSION AND NEXT STEPS

We've expressed throughout this book that onboarding is an experience—for the new hire, the hiring manager, and for the enterprise more broadly. We are certain that this experience shapes outcomes, and it is in the best interest of all parties for the experience to be managed with great skill.

To engineer this experience for optimal outcomes, your enterprise will be well served to (1) adopt design principles, (2) be strategic, and (3) be systemic. Successful Onboarding is far more than traditional orientation in new clothes; it is an innovative strategic program that can boost a company's bottom line and improve its future prospects. By establishing a program covering culture, social networks, early career support, and strategic insight, and integrating onboarding into the infrastructure and processes of a company, you can reduce time to productivity, increase level of productivity, and lower attrition (specifically, regrettable attrition). These measures in turn lead to a clear financial gain—the Onboarding Margin. Tailoring the day-to-day experience of new hires through their first anniversary date, strategic onboarding can produce more satisfied employees and a more productive workforce better aligned with company objectives. In the process, it can produce a stronger, more dynamic, more profitable organization.

With very few exceptions, onboarding remains an untapped promise in business. To realize this promise, the leaders in an organization need to think of onboarding in new ways. HR leaders need to grasp the full opportunity they have before them. The programs need to be focused on far *more than* efficient administration of paperwork, compliance, and distribution of the tools of the trade; it is a substantial, year-long investment in one of a firm's greatest assets—its human capital—with raised expectations for return on investment. Hiring managers need to treat onboarding as a real chance to help an organization create the quality workforce it wants and needs. We hope hiring managers reading this book begin to recognize the great opportunity onboarding offers to break the cycle of "hire, attrit, hire" and transform it into "hire, invest, improve, and grow" (personal growth and enterprise growth). Finally, and arguably most important, we hope that business leaders outside of the human resource function will embrace strategic onboarding and pursue the Onboarding Margin with the same passion that they pursue lean manufacturing, six-sigma programs, and other leading management disciplines.

With global business moving ever deeper into a knowledge-based economy, the knowledge worker has become the company's key asset—more important than production processes and traditional capital investments, especially given that it is the knowledge worker who will help drive the smart investments in new markets, customer service, improved production processes, and capital projects. Business leaders seem to recognize this fact—they *talk* about people as their most important asset—but they don't always put their money behind this idea. Onboarding is the neglected stage in the employee life cycle, and it is the most important area deserving of budget today. By pursuing intelligent designs based on proper diagnostics, companies can redefine the employer-employee compact to a mutually beneficial state that supports the modern enterprise in our modern economy that demands flexibility, responsiveness, and continuous improvement at ever-increasing rates.

Realizing the Onboarding Margin throughout an organization is no small task. Yet it's not a mountain to climb, either. We'd like to conclude by emphasizing that individual hiring managers can make a real difference with onboarding, whether or not their superiors in the organization buy in. Hiring managers can take pieces of the firm-wide onboarding programs we've described and implement them on a smaller scale in their departments or divisions. Onboarding doesn't have to happen all at once, and if worse comes to worse, it doesn't have to happen everywhere at once.

Take heart. And take charge. With an understanding of onboarding in your back pocket, you can become an effective change agent in your organization. You can empower your employees to put their best selves forward at work, progress their careers, and in the end, drive your business further.

ENDNOTES

Introduction

1. *Development Dimensions International and Monster Intelligence 2006.* Global study of more than 3,700 job seekers and 1,250 hiring managers.
2. *BusinessWeek.* September 19, 2008.

Chapter 1

1. According to the Mellon Financial Corporation, average times to full productivity are: eight weeks for clerical jobs, 20 weeks for professionals, and 26 weeks for executives.
2. William A. Kahn provides a definition of Employee Engagement that we especially like, as the situation in which "… people employ and express themselves physically, cognitively, and emotionally during role performances," and also as "… the extent to which workforce commitment, both emotional and intellectual, exists relative to accomplishing the work, mission, and vision of the organization." Psychological Conditions of Personal Engagement and Disengagement at Work. *The Academy of Management Journal,* 33(4), 1990, 692–724.
3. *Engage Employees and Boost Performance.* Philadelphia: Hay Group, 2001.
4. ASTD 2008 BEST Award. *T+D,* October 2008.
5. *http://www.examiner.com/x–828-Entry-Level-Careers-Examiner~y2008m 9d10-Networking-as-a-job-search-tool-part–5-Find-a-mentor.*
6. United States Department of Labor, August 2007.

Chapter 3

1. Names in this example have been changed to protect the interests of the real client in which these events occurred.

2. Procter & Gamble as part of its submission and winning of KM World's 2009 KM Reality Award (for Knowledge Management solution implementation).

3. Frank Rose. The End of Innocence at Apple. *Wired*, April 24, 2009.

4. John P. Kotter. Leading Change: Why Transformation Efforts Fail. *Harvard Business Review*, January 2007.

5. Ram Charan. Home Depot's Blueprint for Cultural Change. *Harvard Business Review*, April 2006.

6. Entry posted by this new hire on his personal blog, 2009.

7. ASTD 2008 BEST Award. *T+D*, October 2008.

Chapter 4

1. Del Jones. Best Friends Good for Business. *USAToday.com*, November 30, 2004.

2. Rodd Wagner and Gale Muller. *Power of 2: How to Make the Most of Your Partnerships at Work and Life*. New York: Gallup Press, 2009, p. 4.

3. Jason Lehrer. The Buddy System. *Wired*, 17(10), September 12, 2009.

4. Best Buy's corporate headquarters features "the Hub," a large (215,000 sq. ft.) area.

5. Mercer Delta Consulting. Executive Onboarding Research Report, 2006.

6. Mercer Delta Consulting. Executive Onboarding Research Report, 2006.

7. Amy Lyman. *Building Trust by Welcoming Employees*. A Report from the Great Place to Work Institute, Inc., 2007.

8. Amy Lyman. *Building Trust by Welcoming Employees*. A Report from the Great Place to Work Institute, Inc., 2007.

9. ASTD BEST Awards 2008. *T+D*, October 2008, 73.

10. Martin Lamonica. IBM Breaks Ground in Second Life. *CNET News*, October 19, 2006.

11. Amy Lyman. *Building Trust by Welcoming Employees*. A Report from the Great Place to Work Institute, Inc. (2007).

Chapter 5

1. Denise R. Hearn. *Education in the Workplace: An Examination of Corporate University Models*. Edited May 10, 2002.

2. Susan M. Heathfield. Training: Your Investment in People Development and Retention. *About.com.*

3. Jill Casner-Lotto, Elyse Rosenblum, and Mary Wright. The Ill Prepared U.S. Workforce: Exploring the Challenges of Employer-Provided Workforce Readiness Training. *The Conference Board*, 2009.

4. Tamara J. Erickson and Lynda Gratton. What It Means to Work Here. *Harvard Business Review*, March 2007.

5. Robert H. Waterman, Jr., Judith A. Waterman, and Betsy A. Collard. Toward A Career-Resilient Workforce. *Harvard Business Review*, July-August 1994.

6. Denise Dubie. CIOs Fear Mass IT Exodus following Economic Recovery. *Networkworld.com News*, 2009.

7. Employee Discontent Expected to Reach Crisis Level Next Year. *PR Newswire*, November 19, 2009.

8. Sylvia Ann Hewlett. *Top Talent: Keeping Performance Up When Business Is Down*. Boston: Harvard Business Press, 2009.

9. Sylvia Ann Hewlett. *Top Talent: Keeping Performance Up When Business Is Down*. Boston: Harvard Business Press, 2009.

10. Sylvia Ann Hewlett, Laura Sherbin, and Karen Sumberg. How Gen Y & Boomers Will Reshape Your Agenda. *Harvard Business Review*, July-August 2009.

11. Martha Irvine. Recession Intensifies Gen X Discontent at Work. *Associated Press*, November 15, 2009.

12. Teresa M. Amabile and Steve J. Kramer. What Really Motivates Workers. *Harvard Business Review* 88(1), January-February 2010, 44–45.

13. Elizabeth Craig, John Kimberly, and Hamid Bouchikhi. Can Loyalty Be Leased? *Harvard Business Review*, September 1, 2002.

14. ASTD 2008 BEST Award, *T+D*, October 2008.

15. J.A. Conger and B. Fishel. Accelerating Leadership Performance at the Top: Lessons from the Bank of America's Executive On-Boarding Process. *Human Resources Management Review* 17, December 2007, 442–454.

16. Wells Fargo: The First Six Months. *Allbusiness.com*, August 1, 2002.

Chapter 6

1. Gerry Johnson, Kevan Scholes, and Richard Whittington. *Exploring Corporate Strategy: Text and Cases*, 8th ed. Upper Saddle River, NJ: Prentice Hall, 2008, p. 3.

2. Yuzo Yasuda. *40 Years, 20 Million Ideas: The Toyota Suggestion System.* Florence, KY: Productivity Press, 1990.

3. Fast Company, "The World's Most Innovative Company."

4. ASTD BEST Award 2008. *T+D*, October 2008.

5. Peter Drucker. *The Effective Executive*. New York: Harper & Row, 1967.

Chapter 7

1. Amy Lyman. *Building Trust by Welcoming Employees*. A Report from the Great Place to Work Institute, Inc. (2007).

2. ASTI Best Award 2008, *T+D*, October 2008, 72.

Chapter 8

1. Jane Porter. Acclimating Newcomers to the Office. *The Wall Street Journal*, October 20, 2009.

Chapter 9

1. These awards include being named by *Fortune* magazine to its 2010 list of "The 100 Best Companies to Work For," and earning a #5 listing by *Consulting Magazine* in its "Best Firms to Work For" in 2009, among others.

INDEX